D0058216

HANDBOOK OF PROGRAMMING LANGUAGES, VOLUME IV

Functional and Logic Programming Languages

Peter H. Salus, Series Editor in Chief

MACMILLAN
TECHNICAL
PUBLISHING
U·S·A

Handbook of Programming Languages, Volume IV: Functional and Logic Programming Languages

Peter H. Salus, Series Editor in Chief

Published by:
Macmillan Technical Publishing
201 West 103rd Street
Indianapolis, IN 46290 USA

International Standard Book Number: 1-57870-011-6

Library of Congress Catalog Card Number: 97-81204

01   00   99   98   4   3   2

Interpretation of the printing code: The rightmost double-digit number is the year of the book's printing; the rightmost single-digit, the number of the book's printing. For example, the printing code 98-1 shows that the first printing of the book occurred in 1998.

Composed in Sabon and MCPdigital by Macmillan Technical Publishing

Printed in the United States of America

Trademark Acknowledgments

All terms mentioned in this book that are known to be trademarks or service marks have been appropriately capitalized. Macmillan Technical Publishing cannot attest to the accuracy of this information. Use of a term in this book should not be regarded as affecting the validity of any trademark or service mark.

Warning and Disclaimer

This book is designed to provide information about functional and logic programming languages. Every effort has been made to make this book as complete and as accurate as possible, but no warranty or fitness is implied.

The information is provided on an as-is basis. The authors and Macmillan Technical Publishing shall have neither liability nor responsibility to any person or entity with respect to any loss or damages arising from the information contained in this book or from the use of the discs or programs that may accompany it.

Permissions

Chapter 1 is reprinted with permission from McCarthy J., P. W. Abrahams, D. J. Edwards, T. P. Hart, and M. I. Levin. 1965. *LISP 1.5 programmer's manual*. Cambridge, MA: MIT Press.

Publisher
Jim LeValley

Managing Editor
Caroline Roop

Executive Editors
Linda Engelman
Tom Stone

Acquisitions Editors
Jane K. Brownlow
Karen Wachs

Development Editor
Kitty Wilson Jarrett

Project Editor
Brad Herriman

Copy Editor
Kristine Simmons

Indexers
Chris Cleveland
Bront Davis

Team Coordinator
Amy Lewis

Manufacturing Coordinator
Brook Farling

Book Designer
Gary Adair

Cover Designer
Karen Ruggles

Production Team Supervisor
Daniela Raderstorf

Production
Mary Hunt
Laura A. Knox

Overview

Table of Contents

Foreword to *the Handbook of Programming Languages*

The aim of the *Handbook of Programming Languages* is to provide a single, comprehensive source of information concerning a variety of individual programming languages and methodologies for computing professionals. The *Handbook* is published in multiple volumes and covers a wide range of languages, organized by type and functionality.

The *Handbook* includes four volumes:

Volume I: Object-Oriented Programming Languages

This volume contains chapters on Smalltalk, C++, Eiffel, Ada95, Modula-3, and Java.

Volume II: Imperative Programming Languages

This volume contains chapters on Fortran, Pascal, Icon, and C, as well as a chapter on intermediate languages by Ron Cytron.

Volume III: Little Languages and Tools

This volume contains chapters on little languages and domain-specific languages, such as troff, awk, sed, Perl, Tcl and Tk, Python, and SQL. It also contains seminal work by Brian Kernighan and Lorinda Cherry as well as Jon Bentley and essays by Paul Hudak and Peter Langston.

Volume IV: Functional and Logic Programming Languages

This volume contains chapters on functional (Lisp, Scheme, Guile, and Emacs Lisp) and logic programming (Prolog) languages.

Natural—human—languages appear to be about 10,000 years old. Symbolic—formal—languages began in Sumer (a civilization of southern Iraq from about 3800 to 2300 BCE), where we find the oldest writing system, cuneiform. It was followed by Egyptian hieroglyphics (about 3000 BCE), the language of the Harappa in the Indus valley, the Chinese shell and bone inscriptions, and (in the Western hemisphere) the language of the Maya.

Writing systems abstract from speech and formalize that abstraction in their symbols. This may be done semantically (for example, hieroglyphs, English numerals, and symbols such as &) or phonologically (for example, alphabetic spelling).

In more recent times, further abstractions have become necessary: warning beacons, flags on sailing vessels, railway telegraph/semaphore, Morse code, and so forth.

Mechanical methods for calculating are very old, but they all involve symbolic abstraction. The abacus is probably the oldest of such constructions. The Chinese and Egyptians had this device nearly four millennia ago. The Mayans possessed it when the Spanish arrived. It was only a few years after Napier's discovery of logarithms (1614), and the use of his "bones" (marked ivory rods) for multiplication, that the slide rule was invented.

In 1642, at the age of 18, Blaise Pascal invented a calculator that could add and carry to aid his father, a tax collector. Almost 30 years later, in 1671, Leibniz took Pascal's machine a step further and built a prototype machine that could multiply using an ingenious device called the *stepped wheel*, which was still in use in mechanical calculators manufactured in the late 1940s. Leibniz demonstrated his calculator to the Royal Society in London in 1676.

The first commercially successful calculator was invented by Charles Xavier Thomas in 1820. By 1878, an astounding 1,500 had been sold—nearly 30 per year. They were still being manufactured by Darras in Paris after World War I. The Brunsviga adding machine, based on an 1875 patent by Frank Stephen Baldwin, which substituted a wheel with a variable number of protruding teeth for the Leibniz stepped wheel, sold an incredible 20,000 machines between 1892 and 1912—1,000 per year.

The first keyboard-driven calculator was patented in 1850 by D. D. Parmalee, and Dorr Eugene Felt's Comptometer—the first successful key-driven, multiple-order calculating machine—was patented in 1887.

In 1812, Charles Babbage came up with a notion for a different type of calculator, which he termed a *difference engine*. He was granted support by the British government in 1823. Work stopped in 1833, and the project was abandoned in 1842, the government having decided the cost was too great. From 1833 on, though, Babbage devoted himself to a different sort of machine, an analytical engine, that would automatically evaluate any mathematical formula. The various operations of the analytical engine were to be controlled by punched cards of the type used in the Jacquard loom. Though only a fraction of the construction appears to have been effected, Babbage's notes, drawings, and portions of the engine are in the Victoria and Albert Museum (as is the set of Napier's bones that belonged to Babbage).

The Jacquard loom, a successful attempt at increasing production through automation, was itself the result of several prior innovations: In 1725 Bouchon substituted an endless paper tape with perforations for the bunches of looped string. In 1728 Falcon substituted perforated cards, but attached them to strings, and in 1748, Jacques de Vaucanson combined the bands of perforated paper and the cards. The patterns on the cards were perforated by machines that cut on designs painted on by stencils. The programmed machine was born.

Over 100 years later, Herman Hollerith, a graduate of Columbia College in New York, recalled the existence of those perforated cards. Hollerith had just started work at the Census Bureau at a generous salary of $600 per year. There he was put to work on a survey of power and machinery used in manufacturing. But he also met John Shaw Billings, who was in charge of "vital statistics." One night at dinner, Billings complained about the recently invented but inadequate tabulating device of Charles Seaton, which had been used for the census of 1870. Billings felt that given the increased population, the 1880 census might not be completed in less than seven or eight years, and the 1890 census would still be incomplete in 1900. "There ought to be a machine for doing the purely mechanical work of tabulating population and similar statistics," Billings said. "We talked it over," Hollerith recalled 30 years later, "and I remember...he thought of using cards with the description of the individual shown by notches punched in the edge of the card." Hollerith thought about constructing a device to record and read such information and asked Billings to go into business with him. Billings was a cautious man and said no.

In 1882 Hollerith went to MIT as an instructor in mechanical engineering (he was then 22). Teaching at MIT gave him the time to work on his machine. He first considered putting the information on long strips of paper, but this proved impractical. In the summer of 1883, Hollerith took a train trip west. On the train he saw the "punch photograph," a way for conductors to punch passengers' descriptions onto tickets so they could check that the same individual was using the ticket throughout the trip; in this system things like gender and hair and eye color were encoded.

Hollerith patented his first machine in 1884 and an improved design in 1886, when he performed a trial by conducting the Baltimore census. On the basis of reports of the trial, New Jersey and New York placed orders for machines (to tally mortality rates). Hollerith and some business colleagues bid for the contract for the 1890 census and won it. The government of Austria ordered machines in 1890. Canada ordered five the next year. Italy and Norway followed, and then Russia. The machines were a clear success. Hollerith incorporated his Hollerith Electric Tabulating System as the Tabulating Machine Company in 1896; he reincorporated it in 1905.

Nearly 80 years passed before the computer industry moved beyond several of Hollerith's insights. First, so that operators would have no problem orienting the cards, he cut a corner from the upper right. Second, he *rented* the machines at a reasonable rate (the rental fees for the 1890 census were $750,000; the labor cost in 1880 had been $5 million), but *sold* the patented cards (more than 100 million between 1890 and 1895). Third, he adapted the census-counting to tally freight and passenger data for railroads. Hollerith effectively invented reusability.

Despite the fact that Thomas Watson said (in 1945), "I think there is a world market for about five computers," the first completed was one he had funded. Howard Aiken of Harvard, along with a small team, began in 1939 to put together a machine that exploited Babbage's principles. It consisted, when completed in 1944, of a 51-foot by 8-foot panel on which tape readers, relays, and rotary switches were mounted. Nearly all of the operations of the Harvard Mark I Calculator were controlled by mechanical switches, driven by a 4-horsepower motor.

The first all-electronic computer was the Electronic Numerical Integrator and Calculator. Completed by J. W. Mauchly and J. P. Eckert of the University of Pennsylvania in late 1945 and installed in 1946, it was commissioned by the Ballistics Research Laboratory (BRL) at the Aberdeen (Maryland) Proving Ground. It was—and will remain, I expect—the largest computing machine ever built: It was made up of 18,000 tubes and 1,500 relays. ENIAC was the electronic analogue of the Mark I, but ran several hundred times faster.

ENIAC had offspring in England, too. Maurice V. Wilkes and his group began planning their Electronic Delay Storage Automatic Calculator (EDSAC) in late 1946, on Wilkes's return from Pennsylvania, and began work at the University Mathematical Laboratory in Cambridge early in the new year. It was one fifth the size of ENIAC and based on ideas that John von Neumann had presented in a paper. When it performed its first fully automatic calculation in May 1949, EDSAC became the first electronic machine to be put into operation that had a high-speed memory (store) and with I/O (input/output) devices. Within a few years, EDSAC's library contained more than 150 subroutines, according to Wilkes.

At virtually the same time, in Manchester, a team under M. H. A. Newman began work on a machine that was to embody the EDVAC concepts. F. C. Williams, who invented cathode ray tube storage, I. J. Good, who had worked on the Colossus code-breaking machine with Alan M. Turing, and Turing himself, joined the team. The Manchester Automatic Digital Machine prototype was built in 1948, and the definitive machine ran its first program in June 1949. MADM introduced to computing both the index register and pagination.

In the meantime, IBM had begun work on its Selective-Sequence Electronic Calculator (SSEC). It is important to remember that while EDSAC was the first electronic computer, the SSEC was the first *computer*—it combined computation with a stored program. It was put into operation at IBM headquarters in Manhattan early in 1948, cleverly placed behind plate glass windows at street level so that pedestrians could see it operate. It was a large machine with 13,000 tubes and 23,000 relays. Because all the arithmetic calculations were carried out by the tubes, it was more than 100 times as fast as the Mark I. It also had three different types of memory: a high-speed tube store, a larger capacity in relays, and a vastly larger store on 80-column paper tape. Instructions and input were punched on tape and there were 66 heads arranged so that control was transferred automatically from one to the other. "It was probably the first machine to have a conditional transfer of control instruction in the sense that Babbage and Lady [Ada] Lovelace recommended," wrote B. W. Bowden in 1953. It did work for, among other things, the Atomic Energy Commission, before being dismantled in August 1952.

That very June, von Neumann and his colleagues completed Maniac at the Institute for Advanced Studies in Princeton, New Jersey. It employed the electrostatic memory invented by F. C. Williams and T. Kilburn, which required a single cathode ray tube, instead of special storage tubes.

The next advance in hardware came at MIT's Whirlwind project, begun by Jay Forrester in 1944. Whirlwind performed 20,000 single-address operations per second on 16-digit words, employing a new type of electrostatic store in which 16 tubes each contained 256 binary digits. The Algebraic Interpreter for the Whirlwind and A-2—developed by Grace Murray Hopper for the UNIVAC—are likely the most important of the machine-oriented languages.

The 704, originally the 701A, was released in 1954. It was the logical successor to the IBM 701 (1952, 1953). The evolution of the 701 into the 704 was headed up by Gene Amdahl. The direct result of the

701/704 was the beginning of work on Fortran (which stands for *formula translator*) by John Backus at IBM in 1953. Work on the Fortran translator (we would call it a compiler) began in 1955 and was completed in 1957. Fortran was, without a doubt, the first programming language.

In December 1959, at the Eastern Joint Computer Conference at the Statler Hotel in Boston, the three-year-old DEC unveiled the prototype of its PDP-1 (Programmed Data Processor-1). It was priced at $120,000 and deliveries began in November 1960.

The PDP-1 was an 18-bit machine with a memory capacity between 4,096 and 32,768 words. The PDP-1 had a memory cycle of 5 microseconds and a computing speed of 100,000 computations per second. It was the result of a project led by Benjamin Gurley and was composed of 3,500 transistors and 4,300 diodes. It had an editor, a macroassembler, and an ALGOL compiler, DECAL. It employed a paper tape reader for input and an IBM typewriter for output. The PDP-1 had the best cost/performance of any real-time computer of its generation. It was also the first commercial computer to come with a graphical display screen.

Just over 40 years ago there were no programming languages. In 1954 programming was still a function of hardware. Fortran was invented in 1957. It was soon being taught. By 1960, not only had COBOL and Lisp joined the roster, but so had others, many now thankfully forgotten. Over the past 40 years, nearly 4,000 computer languages have been produced. Only a tithe of these are in use today, but the growth and development of them has been progressive and organic.

There are a number of ways such languages can be taxonomized. One frequent classification is into machine languages (the natural language of a given device), assembly languages (in which common English words and abbreviations are used as input to the appropriate machine language), and high-level languages (which permit instructions that more closely resemble English instructions). Assembly languages are translators; high-level languages require conversion into machine language: These translators are called *compilers*. Among the high-level languages currently in use are C, C++, Eiffel, and Java.

Yet there is no guide for the overwhelmed programmer, who merely wants to get her job done. This *Handbook of Programming Languages* is intended to serve as an instant reference, a life-preserver, providing information to enable that programmer to make intelligent choices as to which languages to employ, enough information to enable him to program at a basic level, and references to further, more detailed information.

Peter H. Salus

Boston, February 1998

General Bibliography

Histories of Programming Languages

Bergin, T. J., and R. G. Gibson (Eds.). 1996. *History of programming languages*. Reading, MA: Addison-Wesley. Proceedings of ACM's Second History of Programming Languages Conference.

Sammet, J. A. 1969. *Programming languages: History and fundamentals*. Englewood Cliffs, NJ: Prentice Hall. An indispensable work.

Wexelblat, R. L. (Ed.). 1981. *History of programming languages*. New York: Academic Press. The proceedings of ACM's First History of Programming Languages Conference.

Reader on Programming Languages

Horowitz, E. 1987. *Programming languages: A grand tour* (3rd ed.). Rockville, MD: Computer Science Press.

Surveys and Guides to Programming Languages

Appleby, D. 1991. *Programming languages: Paradigm and practice*. New York: McGraw-Hill.

Bal, H. E., and D. Grune. 1994. *Programming language essentials*. Wokingham, England: Addison-Wesley.

Cezzar, R. 1995. *A guide to programming languages*. Norwood, MA: Artech House.

Sethi, R. 1996. *Programming languages: Concepts & constructs* (2nd ed.). Reading, MA: Addison-Wesley.

Stansifer, R. 1995. *The study of programming languages*. Englewood Cliffs, NJ: Prentice Hall.

Foreword to This Volume: Functional and Logic Programming Languages

Imperative languages such as C and C++ enable programmers to express algorithms for problem solution. Declarative languages, such as Lisp and Prolog, enable the programmer to specify what has to be computed, not how the computation is to be done.

There are two kinds of declarative languages: functional languages (the various Lisps and Lisp-like languages) and logic languages (e.g., Prolog). By and large, declarative languages are harder to implement efficiently, but this may be because the implementations are less efficient—they are certainly "younger" by a generation.

John McCarthy's LISP (now capitalized Lisp) was the first functional language. It was created at MIT in 1958, soon after the publication of Fortran, and was originally intended as an artificial intelligence (AI) language.

Because of its importance, the beginning of the *LISP 1.5 Programmer's Manual* is reprinted here. I have chosen Emacs Lisp, obtainable gratis from the Free Software Foundation, as an example of a contemporary Lisp, Scheme as the example of a Lisp-inspired language, and Guile as a library containing an interpreter for Scheme. As I wrote in Volume I, I have decided to place CLOS (which stands for Common Lisp Object System) in this volume with the Lisps, rather than in Volume I, with the object-oriented languages.

There are many other functional languages; Haskell (1992), Miranda (1986), and ML (1987) are the most salient. ML shows strong influence of APL, a single-data structure programming language, in which the data structures are arrays.

Lisp, Haskell, and Miranda are based on λ-calculus; APL is mathematics based.

Prolog is firmly sited in the tradition of formal logic that runs from Aristotle through de Morgan to Frege. Though developed by Colmerauer and Roussel at the University of Marseilles in 1972, Prolog did not flourish till nearly a decade later. Prolog is not based on λ-calculus, but on Horn logic, which was studied by A. Horn in 1951.

Peter H. Salus
Boston, February 1998

Dedication

This *Handbook* is dedicated to John Backus, James Gosling, Adele Goldberg, Ralph Griswold, Brian Kernighan, John McCarthy, Bertrand Meyer, Dennis Ritchie, Bjarne Stroustrup, and the memory of Joe Ossanna, without whose efforts most of these languages wouldn't exist.

Acknowledgments

Many individuals deserve mention where this enormous *Handbook* is concerned. First of all, Tom Stone, who abetted my thinking and then effected a contract prior to deserting me for another publisher; next, Jim LeValley and Don Fowley at Macmillan, for being willing to take a chance on this project. I'd also like to thank Linda Engelman, Tracy Hughes, Amy Lewis, Jane Brownlow, Karen Wachs, and Kitty Jarrett at Macmillan.

In addition to the many authors, I'd like to thank Lou Katz, Stuart McRobert, Len Tower, and Brent Welch for their advice, patience, and friendship.

My gratitude to the ACM, to Addison-Wesley Longman, to MIT Press, to O'Reilly & Associates, and to the Waite Group for permissions to reprint various materials is enormous.

The errors and omissions are mine.

About the Series Editor

Peter H. Salus

Peter H. Salus is the author of *A Quarter Century of UNIX* (1994) and *Casting the Net: From ARPANET to Internet and Beyond* (1995). He is an internationally recognized expert and has been the keynote speaker at Uniforum Canada, the UKUUG, the NLUUG, and the OTA (Belgium) in the past few years. He has been executive director of the USENIX Association and of the Sun User Group and vice president of the Free Software Foundation. He was the managing editor of *Computing Systems* (MIT Press) from 1987 to 1996. He writes on a variety of computing topics in a number of magazines. His Ph.D. in linguistics (New York University, 1963) has led him from natural languages to computer languages.

About the Authors

Paul W. Abrahams

Paul W. Abrahams is a consulting computer scientist and past president of the Association for Computing Machinery. He specializes in programming languages, design and implementation of software systems, and technical writing. He is one of the designers of the first LISP system and also the designer of the CIMS PL/I system, which he developed while a professor at New York University. He also participated in the design of the Software Engineering Design Language (SEDL), developed at the IBM T.J. Watson Laboratories. In 1995 he was honored as a Fellow of the ACM. Paul resides in Deerfield, Massachusetts, where he writes, hacks, hikes, hunts wild mushrooms, and listens to classical music.

James H. Andrews

James H. Andrews is a Canadian who received his doctorate in 1991 from the Department of Computer Science at the University of Edinburgh, Scotland. His dissertation, "Logic Programming: Operational Semantics and Proof Theory," won a 1991 British Computer Society Distinguished Dissertation Award and is published by Cambridge University Press.

Jamie is currently an assistant professor in the Department of Computer Science at the University of Western Ontario in London, Ontario. His research concerns software engineering and the semantics of programming languages.

Jim Blandy

Jim Blandy (jimb@red-bean.com) has extensive experience working with interpreted languages. He has maintained Guile for Project GNU since spring 1996. In the early 1990s, he worked on GNU Emacs for the Free Software Foundation; he and Richard Stallman were responsible for releasing Version 19 of Emacs. He lives in the Boston area with his cat, Foo.

Robert J. Chassell

Robert J. Chassell grew up in Stockbridge, Massachusetts, on property where, as he says, a recent archeological dig found human traces going back 6,000 years. He studied at St. John's College (Santa Fe, NM) and Cambridge University. As a student volunteer, he worked on an archeological site in Dylan Thomas's hometown in south Wales, digging remains from 50,000 years ago.

More recently, he has written *Programming in Emacs Lisp: An Introduction*, an elementary introduction for people who are not programmers.

He was the founding secretary/treasurer and chief financial officer of the Free Software Foundation, Inc., as well as a director. Before that he was part of a project working on expert systems at Lisp Machine, Inc. (Cambridge, MA), a computer manufacturer.

In addition to his abiding interest in social and economic history, Chassell is an avid amateur astronomer; he is an FAA certified flight instructor and a commercial and instrument-rated pilot, and flies his own airplane.

Brian Harvey

Brian Harvey is a lecturer in the Computer Science Division at the University of California at Berkeley, where he has been teaching Scheme-based courses since 1987. He is co-author of the text *Simply Scheme: Introducing Computer Science*. He is also involved in precollege education as lead developer of the freeware Berkeley Logo interpreter and author of the three-volume *Computer Science Logo Style*.

John McCarthy

John McCarthy is a professor of engineering and a professor of computer science and electrical engineering at Stanford University. One of the founders of artificial intelligence research, McCarthy invented LISP while an assistant professor at MIT. He was also involved in the development of ALGOL 58 and ALGOL 60. John McCarthy was awarded ACM's Turing Award in 1971. He received the First IJCAI Research Excellence Award in 1985. He also received the National Medal of Science in 1990, and is a fellow and past president of AAAI.

Jim Veitch

Jim Veitch is vice president of engineering for Franz Inc., a leading supplier of Lisp in the computer industry. Jim has been involved in developing Franz's Allegro CL CLOS system for over 10 years. He has been involved in designing several user interfaces, designed and built a C/Lisp "Foreign function" interface, ported the Lisp system to various UNIX systems, and wrote an incremental loader for UNIX System V. He built a window system (Allegro Common Windows) for NeWS and for Sunview. Prior to joining Franz, Jim did research at AT&T Bell Laboratories and at Princeton University.

Jim has a Ph.D. in statistics from University of California, Berkeley, and received a B.Sc. in mathematics from Flinders University, Australia. Jim was a Fulbright scholar.

PART I
Lisp

CHAPTER 1

The LISP Language[1]

by John McCarthy, Paul W. Abrahams, Daniel J. Edwards,
Timothy P. Hart, and Michael I. Levin

The LISP language is designed primarily for symbolic data processing. It has been used for symbolic calculations in differential and integral calculus, electrical circuit theory, mathematical logic, game playing, and other fields of artificial intelligence.

LISP is a formal mathematical language. It is therefore possible to give a concise yet complete description of it. Such is the purpose of this first section of the manual. Other sections will describe ways of using LISP to advantage and will explain extensions of the language which make it a convenient programming system.

LISP differs from most programming languages in three important ways. The first way is the nature of the data. In the LISP language, all data are in the form of symbolic expressions usually referred to as *S-expressions*. S-expressions are of indefinite length and have a branching tree type of structure, so that significant sub-expressions can be readily isolated. In the LISP programming system, the bulk of available memory is used for storing S-expressions in the form of list structures. This type of memory organization frees the programmer from the necessity of allocating storage for the different sections of his program.

The second important part of the LISP language is the source language itself, which specifies in what way the S-expressions are to be processed. This consists of recursive functions of S-expressions. Since the notation for the writing of recursive functions of S-expressions is itself outside the S-expression notation, it will be called the *meta-language*. These expressions will therefore be called *M-expressions*.

[1]This chapter is reprinted with permission from McCarthy J., P. W. Abrahams, D. J. Edwards, T. P. Hart, and M. I. Levin. 1965. *LISP 1.5 programmer's manual*. Cambridge, MA: MIT Press.

Third, LISP can interpret and execute programs written in the form of S-expressions. Thus, like machine language, and unlike most other higher level languages, it can be used to generate programs for further execution.

CHAPTER 2

Emacs Lisp: A Short Description

by Robert J. Chassell

GNU Emacs Lisp is a full-featured, platform-independent, interpreted, dynamically scoped programming language with special features for use in GNU Emacs, an integrated computational environment.[1]

Emacs Lisp is a simple, albeit complete, language. Not only does it contain the usual features of a programming language, Emacs Lisp also contains special features for use in Emacs's extensible, integrated computational environment: features for scanning and parsing text and also for handling files, buffers, displays, and subprocesses. Moreover, editing commands are functions that can easily be called from Lisp programs; customization parameters are ordinary Lisp variables.

Most of the GNU Emacs environment is written in Emacs Lisp. The language is used by people who write extensions to Emacs, by students who are learning to program, and by programmers to create applications that use the extensive Emacs libraries.

Emacs Lisp is an interpreted language. However, it can be byte compiled to run quickly in a virtual machine. It runs on numerous platforms—more than 40 at last count.

GNU Emacs includes two debuggers, which you can use to examine the runtime stack, step through sources, display a backtrace, and the like.

The antecedents of Emacs Lisp spring from the beginnings of modern-day computing; the language was inspired by MacLisp, which grew out of MIT's Project MAC of the 1960s. (Lisp itself was first developed in the late 1950s for research in artificial intelligence.) Emacs Lisp was also somewhat influenced

---

[1]GNU Emacs (including Emacs Lisp) consists of freely redistributable software. This means you can use, copy, and modify it. You may redistribute the same or modified copies, giving them away or charging for the act of transferring copies, so long as you pass on to others the same rights that you have. Your rights and responsibilities are described in the *GNU General Public License* that comes with GNU Emacs.

by Common Lisp. However, Emacs Lisp is much simpler than Common Lisp. If you know Common Lisp you should be careful: Sometimes the simplifications are so drastic that they confuse an unwary expert in Common Lisp.

The whole GNU Emacs environment, including Emacs Lisp, was first written by Richard Stallman in the early 1980s. Since then, many people have extended the system and contributed new applications, such as Calc mode for calculus and other computations, Calendar mode for Mayan, Coptic, and more conventional calendars, W3 mode for browsing the Web, and ange-ftp for treating remote file systems as if they were local. All these additions were written in Emacs Lisp.

2.1. GNU Emacs and Emacs Lisp

You can think of GNU Emacs in at least four ways:

- As a set of programs in Emacs Lisp, with a fast running base written in C

- As a Lisp machine that runs on more than 40 different types of hardware

- As an editor

- As a general computational environment

This chapter focuses on Emacs Lisp as a programming language. However, because Emacs Lisp comes with GNU Emacs, this programming language possesses multimode user interface libraries suitable both for slow dial-up terminals and for graphical user interfaces, as well as many other libraries to help you with calendars, forms, mail, news, outlines, C and other programming, compiling, debugging, FTP, phases of the moon, Conway's Game of Life, and a universe of libraries.[2]

---

[2]The most valuable references for Emacs Lisp are *The GNU Emacs Lisp Reference Manual*, which tells about Emacs Lisp, and the *The GNU Emacs Manual*, which tells about Emacs. My *Programming in Emacs Lisp: An Introduction* is for people who are not necessarily interested in programming, but who do want to customize or extend their computing environment. These all come with Emacs and can be read online using Info. Also, you can print these manuals yourself or order printed copies from

Free Software Foundation, Inc.
59 Temple Place, Suite 330
Boston, MA 02111-1307 USA
Telephone: +1-617-542-5942
Fax (including Japan): +1-617-542-2652
Email: gnu@gnu.org
World Wide Web: http://www.gnu.org

GNU Emacs provides two interpreters for Emacs Lisp: the Lisp inter-preter and a byte-code interpreter. These are the programs on your computer that execute the code.

The Lisp interpreter reads and evaluates (that is, runs as code) the printed representations of Emacs Lisp that you are able to read. The second interpreter is automatically called by the first in the appropriate circumstances; it evaluates a special representation called *byte-code* that can be executed more efficiently than code you can read. Humanly readable Lisp code is converted into byte-code with a *compiler*.

Because the byte-compiled code is evaluated by the byte-code interpreter, instead of being executed directly by the machine's hardware (as true compiled code is), byte-code is completely transportable from machine to machine without recompilation. It is, in the jargon, "platform independent." It is not, however, as fast as true compiled code.

In this chapter when I speak of "the Lisp interpreter," I mean either of these two interpreters. Customarily, when you write Emacs Lisp, you work with the printed representation; when you are satisfied with your work and need the extra speed, you can byte-compile it.

Most often, people run Emacs Lisp programs within Emacs. In this chapter, I assume that is what you will do.

However, you can run Emacs in *batch mode* just as you run a standalone awk, perl, sed, or sh script.

For example, just as you might run awk like this:

```
awk -f program-file input-file &> log-file
```

you can run an Emacs Lisp program like this (note the files' order):

```
emacs --batch input-file -l program-file -f save-buffer &> log-file
```

This says to visit input-file, load program-file, which makes changes in the visited file, save input-file, and then exit, with messages or errors placed in log-file.

In this discussion, as I said previously, I presume you are working within Emacs.

This means that you should become somewhat familiar with Emacs as an editor if you are not already. For example, you should know that c-u means to hold down the ctrl ("control") key and at the same time type a u; M-x means to hold down the Meta key (which may have some other name, such as Alt) and type an x at the same time. If you lack a Meta key, type Esc and then the x.

A statement such as c-h f (describe-function) means "type c-h f to invoke the command describe-function."

2.2. Lisp Lists

Lists are the basis of Lisp. The word *Lisp* stands for *list processing*. The programming language handles *lists* (and lists of lists) by putting them between parentheses.

For example, '(pine hickory oak maple) is a list. Whitespace makes no difference to a Lisp list, and the preceding list could have been written like this:

```
'(pine
   hickory
   oak
   maple)
```

The elements of this list are the names of four kinds of trees, separated from each other by whitespace and surrounded by parentheses.

Lists can also have numbers in them, as in this list: (+ 2 2). This list has a plus-sign + followed by two 2s, each separated by whitespace.

Furthermore, a list may have a list inside of it, like this:

```
'(this list has (a list inside it))
```

The components of this list are the words this, list, has, and the list (a list inside it). The interior list is made up of the words a, list, inside, and it.

2.2.1. Parts of Lisp

In Lisp, what I have to this point in the chapter been calling words are called *atoms*. This term comes from the historical meaning of the word atom: indivisible. As far as Lisp is concerned, the words I have been using in the lists cannot be divided into any smaller parts and still mean the same thing as part of a program; likewise with numbers and single character symbols such as +. On the other hand, unlike an atom, a list can be split into parts.

In a list, atoms are separated from each other by whitespace. They can be right next to a parenthesis.

Technically speaking, a list in Lisp consists of parentheses surrounding atoms separated by whitespace, or surrounding other lists, or surrounding both atoms and other lists. A list can have just one atom in it or nothing in it at all. A list with nothing in it looks like this: (). It is called an *empty list*. Unlike anything else, an empty list is considered both an atom and a list at the same time. The empty list is also known as nil, a different representation of exactly the same thing, and is considered false in true-or-false tests.

The lists I have been showing are the *printed representations* of the lists as seen by you or me; these are *not* what the computer sees. Generally speaking, you need not concern yourself with the difference between the internal representation used by a computer and the printed representation as seen by a human. However, sometimes an awareness of the distinction helps in understanding.

The printed representations of both atoms and lists are called *symbolic expressions* or, more concisely, *s-expressions*. The word *expression* by itself can refer to either the printed representation or to the atom or list as it is held internally in the computer. Often, people use the term *expression* indiscriminately. (Also, in many texts, the word *form* is used as a synonym for expression.)

A list in Lisp—any list—is a program ready to run. If you run (or *evaluate*) it, the computer will do one of four things: do nothing except return to you the list itself; send you an error message; repeat an infinite loop; or treat the first symbol in the list as a command to do something. (Usually, of course, it is the last of these four things that you really want!)

The single apostrophe, ', that I put in front of some of the sample lists in preceding sections is called a *quote*; when it precedes a list, it tells the Lisp interpreter to do nothing with the list other than take it as it is written.[3] But if there is no quote preceding a list, the first item of the list is special: It is an instruction for the computer to obey. (In Lisp, these instructions are called *functions*.) The list (+ 2 2) shown previously does not have a quote in front of it, so the Lisp interpreter understands that the + is an instruction to do something with the rest of the list—in this case, to add the numbers that follow.

The art of programming in Lisp is to write lists.

---

[3]The single apostrophe, ', is actually no more than a convenience. 'x is an abbreviation for (quote x), a list that starts with the quote built-in function.

2.3. Example: Two Plus Two

Here is a simple program that illustrates, in a limited way, how Emacs Lisp works. In subsequent sections, I discuss primary concepts in more detail.

In Lisp, a program is a list. For example, (+ 2 2) is a list of three elements, +, 2, and 2. This list is a short program; when evaluated, it adds two plus two.

In Emacs, you can evaluate a program such as this by positioning your cursor after the closing parenthesis and typing c-x c-e. (There are other ways to evaluate a list; this is just one of the ways.)

If you evaluate this expression, the number 4 appears.

The first element of the list, +, is a function, which is to say, a program itself, that takes arguments which in this example are the numbers following the +, 2 and 2.

Here is another simple addition: (+ 2 (+ 1 1))

In this example, the list (+ 1 1) is embedded inside the list whose other elements are + and 2.

When the overall list, (+ 2 (+ 1 1)), is evaluated, the inner list is evaluated first, adding one plus one to produce two. Then the result of the first evaluation is provided as an argument to the outer +.

2.4. Evaluation

Here is what the Lisp interpreter does when it evaluates an expression. First, it checks whether there is a quote before the expression; if there is, the interpreter just gives the expression. On the other hand, if there is no quote, the interpreter checks whether the expression is a list, and if so, it looks at the first element in the list to see whether it has a function definition. If it does, the interpreter carries out the instructions in the function definition. Otherwise, the interpreter prints an error message.

Note that lists are not the only kind of expression in Lisp. The Lisp interpreter can also evaluate a symbol that is not quoted and does not have parentheses around it. In this case, the Lisp interpreter will attempt to determine the symbol's value as a *variable*.

Moreover, some functions are unusual and do not work in the usual manner. These are called *special forms*. They are used for special jobs, such as defining a function, and there are not many of them.

Finally, if the Lisp interpreter is looking at a list that has a list inside it, the interpreter first figures out what it should do with the inside list, and then it works on the outside list. If there is yet another list embedded inside the inner list, it works on that one first, and so on. The result may be used by the enclosing expression.

Otherwise, the interpreter works left to right, from one expression to the next.

2.5. A Function Definition

You can write your own functions in Emacs Lisp using a special form called defun, which stands for *function definition*.

Here is an example of a function definition that upcases the last letter of a word.

```
(defun capitalize-backward ()
  "Upcase the last letter of a word."
  (interactive)
  (backward-word 1)                ; This is a comment.
  (forward-word 1)
  (backward-char 1)
  (capitalize-word 1))
```

This function definition has five parts following the word defun:

- The name of the symbol to which the function definition should be attached, in this case capitalize-backward.

- A list of the arguments that are passed to the function. In this case, there are none, so the list is an empty list.

- Documentation that describes what the function does.

- An expression that makes the function interactive so you can use it by typing M-x and then the name of the function; or by typing an appropriate key or set of keys (a *keychord*). In this case, you could run the function inside of Emacs (after loading it) by typing M-x capitalize-backward.

- The code that instructs the computer what to do: the *body* of the function definition.

In this definition, the code says to move point[4] backward to the beginning of the word point is in, or if point is between words, to move to the beginning of the preceding word; then to move forward to the end of the word; then move back one character; and finally to capitalize the word (that is, the character) following point. (This latter action depends on the specific way capitalize-word works, which is to assume that point is at the beginning of the word, or before it in whitespace, and to uppercase the first non-whitespace character reached by moving forward.)

The body also includes a *comment*, which is text between a semicolon and the end of a line. The Lisp interpreter ignores a comment. (Usually, of course, comments do more than simply announce themselves, as here; comments should be informative.)

That is all there is to it.

To make a definition such as this available for use, you need to evaluate the expression. You can do this by placing your cursor immediately after the closing parenthesis and typing C-x C-e.[5]

Then, to use the definition, type M-x capitalize-backward.

Here, in brief, is a template of the five parts of a function definition:

```
(defun function-name (arguments...)
  "optional-documentation..."
  ;; interactive section is optional
  (interactive argument-passing-info-if-any)
  body...)
```

Both documentation and the interactive section are optional.

As a practical matter, however, you should write documentation for every function you define. It will help you and whoever uses your function or reads your code.

Whether you make your function interactive depends on how it is to be used. If you expect a user will call it, make it interactive; if you expect it will be part of another definition and not called directly by a user, there is no need to make it interactive.

---

[4]*Point* is the location at which editing commands take effect. The cursor shows its position. Point always lies between two characters, although in some cases the shape of a cursor makes it look as if it were on top of a character rather than immediately before it.

[5]You could also use eval-region to evaluate the region of text that makes up the definition, or insert the definition into a file of its own and use load-file or other load function to evaluate the function, or use yet other means. *Load* is another term for evaluate.)

2.5.1. An Example of a Search Within a Buffer

This section describes an example of a function definition that is not interactive; it comes from the source code for GNU Emacs version 19.34. You can find the function in the file texnfo-upd.el. (In Emacs you can use the find-tag command to find the source of a function.)

This file provides various tools for creating and updating menus and nodes in a Texinfo file. *Texinfo* is a markup language used for writing documentation. Manuals written in Texinfo can be converted to HTML and read using a Web browser, converted to Info and read online using one of the Info readers, or printed as a typeset book. The original version of this chapter was written in Texinfo.

The texnfo-upd.el file provides updating commands. One of the necessary actions an updating command must do is locate the beginning of a node, that is, the beginning of a particular stretch of text.

In the texinfo-menu-first-node definition shown next, the Lisp interpreter works within a region of text specified by another function in the same file. Within the region, the texinfo-menu-first-node definition uses a regular expression search, which is a kind of search that looks for a particular pattern.

In this example, I first show the whole definition, as it appears in the Emacs sources, then I describe what each part does:

```
(defun texinfo-menu-first-node (beginning end)
  "Locate first node of the section the menu will be placed in.
Return position; do not move point.
The menu will be located just before this position.

First argument is the position of the beginning of the section
in which the menu will be located; second argument is the position
of the end of that region; it limits the search."

  (save-excursion
    (goto-char beginning)
    (forward-line 1)
    (re-search-forward "^@node" end t)
    (beginning-of-line)
    (point)))
```

The first line contains the symbol defun, which tells the Lisp interpreter that this is a function definition. Next comes the name for this definition. The name is quite long and self-explanatory. Like all other definitions involving Texinfo, it starts with texinfo; this is so neither you nor the computer confuse this definition with another definition for some other markup language.

After the name comes the argument list. This definition has two arguments, which use the somewhat self-explanatory words beginning and end—these words become self-explanatory when you learn that in this sort of programming, they customarily refer to the beginning and end of a region of text.

The following few lines are the definition's documentation. If you use the apropos command on a regular expression that matches the name, you will see the first line of the documentation. If you investigate the definition using C-h f (describe-function), you will see the function's full documentation.

This function definition has no interactive line because the function will be called by other functions, not interactively by a user.

Finally, the last part of the definition is the body, which is the code that does the job. I will repeat it here for your convenience:

```
(save-excursion
  (goto-char beginning)
  (forward-line 1)
  (re-search-forward "^@node" end t)
  (beginning-of-line)
  (point)))
```

The body starts with a parenthesis and a symbol—the body is a list. The first element of the list is a function that is carried out. save-excursion saves point, mark, and the current buffer and then evaluates the arguments to save-excursion. After the evaluations, save-excursion restores point, mark, and the current buffer.

Point is the location at which editing commands take effect and is the location of the cursor. *Mark* is another location; the text between point and mark is called *the region*, and many editing commands operate on such a region. The *current buffer* is where you are working. Emacs does not work on a file directly, but on a copy of it, called a buffer.

In brief, save-excursion makes sure Emacs does not change its focal point, even when it moves away temporarily.

The first thing Emacs does after save-excursion is

```
(goto-char beginning)
```

This means that Emacs moves point, temporarily, to the location recorded by beginning; it "goes to that character."

The next line is another list:

```
(forward-line 1)
```

This moves point forward one line and stops at the beginning of this next line. One consequence of this is that if the location indicated by beginning is in the middle of a line, point ends up at the beginning rather than the middle of the next line.

This forward-line command also means that the very first line to which point moves is not searched. It is not evident here, or even mentioned in the documentation, that the first node, which is what this function is searching for, is *not* on the first line of the section. Indeed, the first line often is the beginning of the *preceding* stretch of text, which is not the one that is wanted. Perhaps the documentation should be clearer, or perhaps it is clear enough if you read the source.

Regardless of the quality of the documentation, (forward-line 1) means to move forward one line.

The next line of code is

```
(re-search-forward "^@node" end t)
```

This tells the computer to undertake a regular expression search for the string of letters spelling @node that start at the beginning of a line, to ignore @node elsewhere in a line, and to extend the search no farther than the location recorded by end. (In Texinfo, @node marks the beginning of a particular type of stretch of text. For information on regular expression searches, see the section "Regular Expression Search" in *The GNU Emacs Manual*.)

The last two lines in the body are

```
(beginning-of-line)
(point)
```

Having found @node, (beginning-of-line) says to move point to the beginning of the line and (point) says to return that location. Finally, after returning the location of the beginning of the line containing @node, save-excursion causes Emacs to restore point to where it was.

Once you become accustomed to Emacs Lisp, it is much easier to read code such as this than to read a long-winded description of what it means. The purpose here has been to introduce you to a number of ideas, as well as to the basic outline of a simple function definition.

2.5.2. An Example: `multiply-by-seven`

Here is a very simple function that is interactive, takes an argument, and presents a message to the user:

```
(defun multiply-by-seven (number)
  "Multiply NUMBER by seven."
  (interactive "p")
  (message "The result is %d" (* 7 number)))
```

This function multiplies the number that is presented to it by seven and displays the answer to the user.

It follows the five-part template described previously.

After the symbol `defun` is the name of the definition, `multiply-by-seven`. Next is the argument list. In this definition, the list consists of one element, `number`. It is good practice to name arguments so they are more or less self-explanatory. You could use any symbol you want, such as `quoox`, but such a symbol, although perfectly clear to the computer, which does not recognize meaning, would be obscure to a human who searches for meaning.

After the argument list, starting on a line of its own (and indented two spaces), is the documentation. This documentation fits all on one line so you can read it all when you use the `apropos` or a similar command. By convention, the definition's argument is shown in uppercase letters so you can recognize it readily.

The third line is the interactive specification. It not only contains the symbol `interactive` but also an argument to that symbol, `"p"`. That argument is one of more than 20 alternative arguments that specify to the definition *how* information is passed to the function. In this instance, a lowercase *p* tells the Lisp interpreter that information will be passed to the function as a prefix argument that is converted to a number.

Thus, to use `multiply-by-seven` to multiply 5 by 7, you first evaluate the definition, and then type

```
C-u 5 M-x multiply-by-seven RET
```

where 5 is the prefix argument, introduced by `C-u`.

If you do this inside Emacs, you see

```
The result is 35
```

in the echo area.

Back to an examination of the function definition.

The body of the definition, the fifth part, is the single line

```
(message "The result is %d" (* 7 number)))
```

This line is a list. The first element of the list is the function `message`.

If you examine the documentation string for `message`, for example, by typing `C-h f message RET`, you find that it says, in part:

```
Print a one-line message at the bottom of the screen.

The first argument is a format control string,
and the rest are data to be formatted under control
of the string.  See 'format' for details.
```

In this case, the first argument to `message` is `"The result is %d"`. `message` displays `The result is` as written; and it substitutes the value computed by the second argument into the format specification, which is `%d`.

The second argument is the list `(* 7 number)`. This list looks very like the first example of adding two plus two! Indeed, it is very similar, except that instead of `+`, it uses `*`, which is the symbol for multiplication. `7` is a number and `number` is the local variable declared on the first line in the argument list to the function definition. When you interactively call `multiply-by-seven` with the prefix argument `5`, `number` takes on that value, so the list `(* 7 number))` becomes `(* 7 5))`. This list is evaluated, resulting in `35`, which is passed to the format specification, `%d`.

`35` replaces `%d` so the message you see at the bottom of your screen is

```
The result is 35
```

2.6. Variables

In Emacs Lisp, a symbol can have a value attached to it just as it can have a function definition attached to it. The two are different. The function definition is a set of instructions that a computer will obey. A value, on the other hand, is something, such as number or a name, that can vary (which is why such a symbol is called a variable). The value of a symbol can be any expression in Lisp, such as a symbol, number, list, or string. (Also, at the same time, a symbol can have two other things attached to it: a property list and its name.)

The following simple program sets the value of the symbol `foo` to `5` (it introduces the concepts of value and variable)[6]:

```
(setq foo 5)
```

---

[6]`foo` is what might be called a *conventional, meaningless symbol*. It is often used as a nonce variable or as the name of a scratch file. `foo` is the first of a series of such-like metasyntactic variables, the second of which is `bar`.

In this instance, the symbol foo is being perceived as a *variable*, that is, as a symbol that holds a value—in this case 5—that can be varied.

We can change the value of foo from 5 to 7 by evaluating this expression:

```
(setq foo 7)
```

After this expression is evaluated, the value of foo is 7. setq is a function that sets the first argument to the value of the second argument.

A variable need not be a number; it can be a string of letters. Such a string must be enclosed in double quotation marks, which tell the Lisp interpreter that the letters are a string.

For example, we can make the value of foo be the string of letters Hello, world by evaluating the following expression:

```
(setq foo "Hello, world")
```

To determine the value of a variable, simply evaluate the variable on its own, not inside parentheses; place your cursor immediately after the variable and type C-x C-e:

```
foo → "Hello, world"
```

where → means evaluates to and points to the value returned to by the expression being evaluated.

2.7. A Chest of Drawers

As we said earlier, the printed representation of Emacs Lisp that you and I read is not the same as the representation seen by the computer.

Indeed, a symbol, such as multiply-by-seven, which we defined previously, or buffer-name, which is a standard part of Emacs Lisp, has four components.

The components can best be understood through a somewhat fanciful representation.

Imagine a chest of four drawers:

- The first drawer has in it a piece of paper with the name of the symbol written on it; this is its *printed representation*.

- The second drawer has in it the definition of the symbol as a function, which is what is created with defun.

- The third drawer has in it the value of the symbol as a variable, which is what `setq` sets.

- The fourth drawer has in it a property list, a component we have not yet described. (See section 2.15.)

A single symbol can have any or all of these components. Almost always, it has its name (otherwise you cannot read it), and either a function definition or a value or both, and often a property list.

Here is an example that sets the value of the symbol `bouquet` to a list when you evaluate the expression:

```
(setq bouquet '(rose violet buttercup))
```

In this case, the name of the symbol, called in this context a variable, is `bouquet`; its value is the list `(rose violet buttercup)`.

Here is a representation of how it is held inside Emacs:

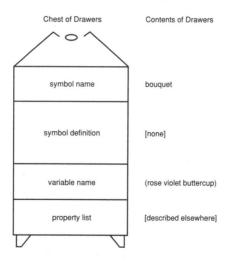

You can determine the value of a variable by evaluating it on its own:

```
bouquet      → (rose violet buttercup)
```

You can also find the contents of the value cell of a symbol—that is, determine its value—by evaluating a list in which the function is `symbol-value` and the first argument is `bouquet`:

```
(symbol-value 'bouquet)
     → (rose violet buttercup)
```

Now let's return to the function from a previous example, `multiply-by-seven`. To review, its function definition is

```
(defun multiply-by-seven (number)
  "Multiply NUMBER by seven."
  (interactive "p")
  (message "The result is %d" (* 7 number)))
```

Also, to illustrate that the same symbol can hold a value, we will set `multiply-by-seven` to the value `49` (we could just as well set it to a string such as `"Goodbye, world"`):

```
(setq multiply-by-seven 49)
```

In a chest of drawers diagram, `multiply-by-seven` looks like this:

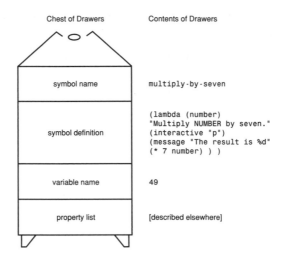

The symbol's name is `multiply-by-seven`, as expected.

The symbol's definition is very nearly like the definition we made using `defun`, except the list starts with `lambda` instead of `defun` and is not properly formatted. The list is not properly formatted to human eyes because the computer does not care; atoms are against parentheses or separated from others by whitespace. (Indeed, in the original, the expression is all on one line, but that would not fit in the diagram, so I fit it onto five lines.)

The list starts with the symbol `lambda`. This indicates that the list represents a function. You may think of the Lisp interpreter as a detective. He finds a chest of drawers hidden in the attic. In the first drawer is a piece of paper with a name on it, `multiply-by-seven`. "Ah ha!" he says, "We have the name of a symbol!" Then he finds in the second drawer a list that starts with `lambda`: "We have a function!" Because that function is in the drawer with the name `multiply-by-seven`, when you evaluate a list that starts with `multiply-by-seven`, its associated function definition is carried out.

A second function, such as `re-search-forward` is associated with a second set of drawers, and has its printed representation in the first drawer and a list, also starting with `lambda`, in the second. The lambda expression for `re-search-forward` is the definition that tells the computer what to do.

You can write a lambda expression on its own, as a list, like the one in the diagram. And you can evaluate it. In this context, the lambda expression is an anonymous function; that is, it is a function that has no name. It becomes a function with a name when the lambda expression is placed in the appropriate drawer of a chest that also has a name in its first drawer.

Returning to that chest of drawers in the diagram—the third drawer has a piece of paper in it with 49 written on it. This is the value associated with the name `multiply-by-seven`.

The fourth drawer in our example is empty; it could contain a property list, which is described in section 2.15.

Each symbol has four components. The four components can be discovered using the four functions `symbol-name`, `symbol-function`, `symbol-value`, and `symbol-plist`.

Here is an example:

```
(symbol-name 'multiply-by-seven)
     → "multiply-by-seven"

(symbol-function 'multiply-by-seven)
     → (lambda (number)
               "Multiply NUMBER by seven."
               (interactive "p")
               (message "The result is %d"
               (* 7 number)))

(symbol-value 'multiply-by-seven)
     → 49

(symbol-plist 'multiply-by-seven)
     → nil
```

nil, you will remember, is another representation of (), the empty list. It means there is nothing in the property list in this example.

2.8. Functions

We have been discussing functions as commands for the computer to do something.

More specifically, to quote the section "What Is a Function?" of *The GNU Emacs Lisp Reference Manual*:

> *A function is a rule for carrying on a computation given several values called arguments. The result of the computation is called the value of the function. The computation can also have side effects: lasting changes in the values of variables or the contents of data structures.*

Emacs Lisp has three kinds of functions: the sort that you and others write in Lisp using defun, the anonymous sort we mentioned previously that begin with lambda, and primitive functions that are written in the C programming language. These latter functions are called *built-in functions* or *subrs* (for subroutine) and are written to provide a low-level interface to operating system services or to run fast.

Technically speaking, a special form, such as defun, is *not* a function because it does not evaluate all its arguments in the usual way.

Likewise, a macro is not a function. A *macro* is a construct defined in Lisp that translates an expression you write into an equivalent expression that the Lisp interpreter evaluates instead. This way, you can do for yourself the sorts of things that special forms can do.

A function that contains an interactive declaration, as shown previously, is called a *command* because a user can invoke it interactively. Such a function can also be called indirectly as part of another function; in this context, the interactive declaration is ignored by the Lisp interpreter.

Finally, we should note that a keystroke command is a command bound to a key sequence. When you type in Emacs, you are calling functions.

2.9. The read-eval-print Loop and Side Effects

To get a better understanding of how Lisp works, let us consider the read-eval-print loop and side effects. Although you can write simple customizations or extensions without understanding this, the concepts clarify some aspects of Lisp that otherwise would be mysterious.

The Lisp interpreter runs as code those expressions that you give it. We say that it "evaluates" those expressions, but that way of describing the process is merely a handy shorthand. In actuality, the Lisp interpreter first *reads* and then *evaluates* the expression. The two activities are separate. Although often linked—often enough linked so we can use *evaluation* as a fair shorthand—they are not the same.

When the Lisp interpreter reads an expression, it first converts the printed representation into the representation used internally. Second, it evaluates the internal representation. This means that it computes the value that the expression returns, and undertakes any other actions, called *side effects*, that the expression may cause. Third, the interpreter sometimes converts the result of the second step into a form that a person can read, and prints that.

The phrase *side effects* may sound peculiar: so-called side effects are often actions that we humans think are important, such as moving the cursor or copying a file. The phrase comes from the notion of a computer as a person or, more recently, a machine for undertaking calculations. It is a sad accident of history that the word *computer*, originally the term for a person who did arithmetic calculations, should come to be the term applied to a type of machine that does all sorts of symbolic transformations, not merely arithmetic.

Initially side effects were other things that a computational machine could do, but were not considered its primary purpose. Moreover, Lisp was based on the premise that what you see as the result of evaluation, the value returned, is what you want. (Or, if you personally do not want to see a value that is an intermediate part of a calculation, the computer does, because it needs that value to complete its calculation.)

For example, when you evaluate the overall expression (+ 2 (+ 1 1)), the first list to be evaluated is (+ 1 1). You, the human reader, do not want to see the result of that; you want to see the result of the whole expression. But for the computer to calculate the whole expression, it has to calculate the (+ 1 1) expression first. Then, instead of passing that value to you, it uses it itself.

However, and this is very important, *you* could have looked at the result of that first expression. Indeed, when you are writing a program, you do look at the parts, and you do look at the values returned, or figure out in general what they will be. This is how you build programs, small part by small part into bigger wholes.

The expression (+ 2 (+ 1 1)) does not have any side effects. It only returns the number 4.

If you evaluate the expression, the number 4 is printed; then the Lisp interpreter waits to read an another expression, convert it to its internal form, so it can compute its value, and print that. Hence the term *loop* in the phrase, read-eval-print loop.

But that is not all. In addition to returning values, the one-time primary task of a Lisp interpreter, it has another job, which is to do other actions, all sorts of other actions: copy files, move the cursor, delete text from the screen, and so on.

For example, when you evaluate (or the computer evaluates for you) the expression:

```
(re-search-forward "^@node" end t)
```

the value that the expression returns is the location in the buffer that is the end of the occurrence found. At the same time, as a side effect, the expression causes the computer to move point to that location.

You do not always want a side effect. In the program discussed previously, texinfo-menu-first-node, the save-excursion expression is used to undo this side effect caused by re-search-forward: save-excursion causes Emacs to save point's initial location and later to return it there. In addition, texinfo-menu-first-node is designed to return the location of the beginning of the line containing the @node, so the last two lines of the definition move point to the beginning of the line and then return that location. This is an example of a function where you mostly do *not* want side effects, and Emacs makes an effort to avoid them.

On the other hand, many times you do want the side effects and not the returned value. For example, when you use Emacs as an editor, you create, move, change, delete, and save text of one sort or another, whether it be a novel, a mail message, or a program. Most of what you see are the results of side effects. When you type M-f to move forward word by word, you hope to see the cursor move forward; you are not interested in the value returned. When you use sort to alphabetize a list, you do not want the value returned, but you want the alphabetized list.

In those many situations in which you do not want to see the value returned, but only the consequences of the side effect, Emacs prevents clutter and does not show you the value returned.

As a practical matter, when writing Emacs Lisp, it is fairly easy to learn when to and when not to use side effects. `re-search-forward` moves point to the end of the occurrence found. If you want to see point moved to that location, fine, leave point there; if you do not want point moved, then use `save-excursion`, as illustrated previously.

In brief, Lisp has two aspects: that understood through the `read-eval-print` loop, in which computations return a value; and that understood through side effects, in which the computer does something else beside compute.

2.10. Types of Variables

A *variable* is a name used in a program to stand for a value. A variable has a standard place in which its current value is always found—the value cell of a symbol. (Earlier, we described this value cell as one of the drawers in our chest of drawers metaphor.)

Emacs Lisp has three different types of variable: global variables, local variables, and buffer-local variables.[7]

Global variables are, as the name suggests, in effect throughout your Lisp system, except when overridden locally. Thus, if you set the value of `bar` to `"Better Living With Lisp!"`, `bar` has that value everywhere in your Lisp system, unless it is superseded locally.

Local variables exist in just a part of a program; hence the name. They are used temporarily. When you define a local variable with the same name as a global variable, the value of the global variable is saved and stashed away; the new value takes its place in the symbol's value cell. In the jargon, the new value *shadows* the old value, so it is *not visible*. When the local value ceases to be, the global value is placed back into the value cell; that value is restored to the variable.

---

[7]There are a few variables of a fourth type, whose values are local to the current terminal; you will not come across these terminal-local variables unless you run Emacs on more than one X Window display. See the section "Multiple Displays" in *The GNU Emacs Lisp Reference Manual.*

Buffer-local variables apply only to one buffer. They provide an important means for creating custom modes. For example, both C mode and Lisp mode set the variable paragraph-start to a value different from Text or Texinfo mode. They make the variable buffer local and set it to the value for that mode. Two ways to make a variable buffer local are to use make-local-variable, which only affects the current buffer, leaving all others to continue to share the global value, and make-variable-buffer-local, which makes a variable buffer local in all buffers, but starts out with the global value of the variable.

While global and local variables are found in most programming languages, buffer-local variables are much less common.

2.10.1. defvar and defconst

Commonly, you specify the initial value of a global variable with the special form defvar, as in this example from the source for ada-mode.el:

```
(defvar ada-language-version 'ada95
  "*Do we program in 'ada83' or 'ada95'?")
```

In this case, ada-language-version is set to ada95, and the variable has documentation written about it that you can access using C-h v (describe-variable).

Moreover, as illustrated in this example, the asterisk at the beginning of the documentation string indicates that the variable is a user option, which means that you can easily set the variable using the commands set-variable, edit-options, or customize.

Interestingly, and confusingly if you are not prepared, defvar does not set a value if the variable already has a value; it only sets a value if the variable is not set, (that is, it is void). This way, you can set a variable yourself ahead of time, before loading the library[8] that uses defvar. Otherwise, you could have your settings changed under you by what you load.

The nearly similar form defconst unconditionally initializes a variable. defconst changes your setting under you. If you want to change the value of a defconst on startup, first load the library containing it before you set your new value.

---

[8]A *library* is a collection of related function definitions and other expressions, often contained in one file, but sometimes in several.

As a practical matter, defconst is for variables that are not normally intended to be changed, that is, for constants. You *can* change a value set with defconst, but normally you would not. Here is an example of a value you would not want to change:

```
(defconst pi 3.14159 "Pi to six places.")
```

On the other hand, also as a practical matter, the source for c-mode.el makes it convenient for users to change the indentation because so many people have strongly held yet different notions of what the constant should be:

```
(defconst c-indent-level 2
   "*Indentation of C statements with respect to containing block.")
```

defvar and defconst themselves serve three purposes. They inform you and other people who read the code that the programmer intends to use certain symbols as variables or constants. They tell this to the Lisp system, while providing default values and documentation. Finally, they provide information to utilities such as etags and make-docfile, which create databases of the functions, variables, and constants in a program.

2.10.2. setq

Within a function you generally set a variable using setq, unless you are using a let form or passing the value to the arguments of a definition, both of which create local variables. Variables set with setq are global, unless they are local or buffer local.

Here is an example:

```
(setq counter 0)              → 0
```

This sets the value cell of the symbol counter to 0. The following sets the value cell of the symbol counter to 1 plus whatever the value of counter was earlier; in this case, the earlier value was 0:

```
(setq counter (+ 1 counter))   → 1
```

The following sets the value cell of the symbol counter to 1 plus the previous value; in this case, the previous value was 1:

```
(setq counter (+ 1 counter))   → 2
```

In more detail, here is what happens when you evaluate:

```
(setq counter (+ 1 counter))
```

The Lisp interpreter first evaluates the innermost list; this is the addition. To evaluate this list, it must evaluate the variable counter and the number 1. When it evaluates the variable counter, it receives its current value. It passes this value and the number 1 to the +, which adds them together. The sum is then returned as the value of the inner list and passed to setq, which sets the variable counter to this new value.

2.10.3. Passing an Argument

When you pass an argument to a definition, you create a local variable.

Thus, when you define a function:

```
(defun add-37 (number)
  "Add 37 to NUMBER."
  (interactive "p")
  (message "The new number is: %d!" (+ 37 number)))
```

number becomes a local variable, local to the function. You can set the value of number to some other value outside the function, using defvar, defconst, or setq, but inside the function (and inside any functions called by the function, none in this example), the local value of number will shadow the global value.

Here is an example in which number is set to 3, but the local value used by the preceding function definition is 5:

```
(setq number 3)          ; Global value of NUMBER is 3

(add-37 5)               ; Local  value of NUMBER is 5
"The new number is: 42!"
```

2.10.4. A let Expression

Another way to specify a local variable is to use let. A let expression binds variables to values locally, for use within an expression, but then, on leaving the expression, the Lisp interpreter restores the values of the next higher level. (Usually, the next higher level is the level of the global variables, but a let expression may be embedded in a let expression, in which case the enclosing expression becomes the next higher level.)

Here is an example. First, the two symbols location and temperature are set to "Venus" and "hot" as global variables using the built-in function setq. Second, a let expression sets the variables locally to "Pluto" and "cold". Finally, the two symbols are written alone, not within parentheses.

When you evaluate each list in sequence, first you see the value "Venus" for location and then "hot" for temperature. After evaluating the let expression, you see the value "On Pluto, it is cold.". Finally, when you evaluate `location` and `temperature`, you see `"Venus"` and `"hot"`, their global values. (Here, as usual, `->` may be read as *evaluates to*; the glyph points to the value returned by evaluating the expression.)

```
(setq location "Venus")    → "Venus"
(setq temperature "hot")   → "hot"

(let ((location "Pluto")
      (temperature "cold"))
   (format "On %s, it is %s." location temperature))
                           → "On Pluto, it is cold."

location                   → "Venus"
temperature                → "hot"
```

In this example, `location` and `temperature` are first set as global variables. Then the `let` expression binds `location` to `"Pluto"` and `temperature` to `"cold"` as local variables within it. When the `format` function creates a string, using `location` and `temperature` as arguments, the values they hold are `"Pluto"` and `"cold"`, which are the local values. Finally, when the Lisp interpreter evaluates `location` and `temperature` *outside* the `let` expression, it returns their values as global variables.

Technically speaking, a `let` expression is a list of three parts. The first part is the symbol `let`. The second part is a list, called a *varlist*, each element of which is either a symbol by itself or, as in the example, a two-element list, the first element of which is a symbol. The third part of the `let` expression is the body of the `let`, in this case a `format` expression. The body usually consists of one or more lists.

The symbols in the varlist are the variables that are given initial, local values by the `let` special form. Symbols by themselves are given the initial value `nil`, and each symbol that is the first element of a two-element list is bound to the value that is returned when the Lisp interpreter evaluates the second element.

A template for a `let` expression looks like this:

```
(let varlist body ...)
```

In programming, you will use `let` expressions frequently.

2.10.5. Buffer-Local Variables

Buffer-local variables are frequently used to customize a mode, which sets up Emacs for work of a particular sort. For example, C mode makes it easier to write code in the C programming language. Ada mode makes it easier to write code in the Ada programming language. Calc mode provides a sophisticated calculator and mathematical tool. Calendar mode provides astronomical (Julian) day numbers and other conventional calendars. Mail mode is for mail. W3 mode is for Web browsing. Gnus mode is for reading net news and mail. Emacs has a rather large number of different modes.

Each buffer has one major mode at any time (but may have several minor modes). The simplest mode is Fundamental, which has no mode-specific redefinitions or variable settings. In Fundamental mode, each option is in its default state.

Consider Perl, which helps you write Perl scripts. You can change a buffer to Perl mode by typing M-x perl-mode or arrange to enter Perl mode automatically with certain files.[9]

When you type M-x perl-mode, or otherwise start Perl mode, the first thing Emacs does is kill all existing local variables, which switches the buffer to Fundamental mode. Perl mode builds on top of this foundation.

Perl mode sets the mode-name buffer-local variable to the string "Perl" and the major-mode buffer local variable to the symbol perl-mode. It makes comment-start a buffer local variable with the expression

```
(make-local-variable 'comment-start)
```

and sets its value with the expression

```
(setq comment-start "# ")
```

You will note that despite the name, make-local-variable makes a variable *buffer local*; it does not create what is called a local rather than a buffer-local variable. The word *buffer* was left out of make-local-variable in order to make the function name shorter.

Also, because comment-start is used in more than 20 different modes, it might have been better to have used the function make-variable-buffer-local just once when Emacs was first written; but Emacs grows incrementally, and each person who wrote a new mode decided to be careful and make comment-start a local variable.

---

[9]One way to enter Perl mode automatically is to add # -*-Perl-*- to the first line of your Perl script so it looks like this:

```
#!/usr/bin/perl--# -*-Perl-*-
```

A second way is to arrange that Emacs recognize an appropriate filename suffix, such as .pl, as indicating a file to be visited in Perl mode. Similarly, .c indicates a file to be visited in C mode. The source file, perl-mode.el explains how to do this. (And because you have Emacs, which you need to run Emacs Lisp, you have access to this source file, an advantage of the form of distribution used by Emacs.) You can also consult the section "How Major Modes Are Chosen" in *The GNU Emacs Lisp Reference Manual*.

In Perl mode, `comment-start`, `comment-end`, and others are all buffer-local variables. You can examine how buffer-local variables are created and used in more detail by looking at your copy of the `perl-mode.el` file or another mode-creating source file.

2.11. Sequencing

Most commonly, in Emacs Lisp, the Lisp interpreter evaluates expressions in the order in which they appear in the text, that is, left to right, top to bottom. However, inner expressions are evaluated first because the results they produce may be needed by the enclosing expression. Some forms, such as conditionals, evaluate enclosed expressions in uncommon ways.

To ensure that a series of expressions is evaluated in sequence, use the `progn` special form. Its template looks like this:

```
(progn first-expression second-expression ...)
```

Each expression is evaluated in turn—first, second and so on, in that order. The value of the last expression becomes the value of the entire `progn`.

`progn` is often used in the `then` part of an `if` expression, because that part can consist of only one list; a subsequent list or lists, if any, belong to the `else` part.

2.12. Conditionals

Conditionals provide choice. In a conditional, depending on circumstances, one expression or another will be evaluated.

Emacs Lisp has two conditional forms: `if` and `cond` (which comes from *conditional*).

The basic idea behind an `if` special form is:

> *if* a test is true,
>> *then* an expression is evaluated.
> *or else,* if the test is not true,
>> evaluate a different expression.

The words `then` and `else` are not part of the Lisp expression, but you can read the expression as if they were there.

The template is

```
(if true-or-false-test
    action-to-carry-out-if-the-test-returns-true)
  action-to-carry-out-if-the-test-returns-false)
```

For example, in the following, the test determines whether the value of the variable equals the symbol fierce. If it does, Emacs displays the message about the tiger; if not, Emacs displays a message saying "It's not.":

```
(if (equal characteristic 'fierce)      ; if part
        (message "It's a tiger!")        ; then part
    (message "It's not."))               ; else part
```

Of course, the value of the variable characteristic must be set before the test can occur. An if is part of a larger context.

The second, less frequently used, conditional in Emacs Lisp is cond, which is a generalized case statement.

cond provides a choice among any number of alternatives, only one of which is chosen.

The template for cond looks like this:

```
(cond
  ((first-true-or-false-test first-consequent)
   (second-true-or-false-test second-consequent)
   (third-true-or-false-test third-consequent)
   ...)
```

When a cond expression is evaluated, each test is subject to being evaluated, in textual order. If a test returns a value that is true (that is, any value that is not nil), then the consequent of that test is evaluated. Otherwise, the consequent is not evaluated, but is ignored. After a test returns true and its consequent is evaluated, the remaining tests and consequents are ignored—they are not evaluated. The Lisp interpreter evaluates each test in turn, until one returns true; then it evaluates its consequent and disregards the rest.

Here is an example:

```
(cond
  ((equal characteristic 'fierce)
   (message "It's a tiger!"))
  ((equal characteristic 'cuddly)
   (message "It's a pussy cat!"))
  ((equal characteristic 'barks)
   (message "It's a dog!")))
```

Suppose you set the value of characteristic to cuddly by evaluating:

```
(setq characteristic 'cuddly)
```

Then you evaluate the conditional. First the Lisp interpreter tests whether the value of characteristic evaluates to fierce, but that is false, so it ignores the message about the tiger. Then it tests whether the value of characteristic evaluates to cuddly; that is true, so it evaluates the expression saying "It's a pussy cat!". The interpreter ignores the test about barking and the expression about the dog.

2.12.1. and, or, and not

and, or, and not are often used together with if and cond to express complicated conditions; they can also be used alone.

When the Lisp interpreter sees and, it evaluates the arguments to and in order. If all the arguments return a value that is true (any non-nil value), then the and expression as a whole returns the value of the last argument. But if any argument is false (returns nil), the interpreter does *not* evaluate any remaining arguments and returns nil (for false) immediately for the whole expression.

or is, so to speak, the reverse of and. When the Lisp interpreter sees or, it evaluates the arguments to or in order. If any argument returns a true value, then the or expression returns that value and none of the remaining arguments is evaluated. If all the arguments return false, then the or expression returns nil.

not tests whether its argument returns a true value; if so, it returns nil; but if the test returns a nil value, the not expression returns t.

Here is an example of and taken from the code for the function forward-paragraph, which is in the Emacs Lisp source file paragraphs.el.

The forward-paragraph command moves the cursor forward to the end of the current paragraph (this is the outcome we want, yet it is called a side effect).

The and expression is part of the varlist of a let* expression. (A let* expression is like a let expression, except that each element in the varlist is evaluated in sequence, and the values resulting from an earlier evaluation can be used later in the varlist.)

In the function definition for forward-paragraph, a variable called fill-prefix-regexp is given a value if and only if

- A fill-prefix exists[10]

- It is a string of letters

- It should be not be ignored

---

[10] A fill-prefix consists of characters at the beginning of a line that are similar for all lines for a paragraph, such as blanks for an indent, or angle brackets for one form of email quotation. The use of a fill-prefix in forward-paragraph means that you can jump to the end of an indented paragraph, or the end of one marked on each line with > or another prefix.

Later in the function definition, the variable is used in an `if` expression, and, if it is not `nil`, the variable is also used to tell the command which lines are part of the paragraph and which are not.

Here is the `and` expression:

```
(and fill-prefix
     (not (equal fill-prefix ""))
     (not paragraph-ignore-fill-prefix)
     (regexp-quote fill-prefix))
```

Here is what the parts mean:

- `fill-prefix`—When this variable is evaluated, the value of the fill-prefix, if any, is returned. If there is no fill-prefix, this variable returns `nil`. This is to check whether there is a fill-prefix.

- `(not (equal fill-prefix ""))`—This expression checks whether an existing fill-prefix is an empty string, that is, a string with no characters in it. An empty string is not a useful fill-prefix.

- `(not paragraph-ignore-fill-prefix)`—This expression returns `nil` if the variable `paragraph-ignore-fill-prefix` has been turned on by being set to a true value such as `t`.

- `(regexp-quote fill-prefix)`—This is the last argument to the `and` function. If all the arguments to the `and` are true, the value resulting from evaluating this expression is returned by the `and` expression and bound to the variable `fill-prefix-regexp`.

The result of evaluating this `and` expression successfully is that `fill-prefix-regexp` is bound to the value of `fill-prefix` as modified by the `regexp-quote` function. `regexp-quote` reads a string and returns a regular expression that exactly matches the string and matches nothing else. This means that `fill-prefix-regexp` is set to a value that exactly matches the fill-prefix if the fill-prefix exists. Otherwise, the variable is set to `nil`.

An `or` expression is often used in a manner that is quite like an `if` expression. Here, for example, is an extract from the source for the `insert-buffer` function definition. `insert-buffer` is a command whose source is found in the `simple.el` file; the command inserts the contents of a second buffer into the current buffer.

The documentation says

```
"Insert after point the contents of BUFFER.
Puts mark after the inserted text.
BUFFER may be a buffer or a buffer name."
```

The or expression checks whether the argument you pass to insert-buffer, which is the variable buffer, is a buffer or the name of one. (Note that the same symbol, buffer, is being used in two ways in this instance—either as a buffer or as a name. If you are confused by the distinction between a buffer and its name, consider the difference between you personally being introduced to the editor of this volume and your name being mentioned to him. The former is you, the latter is a reference to you.)

The or expression in insert-buffer looks like this:

```
(or (bufferp buffer)
    (setq buffer (get-buffer buffer)))
```

The first argument to or is the expression (bufferp buffer).[11] This expression returns true (a non-nil value) if the buffer is actually a buffer, and not just the name of a buffer.

If the argument is a buffer, the or expression returns this true value and does not evaluate the next expression—and this is fine because the commands do not want to do anything to the value of buffer if it really is a buffer.

On the other hand, if the value of (bufferp buffer) is nil, which it is if the value of buffer is the name of a buffer, the Lisp interpreter evaluates the next element of the or expression. This is the expression:

```
(setq buffer (get-buffer buffer))
```

This expression returns a non-nil value that is the value to which it sets the variable buffer—and this value is a buffer itself, not the name of a buffer.

The result of all this is that the symbol buffer is always bound to a buffer itself rather than to the name of a buffer. All this is necessary because the next part of the code (not shown here) works only with a buffer itself, not with the name of a buffer.

---

[11]The p in bufferp stands for *predicate*. In the jargon used by early Lisp researchers, a predicate refers to a function that determines whether a property is true or false. bufferp determines whether it is true that its argument is a buffer—hence this use of the naming convention.

As for or being like if, the expression could have been written like this:

```
(if (not (bufferp buffer))
    (setq buffer (get-buffer buffer)))
```

This would have produced the same result, but is longer and less elegant.

2.13. while Loops and Recursion

Emacs Lisp has two primary ways to cause an expression, or a series of expressions, to be evaluated repeatedly: One uses a while loop, and the other uses *recursion*.

Repetition is valuable. For example, to move forward four sentences, you need only write a program that moves forward one sentence and then repeats the process an additional three times.

In Emacs Lisp, while loops are used more frequently than recursion because they tend to be faster. (In some other dialects of Lisp, recursion is as fast as or faster than while loops.)

2.13.1. while

The while special form tests whether the value returned by evaluating its first argument is true or false. If true, the Lisp interpreter evaluates the remaining arguments of the expression and then again tests whether the first argument to while is true or false. If false, the Lisp interpreter skips the rest of the expression (the *body* of the expression) and does not evaluate it.

The template for a while expression looks like this:

```
(while true-or-false-test
    body...)
```

So long as the *true-or-false-test* of the while expression returns a true value when it is evaluated, the body is repeatedly evaluated. This process is called a loop because the Lisp interpreter repeats the same thing again and again.

The value returned by evaluating a while is the value of *true-or-false-test*. Consequently, a while loop that evaluates without error returns nil or false regardless of whether it has looped 1 or 100 times or none at all. A while expression that evaluates successfully never returns a true value! This means that a while loop is always evaluated for its side effects.

A common way to control a while loop is to test whether a list has any elements. If it does, the loop is repeated; but if it does not, the repetition is ended.

Here is an example of a `while` loop:

```
(defun print-elements-of-list (list)
  "Print each element of LIST on a line of its own."
  (while list
    (print (car list))
    (setq list (cdr list))))
```

The `while` loop is the body of a function that prints the elements of a list, one after another, each on a line of its own.

The first four parts of the function definition are the special form `defun`, the name of the function, `print-elements-of-list`, the argument list, with one local variable called `list`, and the documentation string.

The body of the function definition consists of a `while` loop.

The test for the `while` loop consists of just the local variable, `list`. When the `while` expression is evaluated, the Lisp interpreter first evaluates the variable `list`. If the list is empty, it returns an empty list, `()`, which is `nil`, or false. But if the list is not empty, it returns a non-`nil` value, which is understood by the Lisp interpreter as true. Hence, the test part of this `while` loop tests true so long as the list has elements.

The second argument of the `while` loop (which is the first element of its body) is the expression

```
(print (car list))
```

This expression consists of the function `print`, whose intended action is self-explanatory, and the expression `(car list)`, which is not self-explanatory.

To understand `car` and its sibling, `cdr`, it is necessary to take a short detour. This is worth doing since `car` and `cdr` (and a third function, `cons`) are fundamental to Lisp.

2.13.2. car, cdr, cons: Fundamental Functions

In Lisp, `car`, `cdr`, and `cons` are fundamental functions. The `cons` function is used to construct lists, and the `car` and `cdr` functions are used to take them apart: `car` returns the first element of a list, and `cdr` returns the rest of the list.

The name of the `cons` function is not unreasonable: It is an abbreviation of the word *construct*. The origins of the names for `car` and `cdr`, on the other hand, are esoteric: `car` is an acronym from the phrase *contents of the address part of the register*; and `cdr` (pronounced "could-er") is an acronym from the phrase *contents of the decrement part of the register*.

These phrases refer to specific pieces of hardware on the very early computer on which the original Lisp was developed. Besides being obsolete, the phrases have been completely irrelevant for more than 30 years to anyone thinking about Lisp. Nonetheless, although a few brave scholars have begun to use more reasonable names for these functions, such as *first* and *rest*, the old terms are still in use. Because the terms are used in the Emacs Lisp source code, we will use them also.

The car of a list is, quite simply, the first item in the list. Thus the car of the list (rose violet daisy buttercup) is rose. Here is an example:

```
(car '(rose violet daisy buttercup))
     → rose
```

The cdr of a list is the rest of the list, that is, the cdr function returns the part of the list that follows the first item:

```
(cdr '(rose violet daisy buttercup))
     → (violet daisy buttercup)
```

As mentioned previously, car returns the first element of a list, and cdr returns the rest of the list.

cons (which I mention here for completeness) is used to construct lists (that car and cdr can take apart).

Here are three examples of cons expressions:

```
(cons 'maple '())          → (maple)

(cons 'oak '(maple))       → (oak maple)

(cons 'pine '(oak maple))  → (pine oak maple)
```

Starting with an empty list, (), in each example, one element is added, or more precisely, prepended, to the list. The first cons expression returns the one element list (maple); the second cons expression returns the two-element list (oak maple); and the third cons expression returns the three-element list (pine oak maple).

2.13.3. while, Continued

Now we return to our example of a while loop. Here is the function definition again, for review:

```
(defun print-elements-of-list (list)
  "Print each element of LIST on a line of its own."
  (while list
    (print (car list))
    (setq list (cdr list))))
```

The (car list) expression returns the first element of the variable list, if any, and print prints that element.

In the next line, (setq list (cdr list)), the Lisp interpreter interprets the (cdr list) expression first. This expression returns the second and subsequent elements of the list or an empty list if there are no such elements. setq then sets the variable list to this new value; it sets the value to a shorter list than it had before, to the old list minus its first element.

After the Lisp interpreter evaluates the last line of the body, it evaluates the while expression again. But this time the test expression, the first argument to while, has a different value than before; it has the value of the cdr of its previous value. It is a list still, but shortened by one element.

The looping continues until the variable list is an empty list. Then, when it is tested, the empty list, (), is returned. This is equivalent to nil and means false. At this point, the while loop stops looping and exits.

Here is an example:

```
(setq animals '(gazelle lion tiger))
```

First, setq sets the variable animals to a list of three animals. (Presumably, the variable animals is a global variable, but we might have made it buffer local using the make-local-variable or make-variable-buffer-local functions.) We create and set this variable just to give us something to work with.

Next, we evaluate the function definition for print-elements-of-list; this creates (or loads) the definition.

Finally, we evaluate the expression:

```
(print-elements-of-list animals)
```

which returns the following:

```
gazelle
lion
tiger
nil
```

Each element of the list is printed on a line of its own (that is what the function print does) and then the value returned by the function is printed. Because the last expression in the function is the while loop, and because while loops always return nil, a nil is printed after the last element of the list.

Here is what the `while` loop did:

1. The `while` expression tested `list`, which at first had the value (gazelle lion tiger), which is non-`nil`, or true.

2. The Lisp interpreter evaluated the first expression in the body, which printed the first element of the list, `gazelle`.

3. Next, the Lisp interpreter evaluated the second expression in the body, which set the value of the variable to the `cdr` of the list, to (lion tiger).

4. The loop looped. Each time the loop looped, the list became shorter.

5. The list became an empty list, and the loop stopped.

Instead of `cdr`ing down a list, you can write a `while` loop with a numeric counter or some other mechanism that tests true as long as it should test true, and then tests false when the loop should stop.

For an easy introduction to `while` loops, see the section "`while`" in *Programming in Emacs Lisp: An Introduction*.

2.13.4. Recursion

A recursive function contains at least two expressions. In one of them, a test of the argument tells the Lisp interpreter to stop evaluating the function and leave it. In the other expression, the Lisp interpreter evaluates the same function, but provides it with a systematically different argument. The sequence of arguments passed to each call of the function changes in such a way that eventually a test of the argument tells the Lisp interpreter to stop evaluating the function and leave it.

For example, a function may continue to be called as long as a list has elements, but stop when the list is empty. Each call is on a shorter version of the list.

Here is such an example. This functions prints the elements of a list the `while` loop example did:

```
(setq animals '(gazelle lion tiger))

(defun print-elements-recursively (list)
  "Print each element of LIST on a line of its own.
Uses recursion."
  (print (car list))                    ; body
  (if list                              ; do-again-test
      (print-elements-recursively       ; recursive call
       (cdr list))))                    ; next-step-expression

(print-elements-recursively animals)
```

The `print-elements-recursively` function first prints the first element of the list, the `car` of the list. Then, if the list is not empty, the function invokes itself, but gives itself as its argument, not the whole list, but the second and subsequent elements of the list, the `cdr` of the list.

When this evaluation occurs, the function prints the first element of the list it receives as its argument (which is the second element of the original list). Then the `if` expression is evaluated again, and when it evaluates to true, the function calls itself with the `cdr` of the list with which it is invoked. The second time around, this is the `cdr` of the `cdr` of the original list.

Each time the function invokes itself, it invokes itself on a shorter version of the original list. Eventually, the function invokes itself on an empty list. The `print` function prints the empty list as `nil`. Next, the conditional expression tests the value of `list`. Since the value of `list` is `nil`, the `if` expression tests false so the then part is not evaluated. The function as a whole then returns `nil`. Consequently, you see `nil` twice when you evaluate the function:

```
gazelle
lion
tiger
nil
nil
```

2.14. Macros

The `defmacro` built-in function allows you define new features in Emacs Lisp.

A *macro* is defined somewhat like a function, except that instead of telling the Lisp interpreter how to compute a value, a macro definition tells the interpreter how to create a different Lisp expression from its arguments; that new expression computes the value. The new expression is the *expansion* of the macro.

A macro definition has up to four parts:

- Name

- List of arguments

- Documentation

- Body

This sequence is like that of a function definition, except a macro has no "interactive" part.

For example, the following macro definition defines a construct to increment a variable, as in a counter. It adds one to the variable:

```
(defmacro inc (variable)
    (list 'setq variable (list '+ 1 variable)))
```

When evaluated, the macro definition returns inc, which you use as a function:

1. First set a variable:

    ```
    (setq foo 3)     → 3
    ```

2. Then increment the variable:

    ```
    (inc foo)        → 4
    ```

    Note that the action of incrementing is a side effect.

3. Evaluate the variable:

    ```
    foo              → 4
    ```

When a macro is defined, the Lisp interpreter does not return a function definition; instead, it returns an alternate expression, the expansion of the macro.

The macroexpand built-in function shows expansion:

```
(defmacro inc (variable)
    (list 'setq variable (list '+ 1 variable)))

(macroexpand '(inc foo))        -> (setq foo (+ 1 foo))
```

Put another way, the expression (inc foo) is a shorthand for the expression (setq foo (+ 1 foo)); it is the latter expression that the Lisp interpreter ends up evaluating, after first internally expanding the macro.

In any situation where you use a macro, you could have done without, except that a macro often simplifies writing what is otherwise a complex and repeated set of forms.

2.14.1. The list Built-in Function

list, as you might suspect from its name, creates a list out of its arguments. It can take any number of arguments, each of which becomes an element of the list created; or it can take zero arguments.

The lists specified in the body of a macro definition are created using the built-in function `list` or else using the macro backquote (which is described in the next section).

```
(list)                      → nil

(list 'foo 'bar)            → (foo bar)
```

Note that `list` creates a list of its arguments, whereas `cons` prepends its first argument to an already existing list:

```
(list 'blue 'violet)        → (blue violet)

(cons 'green '(blue violet))  → (green blue violet)
```

2.14.2. Backquote

Macro definitions often consist of large list structures that are hard to write and hard to read once written. They would be too complex for use, except for a macro and a special marker that allow you to evaluate the elements of a list selectively.

The macro is called *backquote* and looks like ` rather than like a regular quote '. The special marker looks like a comma ,.

Here is a quoted list; when evaluated, the list is returned as-is:

```
'(red (+ 2 3) orange)       → (red (+ 2 3) orange)
```

Here is a backquoted list, with one element marked with a comma ,; when evaluated, the unmarked parts of the list are returned as-is, but the marked element is evaluated:

```
`(red ,(+ 2 3) orange)      → (red 5 orange)
```

This latter example works exactly as if you had used `list` and then *quoted* (not backquoted) the elements that were to stay the same:

```
(list 'red (+ 2 3) 'orange) → (red 5 orange)
```

In a sense, backquote ` and the special marker , are the "photographic negative" of `list` and quote.

Another special marker ,@ "splices" an evaluated value such that its elements enter the list at the same level as the other elements of the list, rather than as elements inside their own list.

For more information, see the section "Macros" in *The GNU Emacs Lisp Reference Manual*.

2.15. Property Lists

A *property list*, or *plist* for short, is a list of paired elements stored in the property list cell of a symbol. Each of the pairs associates a property name (usually a symbol) with a property or value.

Often, property lists are used to record information about a symbol, such as its documentation as a variable or the name of the file where it was defined.

For example, suppose we want to say that the characteristic of tigers is that they are fierce and the characteristic of dogs is that they bark. We can do that with property lists this way:

```
(put 'tiger 'characteristic 'fierce)

(put 'dog 'characteristic 'barks)
```

Here is the template:

```
(put symbol property value)
```

put puts on the symbol's property a value. The value can be a symbol, a string, or any other kind of Lisp object.

Then, to get the characteristic, evaluate expressions such as the following:

```
(get 'tiger 'characteristic)    → fierce

(get 'dog 'characteristic)      → barks
```

Here is the template:

```
(get symbol property)
```

A more subtle use of property lists is illustrated by the Emacs Lisp code for converting a Texinfo file into Info. In the texnfmt.el file, you can see how the value of a property is extracted from a symbol and then executed as code. Although this may seem at first a rather roundabout way to evaluate a function, its advantage is that the method permits people to add new features to Texinfo easily and safely.

2.16. Keymaps

A *keymap* tells Emacs what definition to call when you press a key or mouse button. Thus, in Text mode, typing the a key runs self-insert-command, which inserts the letter a. Typing the keychord C-a runs beginning-of-line, which moves point to the beginning of the current line.

A key such as C-x 4 b (switch-to-buffer-other-window) is a three-event sequence. The first two events make up the *prefix key*. In this case, the prefix key consists of pressing the C-x key and then the 4 key. The *complete key* consists of the whole sequence.

Often, two or three keymaps are *active* (in use) in a buffer at the same time. First, there is the *global map*, which is shared by all buffers. Second, there is the *local keymap* associated with the buffer's major mode, such as Text mode, C mode, Mail mode, or Calc mode. Finally, there may be a *minor mode keymap*, such as Outline minor mode. Local bindings shadow (overrule) the corresponding global bindings, and minor mode bindings shadow the local and global bindings.

You can set a key in several different ways. Most simply, you can use the global-set-key function in your .emacs initialization file.

Here, for example, we rebind C-h a from the default function command-apropos to apropos:

```
;;; Use 'apropos' instead of 'command-apropos'
(global-set-key "\C-ha" 'apropos)
```

command-apropos shows all the commands, that is, all interactively callable functions, that match a regular expression. This leaves out those functions that are not interactive. apropos, on the other hand, shows *all* bound symbols whose names match a regular expression. If you are using Emacs as a writing environment, command-apropos is appropriate because it helps you find commands you use. But if you are programming in Emacs Lisp, you may find apropos more relevant because it provides more information.

Note that the syntax \C- means that the following character is a control character. Thus, \C-h stands for the prefix key C-h. \M- means that the following character is a meta character.

Instead of the global-set-key expression, you can do the following:

```
(define-key global-map "\C-ha" 'apropos)
```

The global-set-key command is an interactive function that checks whether the key is in the correct format and then evaluates the expression:

```
(define-key (current-global-map) key command)
```

in which key and command are the arguments you pass global-set-key.

The define-key built-in function, on the other hand, does not check format and is not interactive. (You can read the source for global-set-key in subr.el and the source for define-key in keymap.c.)

A function key is specified in brackets, as in the following example. (See the section "Rebinding Function Keys" in *The GNU Emacs Lisp Reference Manual*.) This sets the function key F3 to run the view-buffer command:

```
(global-set-key [f3] 'view-buffer)
```

A mouse click is also listed in brackets, like this:

```
[mouse-2]
```

for a click on the second mouse button, which is usually the middle button. (Mouse button events can be fairly complex, with codes for initial, drag, and repeat events, but you can do simple things simply, as shown in the following example. See the section "Input Events" in *The GNU Emacs Lisp Reference Manual* for more information.)

Here is an example, taken from my .emacs initialization file, of how to bind a middle button mouse click to a command to select the message you click on in your RMAIL-summary buffer:

```
;;; [mouse-2] in 'RMAIL-summary' to goto message
(defun rmail-summary-mouse-select (event)
  "Select the message whose line you click on."
  (interactive "e")
  (goto-char (posn-point (event-end event)))
  (rmail-summary-goto-msg))

(define-key
  rmail-summary-mode-map
  [mouse-2]
  'rmail-summary-mouse-select)
```

First, define an interactive function; this uses the e argument to interactive, which handles events. Then, define the key for the local RMAIL-summary mode map, using define-key.

2.17. Editing Lisp

GNU Emacs has two modes for editing Emacs Lisp: Lisp Interaction mode and Emacs-Lisp mode. Lisp Interaction mode is for an interactive session with Emacs Lisp, and Emacs-Lisp mode is for editing source files of programs to run in Emacs Lisp. The two modes are nearly identical.

Like other modes, the Lisp modes provide help in carrying out a somewhat specialized activity, editing Lisp in the case of the Lisp modes, editing text in the case of Text mode, or working out dates in the case of Calendar mode.

The Lisp modes provide M-C-q (indent-sexp) and M-C-\ (indent-region) to help you format expressions properly, provide M-TAB (lisp-complete-symbol) to automatically complete the name of a symbol, provide M-C-x (eval-defun) to evaluate a function definition, and provide C-x C-e (eval-last-sexp, which works in any mode) to evaluate any expression.

In addition, in Lisp Interaction mode the C-j key or Line Feed key is bound to eval-print-last-sexp. This means you can position point after an expression, press C-j (or the LFD key if your keyboard has it), and the Lisp interpreter reads and evaluates the expression before point and prints the returned value in the buffer. This is like typing C-u C-x C-e, but simpler.

Emacs Lisp mode has several keys for working with Edebug. (See section 2.19.2 for more information.)

Often, you will begin writing code in the *scratch* buffer (the Lisp Interactive mode buffer that appears when you start Emacs) because it is simplest and then save that code in a file for later use.

By convention, Emacs Lisp code is stored in files whose names end in .el, which tells Emacs to enter Emacs-Lisp mode when you visit the file.

In addition to the specialized Lisp commands, the Lisp modes provide all the usual editing features: incremental search, regular expression search, replacement, copy, cut, paste, and so on. See the section "Introduction" in *The GNU Emacs Manual*.

2.18. Help
GNU Emacs provides a wealth of online documentation and help. It is well worth learning to use these riches.

Most functions and variables in Emacs Lisp are written with documentation that you can access using C-h a (command-apropos), M-x apropos, C-h f (describe-function), and C-h v (describe-variable).

The find-tag command locates and takes you to the source for a function, macro, variable, or special form. This is very helpful, both when reading the source code in the Emacs distribution and when working on your own code. (Simply run etags to create your tags tables for your own files.) See the section "Tags Tables" in *The GNU Emacs Manual*.

You can read the online copy of *The GNU Emacs Lisp Reference Manual* that is part of your system with C-h i (info), the built-in hypertext help system. The reference manual describes all of Emacs Lisp in considerable detail. Of course, you can also begin to learn Lisp by using Info to work through *Programming in Emacs Lisp: An Introduction*. Finally, *The GNU Emacs Manual* explains Emacs as a working environment—how to edit, read mail, use the calendar—rather than Emacs Lisp, the programming language.[12]

2.19. Debugging

GNU Emacs has two debuggers, debug and edebug. The first is built into the internals of Emacs and is always available; the second requires that you specially evaluate the functions you want to debug.

2.19.1. The Built-in Debugger

Suppose you miswrote the add-37 function definition discussed previously. Assume you misspelled number as nmber and wrote the definition like this:

```
(defun add-37 (number)
  "Add 37 to NUMBER."
  (interactive "p")
  (message "The new number is: %d!" (+ 37 nmber)))
```

First, you evaluate the definition; no problem is apparent.

Then you evaluate this:

```
(add-37 5)
```

You see this:

```
Symbol's value as variable is void: nmber
```

rather than the number 42.

In practice, for a bug as simple as this, this error message tells you what you need to know: number is a local variable and it has been misspelled. However, suppose you want to learn more. You can turn on the built-in debugger by setting the value of debug-on-error to t. Type this to set debug-on-error interactively[13]:

```
M-x set-variable RET debug-on-error RET t
```

Or evaluate the following expression:

```
(setq debug-on-error t)
```

---

[12]These three manuals are written in Texinfo, which is a documentation system that uses a single source file to produce both online information and printed output. Hence, you can read the manuals in typeset printed form, you can print copies yourself, or you can order copies from the Free Software Foundation.

[13]It goes without saying that you need not type the full name of the command set-variable; just type enough so that autocompletion does the rest. See the section "Completion" in *The GNU Emacs Lisp Reference Manual*.

This causes Emacs to enter the debugger next time it encounters an error. (You can turn off debugging by setting `debug-on-error` to `nil`.)

If you turn on the debugger and evaluate this:

```
(add-37 5)
```

you see the following in an automatically created `*Backtrace*` buffer:

```
---------- Buffer: *Backtrace* ----------
Signaling: (void-variable nmber)
  (+ 37 nmber)
  (message "The new number is: %d!" (+ 37 nmber))
  add-37(5)
  eval((add-37 5))
  eval-last-sexp(nil)
* call-interactively(eval-last-sexp)
---------- Buffer: *Backtrace* ----------
```

Read the `*Backtrace*` buffer from the bottom up; it tells what the Lisp interpreter did that led to the error. In this case, you made an interactive call by typing `c-x c-e` (`eval-last-sexp`), which led to the evaluation of the (`add-37 5`) expression. Each line above tells you what the Lisp interpreter evaluated next.

The interpreter attempted to evaluate this:

```
(message "The new number is: %d!" (+ 37 nmber))
```

To do that, it first attempted to evaluate the inner list,

```
(+ 37 nmber)
```

To evaluate (`+ 37 nmber`), it attempted to evaluate `nmber`.

The interpreter looked in the value cell of `nmber`, expecting to find a value there; but the value cell was empty, or *void*.

As a result, the interpreter signaled a `void-variable` error.

In addition to entering the built-in debugger when there is an error, you can cause the interpreter to enter the debugger when it enters a specified function, or when you signal quit by typing `c-g`.

The `debug` function is described in detail in the section "The Lisp Debugger" in *The GNU Emacs Lisp Reference Manual*.

2.19.2. Edebug

The second debugger, Edebug, allows you to step through a function and much else.

To use Edebug, you need to prepare the function definition in which you are interested by evaluating it with a special Edebug version of eval. Usually, you do this by placing your cursor within the function definition and typing c-x X d, which runs the command edebug-eval-top-level-form. This action causes the Lisp interpreter to insert numerous edebug-before and edebug-after functions into the function definition that is in the function cell of the symbol.

If you want to see what occurs, first evaluate the add-37 function definition shown previously in the normal way with c-x c-e, and then evaluate this:

```
(symbol-function 'add-37)
```

You will see a lambda expression such as discussed previously.

Next, evaluate add-37 for Edebug with c-x X d, and again call symbol-function. You will see the calls to edebug-before and edebug-after inserted in the definition, along with other expressions.

After you have instrumented add-37 by evaluating it with c-x X d, you can evaluate an expression such as

```
(add-37 -7)
```

When you do this, you are popped to the source for the definition, and an arrow appears on the line that contains the next expression to be evaluated. Point moves to the beginning of that expression.

The source buffer looks like this:

```
---------- Buffer: *scratch* ----------
(defun add-37 (number)
  "Add 37 to NUMBER."
  (interactive "p")
=>☆(message "The new number is: %d!" (+ 37 nmber)))
---------- Buffer: *scratch* ----------
```

The definition is in the *scratch* buffer; ☆ indicates the position of point.

When you press the spacebar, point moves to the next expression the Lisp interpreter will try to evaluate. Eventually (or in this example, rather quickly), it reaches the error.

In addition to stepping through an evaluation and stopping before and after each expression, you can use Edebug to set breakpoints, trace slowly or quickly, display expression results and evaluate expressions as if outside Edebug, automatically reevaluate a list of expressions and display their results each time Edebug updates the display, stop when an error occurs, display a backtrace, specify argument evaluation for macros and defining forms, and obtain rudimentary coverage testing and frequency counts.

Edebug is described in the section "Edebug" in *The GNU Emacs Lisp Reference Manual*.

2.20. Backups and Auto-Saving

GNU Emacs can keep either a single backup file or a series of numbered backup files for each file you edit. This means you can go back to earlier versions of files.

Also, from time to time Emacs saves all the files you are visiting without being asked. This is called *auto-saving*; it means you do not lose more than a limited amount of work if your system crashes.

By default, Emacs saves your files every 300 keystrokes, or after around 30 seconds of idle time. You can examine your auto-saved files like any other file, or use the M-x recover-file command to restore them.

2.21. Evaluating or Loading a Whole File

To evaluate, or *load*, a whole file, use the M-x load-file command. This interactive function reads a filename using Emacs's minibuffer and then evaluates the complete contents of that file as Lisp.[14] Incidentally, you can evaluate a whole buffer with the M-x eval-current-buffer command and evaluate a region within a buffer with the M-x eval-region command.

Files of Emacs Lisp are kept in libraries, that is, in directories whose pathname is part of Emacs's load-path. You can easily load such files using the M-x load-library command. Moreover, programs can load such files by calling load-library, or load, two functions that evaluate whole files.

load-path is an Emacs variable like any other variable. You can examine it using C-h v (describe-variable) or set it with setq. Often, you will specify an additional directory by consing the path of that directory onto its existing load-path, like this:

```
(setq load-path (cons "~/emacs" load-path))
```

---

[14]The M-x load-file command reads a file as found on disk, not the text in an Emacs buffer; when you are writing code, be sure to save your edited text so it becomes part of the file on disk.

This expression prepends the emacs directory in your home directory to the existing load-path. (People often keep personally interesting .el files in the emacs subdirectory of their home directory.)

2.22. Byte Compilation

GNU Emacs possesses a program that converts humanly readable Emacs Lisp expressions into an unreadable form that the byte-code interpreter can run more quickly. Byte code is not native code, specific to a particular type of machine, but can run on any machine; it runs faster than humanly readable Emacs Lisp, but more slowly than true compiled code.

Although you can byte-compile an individual function or macro definition, more often you byte-compile whole files of Emacs Lisp, using the byte-compile-file or byte-recompile-directory commands. These commands create new files, with .elc, rather than .el, extensions.

The M-x load-library command, when given a name without an extension, automatically looks for a file with an .elc extension first, and loads that file rather than a file with an .el extension. If the .el file has a newer date, it prints a warning because it is likely that somebody made changes to the .el file and forgot to recompile it.

See the sections "Libraries of Lisp Code for Emacs" in *The GNU Emacs Manual*, and "The Compilation Functions" in *The GNU Emacs Lisp Reference Manual*.

2.23. Your .emacs Initialization File

GNU Emacs is customizable and extensible. This means you can change how Emacs work and add to it. You can place your own customizations and small extensions in a file in your home directory called .emacs. This file is loaded when you start your Emacs; it is loaded after the sitewide initialization file, site-start.el, but before another sitewide initialization file default.el. This means your customizations and extensions will override whatever is in site-start.el, but will be overridden by default.el.

Your .emacs file consists of expressions in Emacs Lisp. Here is an example—first, a comment, after the semicolons; second, a setq expression; and third, an add-hook expression:

```
;;; Text mode and Auto Fill mode
; The next two lines put Emacs into Text mode
; and Auto Fill mode, and are for writers who
; want to start writing prose rather than code.
```

```
(setq default-major-mode 'text-mode)
(add-hook 'text-mode-hook 'turn-on-auto-fill)
```

As a result of these customizations, when Emacs sees a file, it places that file in Text mode, unless it is told otherwise (by, for example, a .c extension to the file name that indicates C mode).

And every time Emacs turns on Text mode, Emacs runs commands hooked onto Text mode, so in this case, Emacs also turns on Auto Fill mode.

Here is a simple extension to Emacs that moves the line point is on to the top of the window when you press the F9 function key:

```
;;; Line to top of window;
;;; replace three keystroke sequence  C-u 0 C-l
(defun line-to-top-of-window ()
  "Move the line point is on to top of window."
  (interactive)
  (recenter 0))

(global-set-key [f9] 'line-to-top-of-window)
```

These examples show how you can use Emacs Lisp to set values in your initialization file and write simple extensions.

And because Emacs Lisp is a complete programming language, you can go much further: You can write calendars, calculators, spreadsheets, flashcards, Conway's Game of Life, and Towers of Hanoi, not to mention C mode, Fortran mode, Gnus mode, Mail mode, and Telnet mode, all in Emacs Lisp.

PART II
Scheme

CHAPTER 3

Scheme

by Brian Harvey

> Programming languages should be designed not by piling feature on
> top of feature, but by removing the weaknesses and restrictions that
> make additional features appear necessary. Scheme demonstrates
> that a very small number of rules for forming expressions, with no
> restrictions on how they are composed, suffice to form a practical
> and efficient programming language that is flexible enough to sup-
> port most of the major programming paradigms in use today.
> (Kelsey, Clinger, & Rees, 1998)

That's the first paragraph of the *Revised⁵ Report on the Algorithmic
Language Scheme*, edited by Richard Kelsey, William Clinger, and
Jonathan Rees.

Many programmers instinctively feel that the expressive power of a programming language must be related to the complexity of its notation. For
example, the popular language C++ was designed to increase the power of
its predecessor C by adding many new syntactic and semantic extensions.
Students are often encouraged to learn C before C++, even if they have no
desire to program in C, because C++ is too complicated to learn all at once.
Languages for beginners, such as BASIC and Hypertalk, are designed by a
drastic elimination of expressive power for the sake of simplicity.

Scheme breaks this perceived relationship; it is both extremely simple and
extremely expressive. Thus, writing a Scheme interpreter in Scheme itself is
commonly assigned in a freshman computer science course. Scheme is
a good language in which to write an interpreter because it can conveniently
manipulate both the text of a program and the procedures that carry out
the program. It is a good source language to interpret because it has hardly
any syntax, so many annoying details of conventional interpreters can be
avoided. You'll see later that Scheme, although it was not designed with

object-oriented programming specifically in mind, allows for the easy implementation of classes, instances, methods, and so on, with no syntactic extensions required.

3.1. Who Uses Scheme?

Most current, real-world programming is done in relatively low-level languages such as C++. But Scheme seems to meet the needs of a remarkably diverse community of users.

Computer science educators have been interested in Scheme as an instructional language since the 1984 publication of *Structure and Interpretation of Computer Programs* (Abelson, Sussman, & Sussman, 1996). This remarkable text set a new standard for the intellectual depth of introductory computer science courses. In the traditional first course, most of a semester is spent on the syntax and specific features of a programming language. Because Scheme has an extremely simple, uniform syntax, and because the procedure call mechanism is used for most of the purposes served by ad hoc constructions in other languages, the language itself takes only a week or two of instruction. The balance of the course can be spent on ideas such as functional programming, object-oriented programming, declarative programming, data-directed programming, synchronization, and compiler writing. Since 1984, several other Scheme-based textbooks have been published in the same intellectual tradition.

Programming language researchers develop Scheme compilers and run-time systems because instead of having to implement a large number of time-consuming but well understood features, they can focus on research issues in the implementation of high-level languages, such as automatic storage management and type inference.

Extensible programs have long used various dialects of Lisp as the extension language; the most famous example is the extensible text editor Emacs. The goals in an extensible program are to provide a user interface that nonprogrammers can use and also allow users who are programmers to extend the capabilities of the program. Some extensible programs use ad hoc extension languages that exist only in a single program, such as the Hypertalk extension language in the Hypercard program. But designing a good language is hard, and ad hoc languages often turn out to be awkward to use. A better choice is to use a language whose design has been perfected over years of general purpose use. Scheme is a good choice for an extension language because its simplicity means that the Scheme interpreter does not add too much to the size and complexity of the overall program. The Free Software Foundation has established Guile, a version of Scheme, as its extension language for all new software.

3.2. Scheme as a Dialect of Lisp

Some of Scheme's expressive power comes from characteristics that it shares with every dialect of Lisp. I start with a brief review of these aspects of the language.

3.2.1. Expressions

In most programming languages, a program consists of a sequence of instructions, each having some effect. Here's an example in a typical but imaginary language:

```
procedure distance {
   read(x, y);                 // First step: read the input data.
   dist = sqrt(x*x + y*y);     // Second step: perform a computation.
   print(dist);                // Third step: print the results.
}
```

Although it is possible to write a similarly structured program in Scheme, a typical Scheme program is not built out of instructions, but out of expressions, each producing a value. The user interacts with Scheme by typing an expression, to which Scheme responds by evaluating the expression and printing the result. The same computation in Scheme looks like this:[1]

```
> (define (distance x y)        ; Define a function
     (sqrt (+ (* x x) (* y y)))) ; whose body is an expression.
DISTANCE                        ; The (define ...) is an expression too;
                                ; this is its value.
> (distance 3 4)                ; Another expression using the function
5                               ; and Scheme's response.
```

The main advantage of an expression-based language is that you are not committed to printing the result of a computation. The same expression can provide an intermediate value in a larger expression:

```
> (+ (distance 3 4) (distance 5 12))
18
```

Many other languages permit the definition of functions, but in Scheme the composition of functions is the primary control mechanism. Also, Scheme's expression model encourages functional programming, which avoids operations with side effects such as changing the value of a variable. Functional programming avoids certain common categories of program bugs and makes the program easier to analyze for purposes such as optimization or verification.

---

[1]The greater-than sign (>) is Scheme's prompt to the user.

3.2.2. Uniform Syntax

In most programming languages, the operations that can be applied to
data are represented by a combination of prefix notation:

```
sqrt(x)
distance(x, y)
```

infix notation:

```
x + y
x*x + y*y
(x+x) * (y+y)
```

and occasionally postfix notation, such as the eponymous c++ increment
operator. In Scheme, every operation is represented in prefix form:

```
(sqrt x)
(distance x y)
(+ x y)
(+ (* x x) (* y y))
(* (+ x x) (+ y y))
```

Avoiding using infix operators also avoids having to learn the precedence
of operators. (Typically, multiplication has precedence over addition, so
that x+y*z means x+(y*z). The C language has 15 levels of precedence!)

It is this syntactic uniformity of Scheme that makes the language both
quick to learn and simple to interpret. In Scheme, the plus sign (+) is just
an ordinary procedure name, exactly comparable to the name sqrt for the
square root procedure. In the examples in this chapter, only the parentheses (and spaces to separate tokens) have a special syntactic role.

Parentheses indicate the invocation of a procedure, except in certain special forms that begin with a special keyword. define is one of those; the
parentheses in (distance x y) on the first line of the definition of distance
do not call the procedure, which doesn't exist yet. With few exceptions,
parentheses surround a sequence of subexpressions where the value of the
first subexpression is a procedure to invoke and the values of the other
subexpressions provide the argument values. Parentheses are never
optional in Scheme; if they're not required, they're not allowed.

3.2.3. Automatic Storage Management

Most programming languages provide the capability of dynamic memory
allocation, but in most languages, it is the programmer's responsibility to
also deallocate the memory. (The allocation operator may be called new or
alloc; the deallocation operator may be delete or free.)

That approach can be problematic if the language allows a block of memory to be shared by multiple data structures—in other words, if the language allows the programmer explicit access to a pointer to the allocated block. In those languages, it is not always easy for the programmer to know whether all uses of a memory block are finished, a situation that gives rise to dangling pointer bugs (attempts to dereference a pointer to a freed block of memory). Similar bugs may arise even for memory automatically deallocated by the language implementation, such as local storage for a procedure call, if the program can retain a pointer to this deallocated area.

In Scheme, keeping track of which blocks of memory are in use is the job of the programming language implementation, not that of the programmer. This makes programs much faster to write, more readable, and much less bug-prone. Automatic storage management is, arguably, the main thing that distinguishes high-level from low-level languages. The Java language recently introduced this capability to the world of mainstream program development. The process by which the language manages memory allocation is called *garbage collection*.

3.2.4. High-Level Data Types

In traditional programming languages, the data types reflect the design of the underlying computer hardware. For example, in C and C++, the integer data type can represent a range of values that varies depending on the computer model. In a 16-bit computer, the range of integers is plus or minus about 33,000; in a 32-bit computer, the range is plus or minus about 2 billion. The designers of Java are proud that their language specification requires the use of 32-bit integers regardless of the underlying hardware. In most implementations of Scheme, there is effectively no limit to the size of an integer; you can compute an exact value for 1000 factorial. (This `bignum` feature is recommended but not required in the Scheme standard.)

Many Scheme implementations also support numeric types that are not part of the underlying computer instruction set: exact rational numbers and complex numbers. In all Scheme implementations, the numeric types are organized in a way that reflects mathematical truth rather than hardware details: An integer is also a real number. (To accommodate the realities of computer representation, any Scheme number, of whatever type, can be *exact* or *inexact*.)

In most programming languages, the preferred mechanism for data aggregation (creating a data structure with several component parts) is the array, a fixed-size block of contiguous computer memory. Several famous computer security holes, as well as ordinary program bugs, have resulted from the deliberate or accidental overrun of an array—trying to store more elements in the array than the programmer allocated.

Although Scheme does provide arrays, the preferred data aggregation mechanism is the list, a dynamically allocated structure that can expand or contract during the running of a program. The programmer need not know anything about the actual layout in memory of the list elements; the language implementation handles that automatically. The elements of a list may themselves be lists, so tree-structured data require no special planning.

In most languages, non-numeric information is handled through the use of a character data type. An English sentence is represented as a string of characters, in which letters, spaces, and punctuation are all encoded as elements of the string. In Scheme, there is a *symbol* data type that represents a word as an atomic unit. An English sentence is naturally represented in Scheme as a list of symbols so that a program can examine the sentence word by word without having to scan through a string for space characters. (Characters and strings are, of course, also available in Scheme for situations in which they are the most natural representation.)

3.2.5. Untyped Variables

In most languages, each variable may hold only values of a particular type, which the programmer must declare in advance. For example, for any numeric value used in a program, the programmer must decide in advance whether the value will always be an integer or may take non-integer values. The requirement to declare variables was initially used to make languages easier to compile; an expression such as x+y must be compiled into one of two different machine language instructions depending on whether fixed-point (integer) or floating-point (real) arithmetic is needed.

Today, advocates of strongly typed languages argue that type declarations help prevent program bugs and that this justification is more important than the one about helping the compiler. Yet, in most languages, the available type declarations still follow the computer hardware categories. Why is the distinction between integer and non-integer values more valuable as a debugging aid than, for example, the distinction between positive and negative values? If the type declarations are meant to prevent bugs, then the programmer should be able to use any arbitrary predicate function as the type. Compiler efficiency is still, in most languages, the unspoken reason driving the design of the type system. (There are exceptions, such as the language ML, in which typing is both more general and more automatic, without the need for explicit declarations, than in traditionally typed languages such as C++ and Java.)

One cost of strong typing is that it's difficult, in many languages, to build a data structure whose elements can be mixed types. For example, most languages allow the programmer to construct an array of integers or an array of reals, but not (without extra effort) an array of some of each. Even more difficult is constructing a hierarchical structure in which an element can be another aggregate, such as this Scheme list:

```
(4 8.3 "hello" (1 1 2 3 5 8) (3.14159 2 4 6) 7)
```

This six-element list includes two integers, a non-integer real number, a character string, and two sublists as its elements.

Many strongly typed languages do provide escape mechanisms so that, with a lot of effort, a programmer can mix data types. The object-oriented programming paradigm has an undeserved reputation as being complicated; most of the complexity of languages such as C++ and Java has nothing to do with their object orientation but comes instead from the type declarations and the mechanisms to work around them. This is a prime example of how Scheme's approach of removing restrictions compares with the "piling feature on top of feature" needed in other languages, such as the C++ template mechanism.

3.3. Scheme as a Dialect of Algol

The Scheme report acknowledges Lisp and Algol as Scheme's intellectual parents. The main ideas that Scheme took from Algol, which are among the main ideas that distinguish Scheme from other dialects of Lisp, are block structure and lexical scope.

3.3.1. Internal Definitions

The following is an iterative Lisp program to compute a power of a number by repeated multiplication:

```
(define (power base expt)
  (power-helper base expt 1))

(define (power-helper base expt result)
  (if (= expt 0)
      result
      (power-helper base (- expt 1) (* result base))))
```

This program is written in Scheme but could work essentially unchanged in any dialect of Lisp. Although the notation may be unfamiliar, this program mirrors the structure that would be used in a C-like language:

```
int power(int base, int expt) {
    int result;

    result = 1;
    while (expt > 0) {
        result = result * base;
        expt = expt - 1;
    }
    return result;
}
```

The procedure named power-helper in the Scheme version implements the while loop in the C version.

It's inelegant to clutter a program with helper procedures that are used only from one calling procedure. Scheme allows the programmer to make the helper procedure internal to the procedure that uses it:

```
(define (power base expt)
  (define (helper base expt result)
    (if (= expt 0)
        result
        (helper base (- expt 1) (* result base)))))
  (helper base expt 1))
```

So far, this is merely a cosmetic advance; it makes the program more self-documenting and reduces the possibility of accidentally writing two conflicting procedures with the same name. Internal definitions become more useful when combined with the other feature that Scheme took from Algol, lexical scope.

3.3.2. Lexical Scope

In the sample exponentiation program, the variable base has the same value in every call to the helper procedure. Scheme allows the helper to inherit that variable from the outer procedure:

```
(define (power base expt)
  (define (helper expt result)
    (if (= expt 0)
        result
        (helper (- expt 1) (* result base)))))
  (helper expt 1))
```

Because the name base is not reused as a parameter to the helper procedure, references to base within that procedure use the value of base in the outer power procedure.

The earliest Lisp interpreters used *dynamic* scope, which means that each procedure has access to the variables of the procedure that called it, rather than to the variables of the procedure inside which it is defined. Lexical scope is easier for a compiler because in a lexically scoped language, the compiler knows which variable any particular use of some name means, whereas in a dynamically scoped language, the same name in the same procedure may mean two different variables depending on which procedure calls it.

In addition to the efficiency advantage of lexical scope, another reason to prefer it over dynamic scope is that it avoids potential "name capture" bugs. If the same name is used in two different contexts, the one that a procedure sees may not be the one that the programmer intended, depending on where the procedure is called. With lexical scope, it is clear from the text of the program which variable is used.

Most Lisp users currently accept lexical scope as the best choice; Common Lisp, the other widely used dialect, has followed Scheme's lead and adopted lexical scope. Two dialects of Lisp that continue to use dynamic scope are Elisp, the Emacs extension language, and Logo, a dialect used in education. Dynamic scope is arguably easier for a novice to understand. In some ways, it makes debugging easier, and there are situations in which a name capture is what the programmer wants. However, lexical scope is preferred for most applications, not only for the efficiency and correctness reasons mentioned, but for a third reason that applies only to a language such as Scheme in which procedures are first-class data. I'll come back to that point shortly.

3.4. Innovations in Scheme

Other innovations, based on recent research in programming languages, are original in Scheme itself. Two of these, first-class procedures and tail call elimination, are simplifying removals of restrictions that clearly demonstrate the power of Scheme's approach to language design. The other two, first-class continuations and hygienic macros, are somewhat more arcane.

3.4.1. First-Class Data

In most programming languages, a procedure is created with a name and can be invoked only with that name. Here's an example:

```
int square(int x) {
   return x * x;
}
```

You can do the same thing in Scheme:

```
(define (square x)
  (* x x))
```

This is similar in spirit to the named function notation used in high school algebra:

$$f(x) = x^2$$

Both in mathematics and in programming, it is possible, but much less common, to use a function without a name. The mathematical notation is

$$x \rightarrow x^2$$

You can't just use x^2 to represent this function because x^2 is an expression whose value is a number, although you don't know which number until you specify the value of x. Also, note that the following are two different functions:

$$x,y \rightarrow 3x + y$$
$$y,x \rightarrow 3x + y$$

In most programming languages, there is no corresponding notation for an anonymous procedure, but in Lisp, you can say

```
(lambda (x) (* x x))
(lambda (x y) (+ (* 3 x) y))
(lambda (y x) (+ (* 3 x) y))
```

Even in most Lisp dialects, however, a procedure can't be used as the value of an ordinary variable; some extra syntax is needed, for example, to write a procedure that takes another procedure as an argument. In Scheme, a procedure is a perfectly ordinary datum. It can be the value of a variable; it can be a member of an array or a list; it can be an argument to or the return value from a procedure. This is what it means for a data type to be first class in a programming language.

In fact, the definition of the procedure square earlier is just an abbreviation for

```
(define square (lambda (x) (* x x)))
```

which is no different in spirit from assigning any other value to a variable, such as this assignment:

```
(define pi 3.141592654)
```

Here is the standard example of a higher-order procedure, one that takes a procedure as one of its arguments. The `map` procedure computes some function of each element of a list, collecting the results in a new list[2]:

```
(define (map procedure values)
  (if (null? values)
      '()
      (cons (procedure (car values))
            (map procedure (cdr values)))))

> (map square '(4 7 3))
(16 49 9)
```

The combination of first-class procedures (more specifically, the capability for a procedure to return a procedure as its value) with lexical scope makes it easy to write a "procedure factory" procedure in Scheme:

```
(define (make-adder num)
  (lambda (x) (+ x num)))

(define plus-three (make-adder 3))

(define plus-five (make-adder 5))
```

Now the expression (plus-three 6) has the value 9, whereas (plus-five 6) has the value 11. Each of these `adder` procedures "remembers" its own value of `num`, namely, its value in the lexical environment in which the `lambda` expression was evaluated.

It is only when combined with `lambda` that lexical scope really meets its potential. In traditional lexically scoped languages, such as Pascal, lexical scope serves only to restrict the variables available to a procedure when compared with dynamic scope. That restriction can be useful both to improve the efficiency of compiled code and to avoid name capture bugs, but there is nothing in a language without `lambda` that's comparable to the way in which lexical scope gives `plus-three` access to a variable, `num`, that is *not* also part of its dynamic environment.

This same ability to export a procedure from a lexical environment also provides, as an automatic consequence, the ability to create local state variables, which, along with local procedures, are the main tools needed in object-oriented programming. I'll return to that topic later.

---

[2] `car` is a function that extracts the first member of a list; `cdr` extracts the sublist with all but the first member. `cons` prepends one additional member to a list. The names have amusing but irrelevant historical roots. The apostrophe (`'`) is used as a quotation mark, indicating that the list following it should be taken as literal data, rather than as an expression asking to invoke 4 as a procedure with arguments 7 and 3.

3.4.2. Tail Call Elimination

Because Lisp uses procedure calling (more specifically, recursion) as its main control mechanism, it has historically had a reputation for inefficiency compared to languages that have special iterative notations such as while or for.

As you saw earlier, in the definition of power and its iterative helper procedure, it is possible to express, using recursive procedure calls, the same iteration usually done with a special notation. power-helper invokes itself once for each iteration. If a loop is followed for 100 iterations, does the Scheme version require 100 procedure calls and 100 procedure returns? These operations are relatively expensive.

Luckily, a compiler or an interpreter can analyze a procedure and determine that a particular procedure call is the last thing this procedure must do before returning a value. In that case, the compiler can generate the same looping code that a more conventional compiler generates for a while or for loop, even though the program seems to demand a procedure call. The Scheme standard requires that every conforming implementation must do this *tail call elimination*. It is unusual for a programming language standard to specify anything about the implementation of the language, as opposed to the meaning of the language's elements. If an algorithm can be carried out in bounded space (that is, without requiring more memory as the size of the program's input data grows), then any Scheme implementation uses constant space for a program that represents the algorithm with tail calling.

The idea of tail call elimination did not originate with Scheme; in fact, it was widely used by assembly language programmers in the days before high-level languages. However, Scheme is the first language to include a guarantee of tail call elimination as part of the language specification. Scheme programmers can confidently write tail calls no matter which implementation they use.

The name *tail recursion* is often used to describe programs that can be run iteratively because tail calling is most important for recursive calls. In fact the compiler or interpreter must eliminate any tail call, whether or not it calls the same procedure in which it appears, in order to handle the case of mutual recursion. (Procedure A tail-calls procedure B, and procedure B tail-calls procedure A.)

3.4.3. First-Class Continuations

Composition of functions implicitly specifies a flow of control. For example, the Scheme expression

```
(+ (* 2 3) 4)
```

implies that the multiplication must be done first and the result of that multiplication passed on to the addition as one of its operands.

An alternative programming style tells each procedure explicitly what to do with its result (this example will seem quite convoluted, compared to the preceding expression, but you'll soon see how this style can be helpful):

```
(define (add a b next)
  (next (+ a b)))

(define (mult a b next)
  (next (* a b)))

(mult 2
      3
      (lambda (result1) (add result1
                             4
                             (lambda (result2) result2))))
```

This code says "Multiply 2 by 3. Add the result to 4. Then return *that* result as the value of the entire expression." The argument named next is called a *continuation*, and this technique is called *continuation passing style* (CPS).

Now suppose you want to multiply together all the numbers in a list. You could write this in conventional style:

```
(define (list-mult nums)
  (if (null? nums)
      1
      (* (car nums) (list-mult (cdr nums)))))
```

Or you could write this CPS version:

```
(define (list-mult nums)
  (define (helper nums next)
    (if (null? nums)
        (next 1)
        (list-mult (cdr nums)
                   (lambda (result) (next (* (car nums) result))))))
  (helper nums (lambda (x) x)))
```

The advantage of the CPS version becomes clear if you want to optimize the procedure by noticing if one of the numbers in the list is zero and avoiding further multiplication. Here's how you'd modify the conventional program:

```
(define (list-mult nums)
  (if (null? nums)
      1
      (if (= (car nums) 0)
          0
          (* (car nums) (list-mult (cdr nums))))))
```

If you call this procedure with the list (2 3 4 0 5 6 7), you avoid multi-plying by 5, 6, and 7, but you don't avoid multiplying by 2, 3, and 4. You are already committed to those operations before noticing the 0. Using CPS, you can avoid all the multiplications:

```
(define (list-mult nums)
  (define (helper nums next)
    (if (null? nums)
        (next 1)
        (if (= (car nums) 0)
            0
            (helper (cdr nums)
                    (lambda (result) (next (* (car nums) result)))))))
  (helper nums (lambda (x) x)))
```

Ordinarily, the helper procedure calls itself recursively with a continuation that extends the continuation next by one more multiplication. The multi-plications are done when the resulting continuation is finally invoked with 1 as its argument. Here is roughly the sequence of events:

```
(list-mult '(2 3 4))
(helper '(2 3 4) (lambda (x) x))
(helper '(3 4) (lambda (result)
                  ((lambda (x) x) (* 2 result))))
(helper '(4) (lambda (result)
               ((lambda (result)
                  ((lambda (x) x) (* 2 result)))
                (* 3 result))))
(helper '() (lambda (result)
              ((lambda (result)
                 ((lambda (result)
                    ((lambda (x) x) (* 2 result)))
                  (* 3 result)))
               (* 4 result))))
((lambda (result)
   ((lambda (result)
      ((lambda (result)
         ((lambda (x) x) (* 2 result)))
       (* 3 result)))
    (* 4 result)))
 1)
((lambda (result)
   ((lambda (result)
      ((lambda (x) x) (* 2 result)))
    (* 3 result)))
 (* 4 1))
((lambda (result)
   ((lambda (x) x) (* 2 result)))
 (* 3 (* 4 1)))
((lambda (x) x) (* 2 (* 3 (* 4 1))))
(* 2 (* 3 (* 4 1)))
(* 2 (* 3 4))
(* 2 12)
24
```

If a 0 is detected, helper returns 0 directly without invoking next. The continuations that would have done the multiplications are never invoked:

```
(list-mult '(2 3 0 4))
(helper '(2 3 0 4) (lambda (x) x))
(helper '(3 0 4) (lambda (result)
                   ((lambda (x) x) (* 2 result))))
(helper '(0 4) (lambda (result)
                 ((lambda (result)
                    ((lambda (x) x) (* 2 result)))
                  (* 3 result))))
0
```

CPS puts the burden of establishing and administering continuations on the programmer. But any computation, in any language, has an *implicit* continuation: What tasks are left to do after this computation finishes? For example, going back to the simple expression

```
(+ (* 2 3) 4)
```

you can see that the implicit continuation of the multiplication is

```
(lambda (result) (+ result 4))
```

If you imagine a compiler producing a machine language program for this expression, after the multiply instruction would come some instructions to add 4 to the result of the multiplication. (Actually, this is overly simplified. The real continuation of the multiplication, supposing that the expression was typed directly at the Scheme prompt, adds 4 to the result, prints the sum, and prompts the user for a new expression to evaluate. So the continuation isn't really the same as the preceding lambda expression.)

Scheme allows the programmer to gain access to these implicit continuations. The Scheme primitive call-with-current-continuation (for which most Scheme implementations provide the abbreviation call/cc) takes one argument, a procedure that itself takes one argument. Scheme calls that argument procedure with the continuation of the call/cc as the argument. That is, in the expression

```
(+ (call/cc (lambda (cont) (cont (* 2 3)))) 4)
```

the symbol cont represents the same continuation, now made explicit, as the continuation of (* 2 3) in the earlier expression:

```
(define (list-mult nums)
  (call/cc (lambda (escape)
             (define (helper nums)
               (if (null? nums)
                   1
                   (if (= (car nums) 0)
                       (escape 0)
                       (* (car nums) (helper (cdr nums))))))
             (helper nums))))
```

Here the `helper` procedure looks almost exactly like the conventional version without continuations; the only complication is that a `call/cc` is wrapped around it, and the resulting continuation is invoked if a `0` is seen. It may look as if the multiplications before the `0` must be carried out, as in the conventional version, but in fact, no multiplication is done at all until the recursion reaches the end of the list; the multiplications are done on the way out. Calling the escape continuation within `helper` avoids all of them.

The `list-mult` example uses continuations as a form of nonlocal exit, such as the `setjmp` and `longjmp` procedures in C or the `catch` and `throw` procedures in traditional versions of Lisp. `call/cc` corresponds to `setjmp` or `catch`, and invoking the continuation that it provides corresponds to `longjmp` or `throw`. Those other nonlocal exit mechanisms have the restriction that the exit (the `longjmp` or the `throw`) can be used only until the computation within the range of the corresponding `setjmp` or `catch` has completed. In Scheme, a continuation provided by `call/cc` is valid forever[3]:

```
> (define my-continuation '())      ; Make a global variable (value
                                    ;irrelevant)

> (+ (call/cc (lambda (cont)
              (set! my-continuation cont)    ; Save this continuation
              (cont (* 2 3)))) 4)            ; Finish the computation
10

> (my-continuation 20)              ; The saved continuation still works
24
```

As a result, Scheme continuations can be used not only for nonlocal exit but to implement any desired control structure. For example, a multi-threaded system can be implemented by using a continuation to remember the status of each thread that isn't running right now.[4]

---

[3]`set!` is Scheme's notation for assigning a new value to a variable.

[4]The dot in the first line of the definition of `together` indicates that it accepts any number of arguments, whose values are presented to the procedure in a list. `let` creates a local variable and specifies its value. The variable exists only within the scope of the `let`; it's not like `set!`, which affects a variable in a scope outside the `let`. The notation

```
(let ((variable1 value1) (variable2 value2)) body)
```

is just an abbreviation for

```
((lambda (variable1 variable2) body) value1 value2)
```

That is, `let` is just a syntactic convenience for creating and invoking a procedure. `for-each` invokes a procedure, in this case `fork`, repeatedly with each element of a list, in this case `tasks`, as the argument.

```scheme
(define the-forks '())              ; list of all suspended forks

(define finisher '())               ; will be continuation to end forking
(call/cc (lambda (cont) (set! finisher cont)))

(define (together . tasks)          ; run several tasks in parallel
  (for-each fork tasks)
  (waiter))

(define (fork process)              ; create a new fork
  (call/cc (lambda (cont)
             (set! the-forks (append the-forks (list cont)))
             (process))))

(define (wait)                      ; suspend this fork, resume another
  (call/cc (lambda (cont)
             (set! the-forks (append the-forks (list cont)))
             (let ((next-to-run (car the-forks)))
               (set! the-forks (cdr the-forks))
               (next-to-run 'okay)))))

(define (exit-fork)                 ; finish this fork, resume another
  (if (not (null? the-forks))
      (let ((next-to-run (car the-forks)))
        (set! the-forks (cdr the-forks))
        (next-to-run 'okay))
      (finisher 'okay)))

(define (waiter)                    ; make sure all forks run to completion
  (if (not (null? the-forks))
      (begin (wait) (waiter))
      'finished))
```

Here's a simple example of threads at work:

```scheme
(define (counter n)
  (if (= (remainder n 20) 0) (exit-fork))
  (display n)
  (newline)
  (if (= (remainder n 5) 0) (wait))
  (counter (+ n 1)))

> (together (lambda () (counter 6)) (lambda () (counter 201)))
6
7
8
9
10
201
202
203
204
205
11
12
13
14
```

```
15
206
207
208
209
210
16
17
18
19
211
212
213
214
215
216
217
218
219
finished
```

It is tempting to think of `call/cc` as analogous to a label in other languages, and the continuation that it returns as a `goto` that jumps to the corresponding label. This idea is partly right and partly wrong. It's right in that continuations can be used to create any desired flow of control, as `goto` can. But continuations are safer and cleaner than `goto` because they don't just jump to another point in the program; they also remember and restore the correct environment—the scope of variables and the procedure call stack—to allow the continued program to run correctly.

3.4.4. Lexical Scoping Rules for Macros

It's annoying that in the thread example, I had to say

```
(together (lambda () (counter 6)) (lambda () (counter 201)))
```

using `lambda` to turn each of the expressions I wanted to compute into a procedure with no arguments. I really want to be able to say

```
(together (counter 6) (counter 201))
```

but if I'd written `together` that way, Scheme would evaluate the two invocations of `counter` serially before running `together`, which sets up the threads.

Every dialect of Lisp provides some way to allow the programmer to extend the syntax of the language. Such a syntactic extension is called a *macro*. Each dialect of Lisp (and even, until recently, each implementation of Scheme) uses a different notation for macros. In the one that's conceptually simplest, a macro is a procedure with two special characteristics. First, the macro is invoked with one argument, whose value is the entire *unevaluated* expression starting with the macro's name. For example, if I write a together macro in the preceding example, it is invoked with a three-element list whose first element is the symbol together and whose other elements are themselves two-element lists, (counter 6) and (counter 201). Second, the macro must return a valid expression, and that expression is evaluated in place of the macro invocation. Here's how you can write a together macro in one version of that notation:

```
(define-macro (together exp)
  (append '(begin)
          (make-forks exp)
          '((waiter))))

(define (make-forks tasks)
  (if (null? tasks)
      '()
      (cons (list 'fork
                  (list 'lambda
                        '()
                        (car tasks)))
            (make-forks (cdr tasks)))))
```

With this definition, what together returns for the example is the list

```
(begin (fork (lambda () (counter 6)))
       (fork (lambda () (counter 201)))
       (waiter))
```

but that returned list isn't printed as the final result; instead, the returned list is evaluated as a Scheme expression.

Although conceptually simple, this mechanism is messy because of the complexity of constructing the expression using cons and append. A more magical-seeming version, but one that's easier to use, looks like this:

```
(extend-syntax (together)
  ((together task ...)
   (begin (fork (lambda () task)) ... (waiter))))
```

This says that an expression beginning with the word together followed by zero or more subexpressions (the tasks) should be replaced by one with begin followed by invocations of fork with the lambda-ized tasks and then (waiter). It is possible, although complicated, to write an extend-syntax macro that translates this new notation into define-macro form.

The trouble with the kinds of macros presented so far is that they reintroduce the sort of name-capture bugs that are possible with dynamic scope but not with lexical scope. For example, suppose you say

```
(define (times n)
  (lambda (x) (* x n)))

(define (multiples x)
  (map (times x) '(1 2 3 4 5)))
```

```
> (multiples 4)
(4 8 12 16 20)
```

There is no conflict between the two variables named x in the two procedures; each has the value it's supposed to have. Watch what happens if
you redefine times as a macro this way:

```
(define-macro (times exp)
   (list 'lambda
         '(x)
         (list '*
                'x
                (cadr exp))))
```

or this way:

```
(extend-syntax (times)
   ((times n)
    (lambda (x) (* x n))))

> (multiples 4)
(1 4 9 16 25)
```

The trouble is that the macro invocation (times x) is transformed into

```
(lambda (x) (* x x))
```

The use of x in the macro has captured the intended use of x in the calling
procedure.

A *hygienic* macro system is one that avoids these possible name captures
by, in effect, invisibly renaming all the variables created within a macro
invocation and renaming all the variables created within the macro
expansion—the expression that replaces the macro invocation—to guarantee that all the names are unique. That is, the macro system reads this
example as if it were written

```
(extend-syntax (times)
   ((times n)
    (lambda (x1) (* x1 n))))
```

but the name shown here as x1 is actually a special name, tagged to indicate that it's separate from any x elsewhere in the program.

The most recent official release of the Scheme reference manual includes
a hygienic macro system. The notation is somewhat different from what
is shown above:

```
(define-syntax times
   (syntax-rules ()
      ((times n)
       (lambda (x) (* x n)))))
```

The empty list after the phrase `syntax-rules` is used to contain *literals*, symbols that appear in the macro pattern that must appear identically in the macro invocation. For example, if you want to define a macro to change the format of `if` to

```
(if <condition> then <consequent> else <alternative>)
```

then the words `then` and `else` are literals in the macro pattern.

Hygienic macros make it straightforward to write syntactic extensions without worrying about the possibility of name capture. Unfortunately, in some cases a deliberate name capture is needed. The standard example is the definition of a looping control structure, such as `for` or `while` in the C family of languages, inside which specific names are used for escape mechanisms, such as `break` or `continue`. In these cases, the word `break` as used in a macro invocation should mean the same thing that `break` means in the macro definition. Therefore, some mechanism is needed to allow name capture when it's wanted. As of this writing, there is no agreement among Schemers about the form that that mechanism will take.

3.5. Functional Programming in Scheme

In most languages, a computer program consists of a sequence of steps. (Some of the steps may be conditional or may be repeated.) A *functional* program is built not as a sequence of steps, but as a composition of functions. Here is a really simple example:

```
(define (second sequence)
  (car (cdr sequence)))

> (second '(Scheme programmers have more fun))
programmers
```

The function `second` is defined as a composition of the functions `car` (the first member of a list) and `cdr` (all but the first member). I am asking for the first member of the sublist containing all but the first member, but the first member of that sublist is the second member of the entire original list.

In principle, a language that has the ability to create procedures (that is, `lambda`) and the ability to invoke procedures does not need any other features. It can carry out any possible computation. You don't even need numbers; they can be represented as functions, and the arithmetic operations can be represented as functions of functions. Of course, you wouldn't want to have to reinvent arithmetic for every program, and so even Scheme, with its minimalist philosophy, provides some built-in (primitive) procedures and has other data types in addition to the procedure.

You don't even need the ability to assign a value to a name. Instead of using `define` to create a procedure named `second`, I could have said this:

```
> ((lambda (second)
     (second'(Scheme programmers have more fun)))
   (lambda (sequence) (car (cdr sequence))))
programmers
```

Even enthusiasts of functional programming usually take advantage of the convenience of `define`, but in functional programming, it is forbidden to *change* the value of a variable. There are no assignments of the x=x+1 sort. Most name/value associations are made not by assignment, but by calling a procedure; the procedure's formal parameters (such as `sequence`) are associated with the actual values given in the procedure call. Calling the same procedure again does not "change the value" of `sequence`. Instead, it creates a new, separate variable that has the same name. (This idea of *local* variables is, of course, not unique to Scheme.)

Functional programming can directly express recurrence relations. For example, in Pascal's triangle, every number is the sum of the two numbers above it, except for the first and last numbers of each row, which are 1.

```
(define (pascal row column)
  (if (or (= column 0) (= column row))
      1
      (+ (pascal (- row 1) (- column 1))
         (pascal (- row 1) column))))
```

This procedure is too slow for large row numbers (it takes exponential time) because it does many redundant calculations of numbers in higher rows. But it is a good starting point and can be elaborated into an efficient version that still represents the underlying mathematical relationship without introducing extraneous variable assignments along the lines of

```
for i = 0 to row  {...}
```

Using procedures as data is also an important part of functional programming. You've already seen `map`, which takes a procedure as one of its arguments and invokes the procedure repeatedly, and `make-adder`, which takes a number as its argument and returns a procedure whose behavior depends on that number. Here's another example:

```
(define (filter procedure values)
  (if (null? values)
      '()
      (if (procedure (car values))
          (cons (car values) (filter procedure (cdr values)))
          (filter procedure (cdr values)))))
```

```
(define (even? number)
   (= (remainder number 2) 0))

> (filter even? '(781 24 15 3 6 49 14))
(24 6 14)
```

The procedure `filter` takes as its first argument a *predicate* procedure—one that returns either `true` or `false`. `filter`'s second argument is a list. `filter` calls the given predicate repeatedly, once for each member of the list argument. It constructs and returns a new list[5] containing only those members of the original list for which the predicate returns `true`.

Here is an example of functional programming in which both the argument and return value are procedures:

```
(define (derivative func)
   (lambda (x) (/ (- (func (+ x 0.0000001))
                     (func x))
                  0.0000001)))
```

This procedure takes a function as its argument and returns another function that is (an approximation to) the derivative of the first function. It's common to see programs that take a function and a number as arguments and compute the numeric value of the derivative at that number, but here the result is the derivative itself, which is another function:

```
(define (f x)
   (+ (* 3 x x) (* 5 x) 6))

(define df/dx (derivative f))

> (df/dx 4)
29.0000004099511
```

In this example,

$$f(x) = 3x^2 + 5x + 6$$

I define `df/dx` to be the derivative of that function, which should be

$$f'(x) = 6x + 5$$

Then $f'(4)$ should have the value 29. Because I used a small finite Δx instead of taking the limit, I get a numeric result that isn't quite correct.

---

[5]"Constructs and returns a new list" implies that the original argument list is not changed. In functional programming, there are no changes to existing data structures.

3.6. Object-Oriented Programming in Scheme

Object-oriented programming (OOP) is currently a popular technique for managing large programming projects. The core idea of OOP is that instead of having one overarching program that manipulates many pieces of passive data, you have intelligent data; each object knows how to carry out certain tasks. What corresponds to a data type in ordinary programming is an object *class*; a particular object of that type is called an *instance*. Each object can have *local state variables*, which are accessible only within the object itself but whose values persist as long as the object exists. Each object can also have *methods*, which are local procedures to carry out the tasks that the object knows how to perform.

Most object-oriented languages have been designed by adding new OOP syntactic forms to an existing, traditional language. You could do that in Scheme, too, and indeed there have been several OOP extensions to Scheme. Here's an example:

```
(define-class (counter)
  (instance-vars (count 0))
  (method (next)
    (set! count (+ count 1))
    count))

> (define c1 (instantiate counter))
> (define c2 (instantiate counter))

> (ask c1 'next)
1

> (ask c1 'next)
2

> (ask c1 'next)
3

> (ask c2 'next)
1

> (ask c1 'next)
4

> (ask c2 'next)
2
```

This example has one class counter and two instances c1 and c2. A counter accepts only one message, next. Each counter has a local state variable count, whose value starts at 0 and is increased by one for each next message that the counter receives.

What makes Scheme different from most languages is that there is no real need for this sort of syntactic extension. First-class procedures and lexical scope provide the necessary tools:

```
(define (counter)
  (let ((count 0))
    (lambda (message)
      (if (equal? message 'next)
          (lambda ()
            (set! count (+ count 1))
            count)
          (error "Unrecognized message")))))

(define (instantiate class)
  (class))

(define (ask object message)
  ((object message)))
```

With these definitions, you can get exactly the same behavior that is provided by the hypothetical define-class syntactic extension. (In fact, define-class can be implemented as a Scheme macro.) Each instance is represented as a *dispatch procedure*, that is, a procedure that accepts a *message* (a word, such as next) as its argument and returns a *method* (a procedure, such as the one created by the inner lambda in this example). ask works by invoking the dispatch procedure to translate the message into a method and invoking the method.

This simple example leaves out many of the bells and whistles of an OOP language: additional arguments to methods, the ability to provide initial values to instance variables while creating an instance, and *inheritance*, the capability that allows one object class to use methods provided in another *parent* class. All of these features can be included in ordinary Scheme, using essentially the technique shown here. The resulting programs are only slightly more complicated.

The fact that Scheme can provide the power of OOP without any need for specifically OOP-related features is perhaps the most dramatic example of the Scheme philosophy of removing restrictions—in this case, the restriction in most programming languages that prevents a procedure from being the return value of another procedure—instead of adding ad hoc features for each new programming style.

3.7. Common Problems for Beginning Scheme Programmers

3.7.1. Function Composition Problems

Many people, when they have trouble writing their first Scheme programs, blame the syntax: "I get confused by all those parentheses." Most people who teach Scheme agree that the blame is misplaced. The most common source of difficulty is trying to fit a functional program into the paradigm of sequential programs.

As a simple example, programmers who are accustomed to reading a program from left to right sometimes misinterpret an expression such as

```
(car (cdr sequence))
```

to mean "first take the car, then take the cdr." You must read the expression from the inside out; it computes (cdr sequence) and then uses the resulting value as the argument to car.

It *is* possible to lose count of parentheses, especially when you need six close parentheses in a row, but every modern text editor has facilities that help dramatically with the notation. The two most important are automatic indentation, so that the editor makes sure the shape of the program matches the grouping of parentheses, and highlighting the matching parenthesis whenever the editor cursor is on a parenthesis.

3.7.2. Attempted Sequential Results

A function returns only once. Suppose you have a list of numbers and want to compute the squares of each of them. It is tempting to write

```
(define (squares nums)      ;; wrong!
  (if (null? nums)
      '()
      (* (car nums) (car nums))
      (squares (cdr nums))))
```

but this attempt to return the square of the first number and then, separately, to make a recursive call for the remaining numbers will fail. Instead, the first square must be *combined* with the result of the recursive call to construct a new list of numbers:

```
(define (squares nums)
  (if (null? nums)
      '()
      (cons (* (car nums) (car nums))
            (squares (cdr nums)))))
```

This correct version uses cons to prepend the first square onto the list of squares generated by the recursive call.[6]

---

[6]A Scheme procedure can return multiple values, but even so, the values must be gathered together and returned all at once. A procedure using values looks just like a procedure that collects the values into one data structure. Values is a compiler efficiency feature, not a return to sequential programming.

3.7.3. Expressions Don't Print

Sometimes the programmer thinks that a procedure prints its results. For example, beginners sometimes write

```
(define (two-words sentence)          ;; wrong!
  (car sentence)
  (car (cdr sentence)))
```

expecting to use it this way:

```
> (two-words '(hello goodbye))
HELLO
GOODBYE
```

In fact the procedure does not print anything; it merely computes values and returns the last of those values. Scheme's interactive user interface prints the value of the expressions you type, which in this case means the value that two-words returns, so what really happens is this:

```
> (two-words '(hello goodbye))
GOODBYE
```

It is possible to tell Scheme explicitly to display a value, but this is almost always bad Scheme style.

3.7.4. No Variable Reassignment

Another mistake is thinking that an arithmetic operation changes the value of a variable. For example, here is an incorrect attempt to compute $f(x) = 3x + 10$:

```
(define (f x)              ;; wrong!
  (* x 3)
  (+ x 10))
```

The correct version works by composition of functions:

```
(define (f x)
  (+ (* x 3) 10))
```

3.7.5. Scheme Isn't English

People who have programmed in other languages usually do not have this problem, but complete beginners sometimes try to make Scheme be English. For example, they may write

```
(equal? argument (or 'yes 'no))        ;; wrong!
```

because they are thinking of the English question "Is the argument equal to yes or no?" Scheme does provide an or operation, but its arguments are true/false values, so the correct form is

```
(or (equal? argument 'yes) (equal? argument 'no))
```

3.7.6. Incomplete Expression Problems

Programmers unfamiliar with `lambda` sometimes try to use incomplete expressions as arguments to higher-order procedures, like this:

```
(map (+ 5) '(6 7 8))     ;; wrong
```

instead of this:

```
(map (lambda (x) (+ x 5)) '(6 7 8))
```

3.7.7. Recursion Problems

For programmers unaccustomed to recursion, there are many possible pitfalls. A recursive procedure must have a base case, and each recursive call must get closer, in some sense, to the base case. The value that the procedure returns in the base case must be in the range of the desired function. That sounds obvious, but sometimes when writing, for example, a procedure that returns a number, it's easy to return an empty list in the base case without thinking about it because the six previously written procedures all returned lists.

3.7.8. cons Problems

The constructor `cons` that creates a list with one new element prepended to an argument list must have the new element first and then the list to be extended. Using `(cons old-list new-element)` doesn't give an error message, but it creates a data structure that isn't a valid list and looks funny when printed. In the thread manager earlier, to add a new element at the end of a list, I used this construction instead:

```
(append old-list (list new-element))
```

3.8. References

Abelson, H., G. J. Sussman, and J. Sussman. 1996. *Structure and interpretation of computer programs* (2nd ed.). Cambridge, MA: MIT Press/McGraw-Hill. For more information, see `http://www-mitpress.mit.edu/sicp/sicp.html`.

Kelsey, R., W. Clinger, and J. Rees (Eds.). 1998. *Revised[5] report on the algorithmic language Scheme*. Cornell University TR 92-1261. Available online from `file://swissnet.ai.mit.edu/archive/scheme-reports/r5rs.ps.gz`, along with much other documentation. Both of these have extensive bibliographies.

PART III
Guile

CHAPTER 4

Guile: An Interpreter Core for Complete Applications

by Jim Blandy

An interpreter for a programming language can form the core of a powerful, flexible, and robust design for large applications. Done correctly, programs designed around an interpreter for an application-specific language are easy to configure and to extend, allow clear access to their central features, and age gracefully. However, a good interpreter is a substantial project in its own right, and it is difficult to design programming languages that age well. Thus, many developers are reluctant to use interpreter-based architectures for their projects.

Guile is Project GNU's attempt to address these concerns. Guile is a library containing an interpreter for Scheme, a clean, economical programming language in the Lisp family. When integrated into an application, Guile provides a neutral base language that developers can customize with functions, syntax, and data types appropriate to the application at hand. Guile allows developers to escape the tasks of language design and implementation, making it easier for them to offer their users a complete and well-defined extension language.

In Guile-based programs, the performance of the interpreter is not critical because the developer does not implement the application *in* the interpreted language. Instead, the developer implements critical algorithms and data structures in C or C++ and exports the functions and types for use by interpreted code. The application becomes a library of primitives orchestrated by the interpreter, combining the efficiency of compiled code with the flexibility of interpretation.

The choice of a Lisp-like language for Guile is controversial; many programmers prefer a more traditional infix notation to Lisp's parentheses-heavy prefix syntax. However, Scheme is powerful enough that Guile can conveniently translate other languages into it. Users may customize and extend Guile-based applications in any language for which a translator exists. The original developer of the application does not need to choose a language for users. At the moment, Guile has a translator for CTAX, a language syntactically very similar to C; I hope the Guile user community will contribute others.

This chapter

- Describes Guile in its natural state

- Presents an example of a Guile-based application

- Points out features that make Guile especially well suited for use as an embedded language

- Provides hints on how to use Guile most effectively

- Compares Guile with two other similar libraries, Tcl and Python

SCWM (scheme window manager) is a window manager for the X Window system based on Guile, currently under development by Maciej Stachowiak and Greg Badros. In this chapter, I frequently use SCWM as a case study, reflecting one way to embed an application's concepts in Guile.

4.1. Pure Guile

In its simplest form, Guile is a command-line interpreter for Scheme. Like a shell, Guile can be used interactively or as an interpreter for script files. Here is a transcript of an interaction with Guile:

```
$ guile
Sum some numbers.
guile> (+ 1 2 3)
6
Define a function.
guile> (define (factorial n)
          (if (zero? n) 1 (* n (factorial (- n 1)))))
Compute 4!.
guile> (factorial 4)
24
Look up an entry in the user database.
guile> (getpwnam "jimb")
#("jimb" ".0krIpK2VqNbU" 4008 10 "Jim Blandy" "/u/jimb"
  "/usr/local/bin/bash")
guile> ^D
$
```

Guile can also be used as a script interpreter. For example, what follows is the code for `httpc`, a trivial client for the HTTP protocol. It takes two command-line arguments: the HTTP operation to perform and the URL to which to apply it. Given these, it performs the request and displays the reply on its standard output.

```
#!/usr/local/bin/guile -s
!#

;;; Get functions from URL and HTTP modules, and prefix
;;; the function names with the module names, for clarity.

;; thanks to Tim Pierce for the WWW library
(use-modules (www url)
             (www http))

;;; All error-checking code omitted, for brevity.
(let* ((args (program-arguments))
       (method (list-ref args 1))
       (url (list-ref args 2)))
  (display (http:message-body
             (http:request method (url:parse url)))))
```

Here is a sample interaction with the script:

```
$ httpc GET http://www.linux.org/
<!DOCTYPE HTML PUBLIC "-//W3C//DTD HTML 3.2//EN">
<HTML>
<HEAD>
<TITLE>Welcome to the Linux Home Page</TITLE>
</HEAD>
<BODY>
... the rest of the Linux.ORG home page follows ...
```

4.2. The Guile Library

Strictly speaking, Guile is an object library, not an executable. We built the interpreter used in the preceding examples by linking the following code against the Guile library `libguile.a`:

```
/* guile.c --- stand-alone Guile shell
   Jim Blandy <jimb@red-bean.com> --- December 1997 */

#include <libguile.h>

void
inner_main (void *dummy, int argc, char **argv)
{
    scm_shell (argc, argv);
}

main (int argc, char **argv)
{
    scm_boot_guile (argc, argv, inner_main, 0);
}
```

All C code using Guile functions must `#include` the header file `<libguile.h>`, which provides prototypes and definitions for Guile's functions, macros, and constants. The program's `main` function invokes `scm_boot_guile`, which initializes Guile, makes a copy of the arguments for Scheme code to use, and then calls its third argument, `inner_main`. (It passes its fourth argument straight through to `inner_main`; this code does not use it.) When `inner_main` returns, Guile terminates the process with an exit status of zero. This initialization procedure is somewhat circuitous, but it allows Guile to use an automatic storage-management technique, which greatly simplifies the handling of Scheme values in C code; I discuss this in more detail later in the chapter.

The code shown here is rather short; the core of the interpreter comes from the library, and you need only write a stub routine to get things started. The last function invoked, `scm_shell`, takes care of interacting with the user or running a script file, as appropriate.

4.3. Domain-Specific Languages

One of the most critical lessons of computer science is simply that *notation matters*. If this were not so, programmers would usually work directly in machine code because most higher-level languages (assembly language included) are merely pretty notations for machine code. Instead, programming languages provide a critical service when they allow the programmer to work in terms of concepts more relevant to the application and manage uninteresting details transparently.

The more a language implementation can assume about the application, the better the error checking and optimizations it can provide. For example, if we make a request in a database query language such as SQL, we would not be surprised if the database engine optimized the query to perform indexed searches first, thus narrowing the list of records to be scanned by less efficient means. However, we would be quite surprised if we expressed the same database query in C and the C compiler performed the same optimizations; the C compiler does not have enough information about which database columns are indexed, or indeed what a database column is, to recognize the value of the change. Because an SQL engine has more information than a C compiler about the application at hand, it can perform optimizations the lower-level notation obscures.

When a language is highly specialized for a given application, we call it a "domain-specific" language (see Chapter 3, "Domain-Specific Languages," in Volume III of this *Handbook*); Guile's primary goal is to simplify the design and implementation of domain-specific languages.

Stachowiak and Badros's SCWM uses Guile as the foundation for a language for managing windows under the X Window system. In typical use, SCWM looks like any other window manager: The user can move or resize windows by dragging their title bars or borders, iconify windows by clicking title bar buttons, choose actions from pop-up menus, and so on. However, SCWM uses Guile as a configuration language and allows the users to associate their own Scheme procedures with menu items, buttons, and keystrokes.

SCWM extends Guile Scheme with objects representing top-level windows, fonts, and menus (among other things) and provides functions to manipulate these objects. Here is a sample interaction with SCWM:

```
At first, there is no window manager running.
Start SCWM, and have it prompt for Scheme expressions to run.
$ scwm -i
What top-level windows are there?
scwm> (list-windows)
(#<window 12583501> #<window 8388621> #<window 12583671>)
Which are iconified?
scwm> (map iconified? (list-windows))
All but one.
(#t #f #t)
Get a list of the non-iconified windows.
scwm> (list-windows #:except iconified?)
(#<window 8388621>)
Store the window in a variable.
scwm> (define win (car (list-windows #:except iconified?)))
What is its title?
scwm> (window-title win)
"xterm"
```

To help users write configurations and procedures that are somewhat independent of the screen size, SCWM provides the procedures %x and %y, which treat their argument as a percentage of the screen size and return the corresponding number of pixels. Using them, we can define a procedure that makes a window as tall as will fit on the screen and bind that procedure to a key:

```
Try out the %x and %y procedures.
scwm> (%x 100)
The screen is 1152 pixels wide ...
1152
scwm> (%y 100)
... and 900 pixels high.
900
This procedure makes a window as tall as will fit.
scwm> (define (full-height win)
         (let ((x (car (window-position win)))
               (width (car (window-size win))))
           (move-to x 0 win)
           (resize-to width (%y 100) win)))
```

```
Apply our new procedure to the xterm window.
scwm> (full-height win)
The xterm window is now full-height.
#t
Bind the function to the F1 key.
scwm> (bind-key 'window "F1"
        (lambda ()
            ;; get-window returns the window in which
            ;; the user pressed the key.
            (full-height (get-window))))
scwm>
```

Because SCWM has a full programming language as its configuration and
extension mechanism, fewer features need to be included in the window
manager as primitives. For example, users often like window controls
that "toggle" some characteristic—whether the window is in front of
other windows, or behind them, whether it is iconified, whether it is
zoomed, and so on. Rather than include these functions as primitives,
SCWM implements them in Scheme, using a higher-order function that
captures the concept of a toggle. The following code appears in the (app
scwm winops) module of the standard SCWM distribution (slightly edited
here):

```
(define (make-toggling-winop pred neg pos)
  (lambda* (#&optional (w (get-window)))
    (if w (if (pred w)
              (neg w)
              (pos w)))))

(define toggle-raise
  (make-toggling-winop raised? lower-window raise-window))
(define toggle-iconify
  (make-toggling-winop iconified? deiconify iconify))
(define toggle-stick
  (make-toggling-winop sticky? unstick stick))
```

The function make-toggling-winop builds toggling commands. Its first argument should be a function that, when applied to a window, indicates
whether the property being toggled is currently true. Its second argument
should be a function that turns the toggle off, and its third should turn it
back on. Given these three functions, make-toggling-winop returns a new
function to toggle the given property, which can be bound to a key, menu
item, or button. Using make-toggling-winop, the functions toggle-raise,
toggle-iconify, and toggle-stick have trivial definitions.

Because SCWM uses a full-fledged language for configuration and extension, it needs fewer primitive procedures in its core and can express the
operations it does provide in simpler terms—in this example, separating
the notion of a toggle from the property being toggled.

To create SCWM, Stachowiak started with the source code for Robert Nation's FVWM window manager and gradually replaced the original home-grown configuration language with Guile. Procedures such as window-position and bind-key are implemented in C and operate directly on the window manager's internal data structures, whereas others such as %x and %y are defined in Scheme. Guile also allows C code to augment the Scheme type system with new data types; the SCWM examples shown previously illustrate how Scheme code may operate on instances of the window type.

Stachowiak describes his experiences replacing the built-in functions of FVWM with Guile equivalents:

> Converting the built-ins themselves was relatively simple for most cases.... However, in doing the conversion, I have often made my Scheme procedures much simpler than the FVWM commands they emulate because the extra features of the FVWM commands could be done by using normal Scheme functionality. As an example, instead of making move-pointer-to (my equivalent of move-cursor) be able to move the pointer either absolutely or relatively, I added a procedure that gets the current pointer position and wrote the relative move version in Scheme using it. As another example, I wrote the Next, Prev, and WindowList command equivalents entirely in Scheme based on very simple primitives. Although a conversion *could* be done almost mechanically, it is a big win to give it deeper thought.[1]

Stachowiak also reports that the code to support the Guile-based configuration commands was typically two thirds to one half the length of the original code, mostly because Guile takes care of parsing on the application's behalf.[2]

SCWM is not only smaller than its predecessor, but also more powerful. FVWM does support user-defined functions that accept arguments, but there are no general control structures, data structures, or global variables. Given the design of FVWM, these are reasonable limitations; implementing a complete, general programming language would be a distraction from the main purpose of the program. However, because SCWM uses Guile, it requires no extra effort on the part of the SCWM developers to support all of these programming features. Guile relieves the programmer of the burden of language design and implementation.

---

[1]Email posted to the Guile mailing list, September 1997.

[2]Personal communication, October 1997.

4.4. Specializing Guile

To encourage customization, Guile provides extensive interfaces, allowing C code to interact with the Scheme world. C code can freely create, access, and mutate Scheme objects; C functions may call Scheme functions and vice versa; C code may add new types to the Scheme world and take advantage of Guile's garbage collector.

After initialization, the application typically calls the appropriate Guile functions to introduce its extensions to Scheme. For example, here are the relevant portions of the SCSH's initialization code:

```
void
main(int argc, char **argv)
{
    gh_enter(argc, argv, scwm_main);
}

void
scwm_main(int argc, char **argv)
{
    ...
    init_scwm_types();
    ...
    init_scwm_procs();
    ...
    HandleEvents();
    ...
}
```

As in the previous Guile shell example, control passes to `scwm_main` once initialization is complete. That function calls `init_scwm_types` to define the new types needed by SCWM, then `init_scwm_procs` to publish SCWM's primitives to the Scheme interpreter, and finally `HandleEvents`, the main event loop of the window manager.

4.4.1. Adding Functions to Guile

Let us consider `init_scwm_procs` first; it is simpler to define new functions than to add new types. Here is SCWM's code, abbreviated:

```
void
init_scwm_procs(void)
{
    ...
    gh_new_procedure("bind-key", bind_key, 3, 0, 0);
    ...
    gh_new_procedure("get-window", get_window, 0, 3, 0);
    ...
    gh_new_procedure("raise-window", raise_window, 0, 1, 0);
    gh_new_procedure("lower-window", lower_window, 0, 1, 0);
    ...
```

```
gh_new_procedure("iconify", iconify, 0, 1, 0);
gh_new_procedure("deiconify", deiconify, 0, 1, 0);
gh_new_procedure("iconified?", iconified_p, 0, 1, 0);
...
gh_new_procedure("menu?", menu_p, 1, 0, 0);
gh_new_procedure("color?", color_p, 1, 0, 0);
gh_new_procedure("font?", font_p, 1, 0, 0);
gh_new_procedure("window?", window_p, 1, 0, 0);
...
}
```

The init_scwm_procs function is actually much longer and consists entirely of calls to gh_new_procedure similar to those shown; I selected a few familiar or interesting entries to show here.

As a simple example, consider the following line:

```
gh_new_procedure("lower-window", lower_window, 0, 1, 0);
```

This defines a new Scheme function called lower-window, implemented by the C function lower_window. The new Scheme function takes no required arguments and one optional argument and does not accept "rest" arguments. Thus, the Scheme expression (lower-window w) causes Guile to call the C function lower_window with the value of w as its sole argument. The complete code for lower_window is as follows, with annotations:

```
/* The SCM type represents a Scheme value.  */
SCM
lower_window(SCM win)
{
    /* Ensure that this function will not be interrupted by the user.  */
    SCM_REDEFER_INTS;

    /* Make sure argument is a valid window object, or was omitted;
       otherwise, raise an error. If omitted, set win to the current
       window. Include the name of this function in the error message.
    */
    VALIDATE(win, "lower-window");

    /* win is a Scheme value; extract the pointer to the SCWM window
       structure from win, then call the function to lower window.  */
    LowerWindow(SCWMWINDOW(win));

    /* Allow interrupts again. */
    SCM_REALLOW_INTS;

    /* SCM_BOOL_T is the Scheme #t value.  */
    return SCM_BOOL_T;
}
```

Notice that, although Guile ensures that the function is passed the correct number of arguments, the function itself must check the types of its arguments. Because Scheme is a dynamically typed language, each value carries an indication of its type; the VALIDATE macro uses that typing information to assure that the argument to lower-window is plausible, and the SCWMWINDOW macro strips it off to yield a pointer to the underlying SCWM window structure. The other functions declared in init_scwm_procs are generally more complex than lower_window, but they have the same essential structure.

The C code of a Guile-based application frequently wants to operate on ordinary Scheme data structures—lists, vectors, symbols, and so on. Guile provides C functions to perform every operation available at the Scheme level and often provides C code direct access to the internal representations. For example, given a Scheme string, the Guile SCM_LENGTH macro returns its length, and the SCM_CHARS macro returns a pointer to the string's contents, an array of characters. Most of the standard Scheme procedures are implemented by C functions, visible to Guile clients; for example, applications can call the C function scm_cons, which is the underlying implementation of the Scheme procedure cons.

4.4.2. Adding Types to Guile

It is often useful to augment Scheme with data types specific to the application, allowing the interpreted code to refer to resources and data structures used by the application. For example, the window values in SCWM are pointers to SCWM's internal window structures, wrapped with enough typing information to keep the interpreter consistent. Scheme functions such as full-height can manipulate them, and SCWM primitive functions such as lower-window can easily extract the underlying data structure.

Smobs are Guile's mechanism for adding new types. (Smob is an abbreviation of *small object*.) The full procedure for defining new smobs is rather involved, so I only sketch it here. Guile's manual describes the process fully, and examples abound in Guile-based packages such as SCWM and in the Guile source code itself.

To implement a new smob type, the user must first write a set of C functions that Guile may call to perform certain essential housekeeping tasks on instances of the type:

- All Scheme values are managed by the garbage collector, so the programmer must provide mark and free functions for it to call as necessary. When the garbage collector determines that a smob is alive, it calls the smob's mark function to discover which other objects the smob refers to and mark them as alive too. If the collector determines that a smob is dead, it calls the smob's free function to deallocate the smob's memory and release any other resources to which it may refer.

- To allow the standard Scheme display and write functions to print instances of the new type, the programmer must provide a printing function.

- The programmer may supply a function equal? that can call to compare two instances of a smob type.

For example, here is SCWM's free_font function, called by the garbage collector to destroy unreferenced font objects:

```
size_t
free_font(SCM obj)
{
  /* OBJ is the font smob to free. Extract the XFont object and the
     font name, free them, and then free the SCWM font object itself.
*/
  XFreeFont(dpy, XFONT(obj));
  free(FONTNAME(obj));
  free(FONT(obj));
  return (0);
}
```

Given the set of housekeeping functions described here, the programmer must initialize a scm_smobfuns structure to point to them. For example, here is SCWM's declaration of the scm_smobfuns structure for the font data type:

```
static scm_smobfuns font_smobfuns =
{
  &scm_mark0,
  &free_font,
  &print_font,
  0
};
```

Because fonts are relatively simple objects, the font_smobfuns structure cites a standard Guile function, scm_mark0, to mark fonts for the garbage collector. The structure lists the free_font function to be called when a font object dies.

Given the initialized `scm_smobfuns` structure, the application calls `scm_news-mob` to register the font smob type with Guile, along with several other new types:

```
void
init_scwm_types(void)
{
   scm_tc16_scwm_font = scm_newsmob(&font_smobfuns);
   scm_tc16_scwm_color = scm_newsmob(&color_smobfuns);
   scm_tc16_scwm_window = scm_newsmob(&window_smobfuns);
   scm_tc16_scwm_menu = scm_newsmob(&menu_smobfuns);
   ...
}
```

When the application creates a new instance of a smob type, it must tag the instance with the value returned by `scm_newsmob`; this allows Guile, given a smob, to find the functions to manage it. For example, here is how SCWM allocates a new font object:

```
SCM
load_font(SCM fname)
{
   ...
   /* Allocate storage for our font structure. */
   font = (scwm_font *)safemalloc(sizeof(*font));
   ...
   /* Create a new Scheme object, tagged as a font smob, and pointing to
      the storage we have allocated. Notice that scm_tc16_scwm_font
      is the tag returned by scm_newsmob.  */
   SCM_NEWCELL(answer);
   SCM_SETCAR(answer, scm_tc16_scwm_font);
   SCM_SETCDR(answer, (SCM) font);

   /* Initialize our font structure.  */
   XFONT(answer) = xfs;
   FONTNAME(answer) = fn;
   ...
   return answer;
}
```

4.5. Cooperation Between Scheme and C

In designing a Scheme interpreter to be embedded in other applications, there are a number of interesting issues to consider. Guile makes a number of concessions in order to coexist comfortably with C code:

- *Scheme implementations must optimize tail calls.* The Scheme language places heavy requirements on function calls; for example, all loops are written in terms of recursive function calls. The language definition requires implementations to detect and optimize tail calls to allow iterative computations to execute in constant space. (Any thorough presentation of Scheme discusses this topic in more detail.)

There are a number of ways to meet this requirement, but most make it difficult to mix Scheme and C functions, a critical goal for Guile. Guile avoids the issue by having the interpreter optimize tail calls between Scheme functions but implement tail calls to and from C functions as ordinary C function calls. This arrangement allows developers to write new Scheme-visible C functions in the obvious way and simplifies interlanguage function calls.

- *Scheme implementations must support* `call/cc`. The notorious `call-with-current-continuation` function (also known as `call/cc`) allows the user to treat continuations as first-class objects. Because Guile allows C functions and Scheme functions to call each other freely, a Guile continuation may include both C and Scheme stack frames. For simplicity, Guile's implementation of `call/cc` copies the entire C stack into the heap; invoking a continuation copies the stack back from the heap and uses the `longjmp` function to reactivate it. This implementation has a number of drawbacks: It is certainly not guaranteed to work by the definition of the C language, and it makes `call/cc` rather slow. However, it has proved portable to a very wide variety of machines in practice, and the performance of `call/cc` does not seem to be critical to most Guile applications. The overwhelming advantage of this approach is that it places no special requirements on the code of Scheme-visible C functions.

- *Scheme implementations must provide garbage collection.* For a Scheme implementation to free the storage occupied by an object, it must prove that the object will never be accessed by the program in the future. If C functions are allowed to hold pointers to Scheme objects in local variables (a very desirable ability), then the implementation must be able to discover all pointers on the C stack to Scheme objects in the heap.

Many languages offering automatic storage management encounter this issue and use a variety of solutions; some interpreters use reference counting, whereas others require C functions to add pointers to their local variables to a linked list upon entry and remove them from the list before returning. In theory these approaches are precise and sufficient, but in practice they are unmaintainable; even expert programmers will forget to adjust reference counts appropriately or neglect to register a local variable with the collector.

To avoid these problems, Guile uses "conservative marking" to find pointers on the stack to Scheme objects. Guile's representation for Scheme objects allows the garbage collector to efficiently and correctly distinguish valid pointers to heap objects from non-pointers. At garbage-collection time, Guile scans the C stack word-by-word, looking for any values that could possibly be valid pointers into the heap, and then traces the possibly referenced objects using ordinary precise marking techniques.

There are a number of objections to this approach: The collector may misinterpret a non-pointer as a pointer and thus retain objects which could be freed, or the C compiler might perform an optimization that creates pointers stored in an unusual format. However, these problems do not seem to arise in practice. Conservative techniques are becoming widely accepted in the industry, and there is extensive literature on their performance.

In the spectrum between purely precise and purely conservative marking techniques, Guile's collector sits at the safer end because it uses precise marking for all pointers in the heap and requires conservative marking only for the stack and continuation objects. In practice, we have found it reliable.

4.6. Hints for Using Guile

Here are a few principles I have found helpful in designing Guile-based applications:

- *Implement performance-critical sections in C.* Scheme code interpreted by Guile is much slower than compiled C code, but in well-designed programs, the interpreter's speed is not critical to the application's overall performance. It is usually straightforward to identify the algorithms or operations that contribute most to the application's running time; those can then be implemented in C and exported to the Scheme level as primitives. The result is a system stratified into efficiently coded primitives and flexible Scheme code.

  The GNU Emacs editor text exemplifies this approach. It provides C primitives for inserting and deleting text, finding line boundaries, and searching for literal strings and regular expression matches. Because these primitives were chosen and implemented carefully, operations on Emacs's text buffers are so efficient that Emacs Lisp programmers frequently choose to use them instead of Lisp's more traditional data structures.

- *Interpreted code should be untrusted.* As a general principle, Scheme code should not be allowed to crash the application. Primitives should verify the types of all their arguments and perform all checks necessary to raise an error instead of performing an illegal operation. For example, SCWM's lower-window primitive, discussed previously, calls the VALIDATE macro to verify that its argument, win, is indeed a live window object. If the user accidentally passes a string to the function, SCWM signals an error, instead of blindly extracting a pointer and wreaking havoc.

- *Borrow Scheme features when possible.* Guile provides a number of broadly useful features; applications should take advantage of them, instead of reinventing them:

  Scheme's read and write functions provide a simple and versatile file format; everything from lists to trees to strings containing arbitrary binary data can be safely written out and restored with minimal effort.

  Using smobs, the garbage collector can manage the application's own internal data structures, as well as the user's.

  When appropriate, let the user provide call-back procedures in Scheme, instead of offering a fixed list of possible responses.

- *Plan for creeping featurism.* Certain applications are especially prone to creeping featurism, the gradual acquisition of more and more features. If something is inevitable, it is best to plan for it. Guile-based applications allow users to implement some features on their own without modifying the core of the application. Whether or not to use such features becomes a matter of personal taste on the user's part, but not a concern for the application's maintainer.

  For example, the TWM window manager has an InterpolateMenuColors option, which allows rainbow-like effects in pop-up menus. In light of this evidence, I consider it safe to say that window managers are prone to creeping featurism. SCWM makes it possible for users to implement features such as interpolated menu colors without specific support from SCWM itself.

4.7. Related Work

Guile is certainly not the first package to promote the concept of an embeddable interpreter. Here I compare it with some notable predecessors:

- *Tcl*—Tcl is a clean, simple language designed for use as an embedded control language. It is usually paired with Tk, a powerful toolkit for building graphical user interfaces. Tcl was first implemented in 1988, making it a very mature system. (Scheme dates back to 1976, but Guile itself was first released in 1993.)

  The fundamental data type in Tcl is the string. Tcl represents lists as strings, using spaces, brackets, and backslashes to delineate elements. Numbers are simply strings of digits, and even Tcl programs themselves are represented as strings. Tcl's evaluation rules and syntax are very consistent but can lead to confusing results at times. The simplicity of the string-based values makes it easy to extend Tcl from C; because Tcl was designed from the beginning to interface with C, the issues discussed previously regarding tail calls, continuations, and garbage collection in Guile do not arise.

  However, Tcl's simplicity has a price: It is very slow. To retrieve the Nth element of a list, Tcl must first completely parse the first N–1 elements. To manipulate values, Tcl spends a good deal of time constructing strings in cases where other languages simply maintain a pointer to the original data. Because numbers are represented as strings, adding two numbers entails parsing the addends, computing the sum, allocating space for the sum, and converting the sum back into text.

  These problems have been partially rectified in Release 8.0 of Tcl, which compiles programs to a byte-code representation and uses more efficient internal representations for data types, automatically converting to and from strings as necessary to maintain the language's semantics. However, to use these improvements in your own code, you must give up the simplicity that made Tcl appealing in the first place. Furthermore, the new data representation relies on reference counts to manage storage, instead of a full garbage collector; as mentioned previously, reference counting is a frequent source of programmer error.

  Tcl requires programmers to follow rather odd circumlocutions to refer to global variables and to pass arrays as arguments. In theory, these rules keep the interpreter simple, but in practice, they create a new class of coding mistake that I (at least) make frequently. Because the interpreter did not stay simple in the long run anyway, this design choice appears to have been a mistake.

Given these weaknesses, you can argue that Tcl has acquired most of the drawbacks of Scheme without matching Scheme's power and simplicity. Guile has a richer and more consistent set of data types and control structures than Tcl, Scheme's variable references work in the obvious way, the conservative garbage collector is simple to use correctly, and Scheme's syntax, although parentheses-laden, has fewer pitfalls than Tcl's.

- *Python*—Python is another interpreted language designed to be incorporated into other applications. It features a clean infix syntax, support for modules and object-oriented programming, and interfaces to a variety of graphical user interface systems.

  Like Tcl, Python provides the traditional suite of control structures. Although it does provide a λ syntax for anonymous functions, Python's λ expressions do not capture references to local variables and may only contain expressions, not statements; Scheme's λ does not have these restrictions.

  Python's allocation system also uses reference counting to manage storage; reference counting is more difficult to use correctly than Guile's conservative garbage collector.

Guile's two main advantages over its competition are these:

- *Guile is easier to extend.* Guile's transparent support for garbage collection makes it easier to write reliable primitives that manipulate dynamically allocated objects than is possible in Python. Tcl's older interface restricts the user to operating on strings, and Tcl's newer interface requires the user to maintain reference counts; neither is an attractive choice.

- *Guile supports translators.* Unlike Tcl and Python, Guile offers users a choice of scripting languages. A user can configure and extend any Guile-based application using any language for which a translator exists.

4.8. Obtaining Guile and Other Packages

Guile and SCWM are still under active development. The examples in this chapter show interactions with the versions current in late 1997; subsequent versions may behave differently. Consult up-to-date documentation for details.

Guile is available via anonymous FTP on `prep.ai.mit.edu` in `/pub/gnu`; as of this writing, the most recent release is `ftp://prep.ai.mit.edu/pub/gnu/guile-1.2.tar.gz`. Nightly snapshots of the Guile development sources are also available; see the Unofficial Guile Home Page at `http://www.red-bean.com/guile/` for details.

The SCWM home page is `http://web.mit.edu/mstachow/www/scwm.html`; it contains news and pointers to the most recent release.

The Tcl/Tk home page is `http://www.tcltk.com/`.

The Python home page is `http://www.python.org/`.

PART IV
CLOS

CHAPTER 5

A History and Description of CLOS

by Jim Veitch

5.1. A Quick History of CLOS

Lisp is one of the oldest programming languages in existence today. In 1956, John McCarthy participated in the Dartmouth Summer Research Project in Artificial Intelligence and began designing the language; an implementation began in 1958 (McCarthy, 1991). Among non-assembler languages, only Fortran is older. Lisp was designed as a test bed for symbolic programming, reflecting the very early artificial intelligence ideas, and Lisp has survived, evolved, and thrived, paving the way for idea after idea in other languages, along the way creating dialect after dialect.

As John Foderaro put it, "Lisp is a programmable programming language" (Graham, 1994). The structure of Lisp lends itself to extending the language, implementing entirely new dialects, and generally experimenting with new language ideas. The reason for this is the uniform syntax, where user-defined functionality looks just like system-defined functionality and new language constructs are easily transformed into regular Lisp syntax.

Using only a small number of Lisp primitives (around a dozen), it is easy to get a Lisp-like language up and running in almost any environment or hardware platform. The uniform syntax makes it easy to implement a new dialect within an existing Lisp. The Lisp syntax allows rapid experimentation on designing and implementing new semantics. Once the semantics are suitable for the domain, a full-scale implementation, including a parser, compiler and so on, can be done.

The ability to extend and adapt the language allowed early experimentation in object-oriented ideas. For example, in the early 1970s, Carl Hewitt and others at MIT (Smith & Hewitt, 1975) built a message-passing system where every component of the program is an actor, or an agent that responds to messages. Gerry Sussman (and his students), also at MIT, turned this around in Scheme, which captured nearly all the aspects of the actor model and which remains a dialect of Lisp widely used for teaching.

By the early 1980s, frame-based languages were being used widely in Lisp. These frame-based languages, such as KRL (Knowledge Representation Language) or KEE (which also incorporated an inference engine) were used to represent objects.

In the early 1980s, the Lisp community got together to form a standard for Lisp. This standard has since gone through the American National Standards Institute (ANSI) process for language standardization and is known as Common Lisp. This includes an object system known as the Common Lisp Object System, or CLOS. Common Lisp is not a pure object-oriented programming language (like Smalltalk or Java). Like C++, but unlike Smalltalk or Java, it extends a procedural paradigm. I hasten to point out that Common Lisp is by no means the only currently widespread Lisp dialect in use today: Other dialects include Scheme, Xlisp, Elisp, Clisp, and EuLisp. In contrast to most of these other dialects, Common Lisp has a large set of libraries and pays a lot of attention to allowing efficient compilation.

CLOS came from widespread experimentation with different object protocols layered into Lisp and was adopted in 1988. Object systems that already existed in various dialects of Lisp extant in the mid-1980s were combined to form CLOS. Symbolics (1985) was using New Flavors (a message-sending object model, like Java today), Xerox was using CommonLoops, Lisp Machines Incorporated was using Object Lisp (Bobrow, 1986), and Hewlett-Packard proposed using Common Objects (Kempf, 1987). The groups vied with each other in the context of the standardization effort going on for Common Lisp at the time and finally settled on a standard based on CommonLoops and New Flavors.

Making Lisp object oriented is easy: You can do it in two pages of code (Graham, 1994). Making object-oriented Lisp as extensible and flexible as the rest of Lisp is more difficult. Although CLOS is a complete object system, CLOS is implemented in an object-oriented fashion. The object-oriented implementation of CLOS is known as the CLOS Metaobject Protocol (or MOP) and permits the object system to be customizable and extensible.

5.2. An Introduction to CLOS

A computer program uses a model to guide the implementation. When implementing the system, it's often convenient to think about the system as objects: entities that have characteristics. Object-oriented programming allows the program to represent as similar in source code entities that differ in details, but are convenient to think about as similar. These entities are known as objects. Objects with the same characteristics are bundled as generic types known as classes. Objects might represent managers, employees, and departments in a business application or might represent events, locks, and windows in a window system.

CLOS makes it easy to model a system using objects. A window system may have many components that conceptually handle the same operations: Window panes and scrollbars both want to support operations such as mouse-in, mouse-out, and mouse-click. The underlying implementation of what a mouse-click does is quite different in a window pane and in a scrollbar, but conceptually, it is a lot simpler to treat them as being the same. CLOS has a rich, flexible, and complete object model.

Like other object systems, CLOS supports separation of implementation from the interface. Objects are known only by their interface, or the set of operations that can be performed on them. Other components of the application use these operations to create and interact with these objects and do not have knowledge of the actual implementation of each underlying object.

The separation of interface from implementation is one of the key benefits of object programming: Objects may be modified, extended, or implemented differently without the rest of the program, which depends only on the interface, needing to be changed. New objects with the same interface may be introduced into the system without the rest of the program needing to be changed.

CLOS makes it easier to design, develop, extend, and maintain a program. The larger the program, the more complex it is, and the more important it is to structure it into modules that minimize the dependencies between them. Use of object-oriented programming in CLOS supports this type of decomposition into separately maintainable and extensible components that interact only using interfaces.

Like the rest of Lisp, CLOS is a completely dynamic language that is runtime extensible without the need for all the source code. In the running application, classes can be redefined or extended, objects can change their class, and methods can be redefined or added. As you shall see later, important applications are built that rely on this feature.

To summarize, using CLOS in Lisp applications adds the following benefits:

- The application source code more directly models the application domain. The code reflects the abstract properties of objects and hides implementation details.

- Modules use interfaces to interact with each other. The interfaces encapsulate the implementation away from modules of the system that use the abstract operations and remain unchanged even when the implementation of a module changes.

- Applications are easily extensible, both in source and at runtime. Applications designed to be extensible allow users to extend a set of classes and operations on those classes. The supplied set of classes are used as a framework of building blocks and predefined abstract behavior that end users can use to create new classes that have application-specific custom behavior.

- CLOS is a standard. Multiple vendors supply CLOS. CLOS (or parts of it) is being used to add object orientation to other Lisp dialects such as EuLisp or Emacs Lisp.

- CLOS is implemented as a documented object-oriented protocol. This object protocol (MOP) allows the implementation of different object-oriented semantics, typically specialized to a problem domain. Language research and embedding other language semantics directly in Lisp are two different such uses of the MOP.

In keeping with the Lisp tradition of extensibility and openness, CLOS makes no attempt to enforce modularity or to hide implementation across module boundaries. Instead, it encourages application programmers to use CLOS to design modular and extensible programs.

5.3. Components of CLOS

CLOS programs consist of classes, instances, generic functions, and methods. CLOS programs are put together with inheritance, method combination, and, of course, regular procedural Common Lisp code. I'll introduce these elements in this section and occasionally contrast the terminology and use against a couple other popular object-oriented languages: C++ and Smalltalk.

For a good introductory book on both CLOS and object-oriented programming, see *Object-Oriented Programming in Common Lisp* (Keene, 1989).

5.3.1. Classes and Instances

In object-oriented programming, the code is organized around *classes*, which represent abstractions of encapsulated data useful in the domain being modeled in the application. At runtime, specific data objects, or *instances*, of these classes are created, initialized, and operated on. In CLOS, classes must be defined before instances can be used or created. This is not always true; other object semantics include taking an existing object as a template and building new objects by customizing the already existing object (sometimes known as a *prototype-based system*). A class definition defines the instance structure, that is, a set of named data types, known as the *named slots*. Named slots are known as *instance variables* in Smalltalk or as *member data elements* in C++. Instances are known as *objects of a class* in C++.

Class definitions also may contain other information, including inheritance, and a great deal of information about each slot (or *slot options*), including the type of data the slot uses, initialization functions, and names of accessor functions. For example, here are CLOS definitions of a class named point:

```
(defclass point ()
    ((x :initarg :x
        :initform 0.0
        :accessor x-coordinate
        :type single-float)
     (y :initarg :y
        :initform 0.0
        :accessor y-coordinate
        :type single-float)))
```

The class definition defines that instances of type point have two slots, one named x and the other named y. Each slot is defined as a list starting with the name of the slot and followed by a set of slot options, defined by keywords (symbols beginning with a colon). For example, the slot named x has four options named by the keywords :initarg, :initform, :accessor, and :type. The first two options are used to specify both an initialization value to the slot at creation time and a default initialization value (in this case, 0.0) if no initial value is specified. :accessor names the operation (called a *generic function* in CLOS) x-coordinate, which is used to look up or set the value in the x slot.

The form

```
(make-instance 'point :x 1.0 :y 1.0)
```

creates and initializes an instance of type point with its x slot and its y slot both set to 1.0.

Note that the x and y slots of point have a type specified (i.e., single-float). CLOS may use type information, if present, but unlike C++, where type information is mandatory, type information is not enforced and in some implementations may be ignored. C++ automatically defines a constructor for objects using the new operator. As in CLOS, C++ has mechanisms for providing initial values as arguments and for default values. For example, in C++, the equivalent class definition might look like

```
class Point {
public:
    Point( float x, float y);
private:
    float _x = 0.0;
    float _y = 0.0;
}
```

and the constructor is

```
Point::Point(float x, float y) {
    _x = x;
    _y = y;
}
```

and initialization would look like

```
new Point(1.0, 1.0);
```

Smalltalk has a slightly different paradigm: As in C++, instances are created by sending the new message to the name of the class, but initial values are always specified. In Smalltalk, you would end up using a creation message as in

```
Point x: 0.0 y: 0.0
```

because default initialization is not specified in Smalltalk class definitions.

By default, CLOS also permits two kinds of slots: *local slots* and *shared slots*. The value in a local slot is unique to each instance, but the value in a shared slot is seen by all instances of the class. I defer discussing shared slots to section 5.4.1.

5.3.2. Class Inheritance

CLOS allows you to incrementally extend other, previously defined classes to create a new class. The new class inherits both structure (or slots) and behavior from the other classes, or *superclasses*. Looked at the other way round, the new class is known as a *subclass* of its superclasses. Smalltalk uses the same terminology, but in C++, a subclass is known as a *derived class*, which inherits from an existing *base class*.

Consider the following example:

```
(defclass circle ()
    ((center :initform (make-instance 'point))
     (radius :initform 1.0)))
(defclass fillable-circle (circle)
    ((fill-pattern :initform 'blue-stipple
                   :initarg :fill
                   :accessor fill-pattern)
     (radius :initform 2.0)))
```

The class `fillable-circle` is a subclass of `circle` and inherits the slots
`center` and `radius` from its superclass, `circle`, plus the newly defined
`fill-pattern` slot for a total of three slots. The `radius` slot has an `:initform`
that overrides the `:initform` specified in the `circle` superclass, so in essence
it is the same slot as in the superclass, but with a different initialization.
This is unlike C++, where there would be two slots named `radius`, indepen-
dently accessible depending on the declared type of the object. In Smalltalk,
it is illegal for subclasses to declare instance variables of the same name as
a superclass. CLOS and Smalltalk are alike, but unlike C++, in that the
slots (or instance variables) in an instance of a class are the union of the
unique slot names in the class and its superclasses.

Longer chains of class definitions are common. For example, you might
have a class chain such as `region` as a superclass of `convex-region`, which is
a superclass of `circle` (note that this would require a redefinition of `circle`
as defined in the previous example to inherit from `convex-region`). In this
case, `circle` inherits directly from `convex-region` and indirectly from `region`.
`convex-region` is called the *direct superclass* of `circle` and a superclass of
`fillable-circle`. Similarly, `fillable-circle` is a direct subclass of `circle`,
which in turn is a direct subclass of `convex-region`.

CLOS supports multiple inheritance: A subclass can inherit from more
than one direct superclass. The typical use of multiple inheritance is to
define *mix-in classes*—that is, classes that encapsulate independent behavior, which allows the programmer to better control the total possible
number of combinations of possible classes. By clearly factoring the problem into independent components in advance, it's much easier to understand how classes of interest in the application relate to each other and
when new classes should be defined. Mix-in classes are not designed to
have instances. Instances are always made from specialized classes that
inherit from the principal class and one or more mix-in classes. To give

an example, you can factor the preceding example into shapes and fill-patterns by using mix-in classes in the following way:

```
(defclass fill-pattern-mix-in ()
    ((fill-pattern :initform 'blue-stipple
                   :initarg :fill
                   :accessor fill-pattern)))
(defclass fillable-circle (fill-pattern-mix-in circle)
    ((radius :initform 2.0)))
```

Note that this example would lend itself to factoring out colors as an independent component as well; you would have a color-mix-in, and fillable-circle would inherit from fill-pattern-mix-in, color-mix-in, and the circle class.

Multiple inheritance is sometimes confusing when the components aren't independent and some of the superclasses have the same named slots. CLOS resolves this using a default rule, which is described in section 5.4.4.

5.3.3. Classes and Operations

Generic operations (known as *generic functions* in CLOS) typically apply to a number of distinct (usually related) classes. The implementation of the generic operation is different for each different class, where each separate implementation is known as a *method*. In C++, the corresponding class-specific implementation of an operation is known as a *member function*. In CLOS, invoking the operation has identical syntax to ordinary Lisp functions. When you call a function, you don't need to know whether the function is defined as an ordinary function or a generic function.

Both Smalltalk and C++ invoke generic operations by attaching the name of the operation to a particular instance of the class (which actually invokes the method on the instance). In Smalltalk, this is known as *sending a message to the instance*, and in C++, *calling a member function of the instance*. Methods in Smalltalk are found by looking up a method table pointed to by each instance of the class; methods in C++ may either be resolved at compile time or be resolved at runtime in a similar manner to Smalltalk (if they are declared to be *virtual*).

For example, the generic function for rendering figures specifies the interface

```
(defgeneric draw (figure surface))
```

This draw protocol is an interface protocol for how to render a figure on a surface. The methods are specialized to classes of interest. For example, the following might be the code that implements draw:

```
(defmethod draw ((figure circle) window))
    (draw-circle (radius figure) (center figure) window)))
```

This method *specializes* on the class of its first argument, which is the parameter figure declared to be of class `circle`. `window` is a parameter name that does not have a specializer. A different type of figure needs a different method implementation, such as the following:

```
(defclass square (convex-region)
    ((lower-left :initform (make-point :x 0 :y 0)
                 :initarg :lower-left
                 :accessor lower-left)
     (upper-right:initform (make-point :x 1 y 1)
                 :initarg :upper-right
                 :accessor upper-right)))
(defmethod draw ((sq square) window)
    (let ((xlow (x-coordinate (lower-left sq)))
          (xhigh (x-coordinate (upper-right sq)))
          (ylow (y-coordinate (lower-left sq)))
          (yhigh (y-coordinate (upper-right sq)))
      (draw-line :from (lower-left sq)
                 :to (make-point :x xlow :y yhigh) window)
      (draw-line :from (make-point :x xlow :y yhigh)
                 :to (upper-right sq) window)
      (draw-line :from (upper-right sq)
                 :to (make-point :x xhigh :y yhigh) window)
      (draw-line :from (make-point :x xhigh :y yhigh)
                 :to (lower-left sq) window)
```

The implementation of the method for `draw` specialized on `square` is quite different from the `circle`. The call to the generic function looks like an ordinary function:

```
(draw c1 *root-window*)
```

If `c1` is an instance of `circle`, this call dispatches to the first of the `draw` methods defined previously. If it were an instance of `square`, it would dispatch to the second `draw` method. In CLOS, unlike in C++, all resolution is done at runtime. Code in the generic function resolves the type of the arguments and looks up the appropriate method to run. Doing it this way permits multiple argument dispatch (or *multimethods*), which are discussed in the next section.

As in the case of slots under multiple inheritance, some of the superclasses may have the same named methods. CLOS resolves this using the same default rule as for deciding which slot to use in the subclass, which is described in section 5.4.4.1. In the absence of any specialization on the subclass, the method that is used is known as the *most applicable method* for the subclass.

CLOS supports customization of methods, including the ability to call the method definition this method customization overrides (the next most applicable method, or the most applicable method computed from the superclasses). To invoke this overridden method, you use `call-next-method` in the code defining the new method. `call-next-method` implicitly uses the same arguments the specializer method takes and returns the value the overridden method returns. For example, the method on drawing a `fillable-circle` might be defined in the following way:

```
(defmethod draw ((circle fillable-circle) window)
    (call-next-method) ; draws the circle
    (fill circle (center circle) (fill-pattern circle) window))
```

This method is specialized on `fillable-circle` and overrides the original method, which draws the boundary of the circle. It uses `call-next-method` to draw the boundary of the circle and then calls a fill function, which floods the circle with the appropriate fill pattern starting from the center of the circle.

Smalltalk is a single-inheritance model, message-passing syntax, so the equivalent call would look like this:

```
c1 draw: window
```

sends the draw message with argument `window` to `c1`. To call the overridden method in the method definition, Smalltalk syntax looks like this:

```
super draw: standardDisplay
```

searches for the method defined in a superclass and sends the message to the object. `super` used in this way is equivalent to the special variable `self`, which Smalltalk uses to call other methods on the object itself within a method definition.

C++ has a somewhat different syntax again: It emphasizes selection of the member function by using the object

```
c1.draw(window)
```

In the function definition, C++ uses the variable `this` to call other member functions. There are two types of member functions: virtual (which can be looked up at runtime) and compile-time resolved (the default type of member function), which do not support object-oriented specialization. To call an overridden virtual function, the qualified name of the super-class (in C++ terms, the *base class*) is used. For example, `circle::draw` invokes the overridden function in the member function defined on `fillable.circle`.

5.3.4. Multiple Argument Dispatch

CLOS is different from most other object-oriented languages because generic functions can dispatch on more than one argument. In this way, the interfaces defined by generic functions do not necessarily belong to just one class. This is quite unlike both Smalltalk and C++,[1] where methods are specific to one class.

For example, you might want to write methods for draw that are implemented differently for different displays. For example, the following defines different subclasses of display types:

```
(defclass display ())
(defclass postscript-printer (display))
(defclass microsoft-window (display))
```

Now the specialized method for draw on circle and postscript-printer would consist of

```
(defmethod draw ((figure circle) (display postscript-printer))
   (code to generate postscript for drawing a circle))
```

and for drawing to microsoft-window:

```
(defmethod draw ((figure circle) (display microsoft-window))
   (code to draw the circle on a Microsoft window))
```

In this case, draw specializes on both arguments: the figure to be drawn and the display to draw it on.

5.3.5. Structure Encapsulation and Slots

A CLOS class consists of slots. Slots can always be accessed through a call to slot-value. This is not the recommended convention for accessing slots. Access options are provided as keyword options in the definition of the class itself, and you've seen these without explanations in prior examples.

In the example of point, the published method for getting the value of the x slot of a point p1 is

```
(x-coordinate p1)
```

which returns the value of the x slot.

---

[1]C++ does implement a form of multiple argument dispatch, but only for built-in C++ operators, where it is known as operator overloading. It is not available for user-defined methods.

In CLOS, the syntax for setting a slot uses the Common Lisp macro `setf`. Setting the value of the x slot of p1 is

```
(setf (x-coordinate p1) 33)
```

which sets the x slot of p1 to 33.

The generic functions for `x-coordinate` (setting and getting) are automatically generated by the keyword `:accessor` in the following code:

```
(defclass point ()
    ((x :accessor x-coordinate)
     (y :accessor y-coordinate)))
```

The accessor functions are defined in terms of the function `slot-value`, which takes the object and the name of the slot as arguments. It defines `x-coordinate` as

```
(defmethod x-coordinate ((p point))
    (slot-value p 'x))
```

Note here that most Common Lisp systems optimize this definition, so this definition may be transformed into an optimization for slot value lookup.

Similarly, when the slot value is modified using the published `setf` function

```
(setf (x-coordinate p1) 33)
```

the system converts this in an internal function that is called to actually set the value. Common Lisp uses the notation `(setf x-coordinate)` for the actual function that sets the value, and this composite name is known as a *function specification*. The following code

```
(setf (x-coordinate p1) 33)
```

sets the value using the following definition:

```
(defmethod (setf x-coordinate) (new-value (object point))
    (setf (slot-value object 'x) new-value))
```

Once again, an actual implementation would normally optimize this definition. It's important to note that this method dispatches on the second argument, not on the first. CLOS generic function syntax, as described in the previous section, permits any combination of dispatching on the arguments.

CLOS supports publishing a `:reader`, which generates only the function to retrieve `slot-value`, `:writer`, which generates only the function to modify `slot-value`, and `:accessor`, (described previously), which generates both the `:reader` method and the `:writer` method.

Unlike C++, where member functions are only visible in the lexical scope of the class, so that member functions in derived classes do not have access to member data elements in base classes, CLOS permits access to slots by name at all times and in any context. In CLOS, the convention of defining accessors is just that: a convention. However, it is strongly recommended that CLOS programmers use this convention; otherwise, it is too easy to break encapsulation and introduce unwanted dependencies on implementation details. C++ solves the problem of making names available using the protected and public specifiers, but usual C++ conventions recommend making public access only available through user-defined virtual functions (for the same reason as CLOS programmers are recommended to use defined accessors).

By contrast, Smalltalk enforces public access to instance variables only through user-defined methods. Instance variable names are visible only to methods defined in the same class (or in a subclass) that the instance variable is defined in.

By providing the mechanisms for accessors, CLOS encourages publishing access to slot values using interfaces defined by the accessor names but does not enforce it. This is unlike Smalltalk, or, to a lesser extent, C++.

5.3.6. Standard Method Combination

CLOS permits generic functions to be split into several interacting components. A *primary* method performs the main work of the computation. All the methods defined so far in the examples are primary methods. The primary method can be augmented by auxiliary methods: before methods, after methods, and around methods. For example, suppose you are plotting points. The primary method for plotting the point might have the following implementation:

```
(defmethod draw ((p point) window)
    (move-to window (x-coordinate p) (y-coordinate p))
    (draw-point window))
```

As part of this protocol, you might want to notify another part of the system that fits a line to a set of already plotted points. We would like to add a specialization that encapsulates this particular behavior without interfering with the primary draw method. We can do this by adding an after method, which does the notification after the point is plotted:

```
(defmethod draw :after ((p point window))
    (fit-new-line (add-to-point-set p) window))
```

Using auxiliary methods is convenient. It is typically used to establish initial conditions (as a before method) and cleanup conditions (as an after method). They are also commonly used to add triggers (or notifications) to operations, as in the example given here. Building systems such as blackboards, where components interact solely by posting results to a common area (called a *blackboard*) and where the other components read results off it, use triggers to make sure the component doing the writing notifies other components that the results are available for reading.

CLOS supports multiple before methods and multiple after methods. When the generic function is called, all before methods are run, then the most applicable primary method, followed by all the after methods. This pattern of calling is known *as standard method combination*, although CLOS supports other combinations described in section 5.4.7. Standard method combination has other features, described in section 5.4.6, where the detailed rules for standard method combination are also given.

5.3.7. The Metaobject Protocol

One way CLOS is different from any other object-oriented language today is that CLOS supports an object-oriented protocol (the MOP) for customizing the actual object protocol implemented for standard CLOS. Using the MOP permits programmers to extend CLOS by overriding the standard CLOS semantics I have been describing. You can add persistent classes, new protocols for accessing slots, or custom behavior for methods.

In C++, classes specify the layout of an object in memory and specify the names used in the source code to manipulate components of the object. Once the code is compiled for execution, the class information is gone. In CLOS and in Smalltalk, the compiled code contains an object that retains the class information at runtime. This object is the runtime representation of the class definition in the source code and is known as an *instance*. In Smalltalk (as in Java), the layout of the object representing a class is fixed, corresponding to the semantics of the object system. In Common Lisp, however, the object system can represent objects in multiple ways and has the ability to add more by customization via the MOP.

Common Lisp contains more than CLOS classes; it has a pure procedural component with built-in, non-extensible, data types (known as built-in class) such as streams, and also a simple object system (known as *structures* and defined by defstruct). Because there is more than one type of class, the system must not only have a runtime representation of the classes, but it must also keep track of each type of class. The type of a class is known as the metaclass and is represented as an object available at runtime. The system uses the information in a class object's metaclass to decide how to handle it. Regular CLOS classes are instances of `standard-class`.

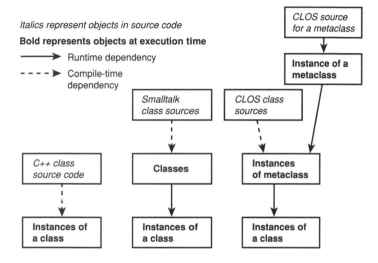

Similarly to classes, other elements of CLOS programs such as slots, generic functions, methods, and method combination all have their metaclasses. In the MOP, this set of metaclasses is called *metaobject classes*. Having all these objects exist in the runtime makes CLOS programs runtime extensible. New classes can be defined at any time (using the class metaobjects or metaclasses), new methods can be added (using the method metaobjects), and so on.

For example, standard CLOS classes specify slots that are implemented as a set of named locations in an instance laid out in the memory of the computer. This is a highly efficient implementation along the lines of most object-oriented languages. Calling `slot-value` retrieves the value by looking in this memory location and returning the value. However, there are other semantics. You can subclass `standard-class` to customize `slot-value` to do something different. For example, you might decide that setting the value in memory should trigger custom behavior (such as checking security access privileges). You might decide that the value isn't really in memory at all; calling `slot-value` instead returns the result of a calculation even though it is convenient in the program source code to think about the attribute as if it were there in memory. For example, the value might depend upon accessing a database. I'll give some examples of this type in section 5.4.9.1 because customizing `slot-value` turns out to be a powerful programming paradigm.

The MOP is subtle and discussing it is difficult because it is easy to get mixed up between the objects in the typical object-oriented programs and the metaobjects used in CLOS. However, consider the following:

- Every Lisp object is an instance of a class. Given an object, calling `class-of object` returns the object's class.

- The class of the object determines its structure and behavior by specifying its slots and their properties. Every instance of a particular class has the same set of slots and properties. Any method that specializes on a given class applies to every instance of the class.

- The class has a set of superclasses from which it inherits structure and behavior. Slots are inherited from the superclasses, as are methods.

In the metaobject programming,

- A class is itself an object. Given a class, `class-of class` returns the metaclass. Instances of metaclasses are class objects.

- The metaclass determines the structure and behavior of any class that is an instance of the metaclass. The MOP is the set of structure and behavior that applies to `standard-class`, the root metaclass that implements default CLOS behavior.

- Custom object systems are typically built by subclassing `standard-class` and overriding the default behavior. This way, you can override some aspects of the behavior while inheriting the rest of it.

It's worth adding a note on efficiency. It seems that the MOP might add a tremendous amount of overhead into the object system. However, implementations of Common Lisp normally implement a large number of optimizations specific for the semantics of `standard-class`. If you start using the MOP to build custom metaclasses, then some of the optimizations applied to `standard-class` are overridden by the custom behavior. In some cases (e.g., in the case of lazy evaluation and dependency tracking discussed in section 5.4.9.1), the custom behavior is more efficient for the type of problem being solved. In all cases clarity, maintainability, and extensibility of the source code are dramatically improved.

5.4. Programming in CLOS

This section gives some of the more detailed rules for CLOS programming and delves into areas where CLOS is somewhat different from most other object-oriented languages.

5.4.1. Slot Properties

There are two default types of slots: Slots may be local, in which case they are of type *instance,* or they may be of type *class,* in which case they are shared by all instances of the class.

To give an example, I'll redefine the class square:

```
(defclass square (convex-region)
    ((number-of-sides :initform 4 :allocation :class)
     (lower-left :initform (make-point :x 0 :y 0)
                 :initarg :lower-left
                 :accessor lower-left)
     (upper-right:initform (make-point :x 1 y 1)
                 :initarg :upper-right
                 :accessor upper-right)))
```

number-of-sides is declared as a class-allocated slot. All instances share this slot. A diagram of the situation is

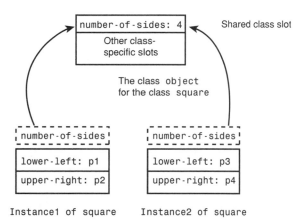

5.4.2. Accessors and slot-value

The implementation of accessors is always done by using slot-value. slot-value accesses the slot directly, without calling the accessor methods. As discussed previously, exposing this as part of the interface makes it easy to break the interface when the internal representation changes. In standard CLOS programming, user code only uses slot-value for a couple reasons: defining custom accessors and debugging.

5.4.2.1. Using with-accessors and with-slots

CLOS provides two convenient macros for accessing slots in code bodies by treating the slots as variable names: with-accessors and with-slots.

We discuss `with-accessors` first. In code composing the body of a `with-accessors` macro, using a variable has exactly the same effect as calling the corresponding accessor function:

```
(defgeneric area (figure)
    ;; returns the area of a figure
    )
```

is an interface defined to calculate the area of a figure. You can define the area method on a square as follows:

```
(defmethod area ((square square))
    (with-accessors ((l lower-left)
                     (u upper-right))
                    square
        (let ((xlow (x-coordinate l))
              (xhigh x-coordinate u))
              (ylow (y-coordinate l))
              (yhigh (y-coordinate u)))
            (* (- xhigh xlow) (- yhigh ylow)))))
```

is exactly equivalent to

```
(defmethod area ((square square))
    (let ((xlow (x-coordinate (lower-left square))
          (xhigh x-coordinate (upper-right square))
          (ylow (y-coordinate (lower-left square))
          (yhigh (y-coordinate (upper-right square)))
        (* (- xhigh xlow) (- yhigh ylow)))))
```

As another example,

```
(defgeneric grow-figure (figure amount)
    ;; grows the area of a figure by a relative amount
    )
```

is an interface to return a new figure with its area increased by `amount`. The implementation for a method specialized on a square using `with-accessors` is

```
(defmethod grow-figure ((square square))
    (with-accessors ((l lower-left)
                     (u upper-right))
                    square
        (let ((xlow (x-coordinate l)
              (xhigh (x-coordinate u))
              (ylow (y-coordinate l))
              (yhigh (y-coordinate u))
              (adj (sqrt amount)))
            (setf u (make-point :x (+ xlow (* (- xhigh xlow) adj))
                                :y (+ ylow (* (- yhigh ylow) adj))
                )))))
```

Inside `with-accessors`, the form

```
(setf u expression)
```

is exactly equivalent to

```
(setf (upper-right square) expression)
```

The macro with-slots is exactly analogous to with-accessors. The following:

```
(defmethod distance ((p point))
  (with-slots (x y)
          p
    (sqrt (+ (* x x) (* y y)))))
```

is equivalent to this:

```
(defmethod distance ((p point))
    (sqrt (+ (* (slot-value p 'x) (slot-value p 'x))
             (* (slot-value p 'y) (slot-value p 'y)))))
```

5.4.3. Multiple Inheritance: Using Mix-ins to Get Modularity

This section shows how multiple inheritance using mix-in classes permits you to write clean, modular code. In general, multiple inheritance has a bad reputation, probably arising from its implementation in C++. In C++, if different classes inherit from the same superclass and a subclass inherits from both of the derived classes, then instances of the subclass contain two copies of the data members of the original superclass. This is not the case in CLOS, which supports a cleaner and more intuitive form of multiple inheritance.

Multiple inheritance is useful because it allows the new classes to be constructed by putting together orthogonal components. As an example, suppose you are modeling ice cream varieties in an ice cream store. You break up the types of ice cream into plain flavors, mix-ins that are added into any of the flavors, and sprinkles that get added on top of the ice cream.

The possible combinations have been broken down:

```
(defclass edible ()

(defclass ice-cream (edible))

(defclass vanilla (ice-cream))
(defclass chocolate (ice-cream))
(defclass strawberry (ice-cream))

(defclass basic-mix-in (edible))

(defclass marshmallows (basic-mix-in))
(defclass chocolate-chip (basic-mix-in))
```

```
(defclass oreos (basic-mix-in))
(defclass almonds (basic-mix-in))

(defclass sprinkles-mix-in (edible))

(defclass sugar-sprinkles (sprinkles-mix-in))
(defclass chocolate-sprinkles (sprinkles-mix-in))
```

Ice cream is modeled as a series of variant flavors with two different types of mix-ins. Complex flavors can be easily defined by using multiple inheritance to combine the components:

```
(defclass cookies-n-cream (vanilla oreos))

(defclass rocky-road (chocolate marshmallows almonds))
```

To make `cookies-n-cream`, `basic-mix-in` might have a standard interface: `do-mix-in`. On the mix-in `oreos`, `do-mix-in` is done with a machine at the store:

```
(defmethod do-mix-in ((m cookies-n-cream))
    (format nil "take vanilla ice-cream and mix-in in oreos"))
```

Clearly, it is possible to easily extend this structure, which has three orthogonal behavioral components, to include many more flavors, sprinkles, and basic mix-ins. Note that flavor is conveniently modeled as subclasses rather than as another mix-in because the ice cream must have a flavor but need not have any other mix-in types. However, it is easy to see that flavor could have been easily modeled as just another mix-in type.

Using single inheritance only, the model is different. A single inheritance implementation of `cookies-n-cream` might look like this:

```
(defclass ice-cream ()
    ((basic-mix-in)
     (sprinkles-mix-in)))

(defclass vanilla (ice-cream))
```

This is a delegation model, but it hides the basic structure of the problem. `cookies-n-cream` now no longer appears as a distinct entity. `do-mix-in` must be implemented as a function that takes an ice cream flavor as an argument and calls a second method based on the value in the `basic-mix-in` slot.

An alternative would be to subclass `vanilla` to get `cookies-n-cream`, but this won't scale. This is even worse than the delegation model. Using multiple inheritance, the system represents objects as an orthogonal breakdown of several different types of mix-in classes. The code need only consider the sum total of all the basic mix-in types, and this alleviates the fact that the number of possibilities is actually the product of the number of distinct mix-in subclasses per mix-in type. Using single inheritance to achieve the same thing means that the organization into mix-in types is lost and the programmer is faced with a large number of classes without any obvious organizing principles.

5.4.4. Inheritance Rules: Precedence

In complex inheritance structures, there may be multiple possibilities from which to inherit either methods or slots.

Suppose you have a class structure as in the previous example:

```
(defclass edible ()
    ((fat-content)
     (type :accessor type :initarg :type)))

(defclass ice-cream (edible))

(defclass basic-mix-in (edible))

(defclass vanilla (ice-cream)
    ((fat-content 'high)))

(defclass oreos (basic-mix-in)
    ((fat-content 'low)))

(defclass cookies-n-cream (vanilla oreos))
```

In this case, you can see that cookies-n-cream inherits the fat-content slot from two different possibilities: vanilla and oreos. Both of these have fat-content slots that override the fat-content slot of edible. CLOS has a default rule that decides which slot cookies-n-cream uses. CLOS builds a *precedence list*: an ordering of the class and its superclasses by a convention known as *most specific* to *least specific*. This is a *linearization* of the inheritance tree class and its superclasses. CLOS makes a list of all super-classes to control inheritance: Slots appearing early in the list always shadow similarly named slots later in the list. For each slot in the class, CLOS chooses the first slot it finds in the precedence list to inherit from. In CLOS terminology, it uses the most specific class definition to inherit the slot from.

I demonstrate the rule that CLOS uses by using a diagram: The class structure for cookies-n-cream is a class hierarchy as follows:

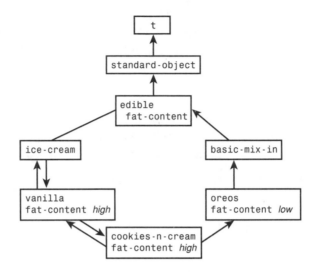

Here's how you linearize the class and its superclasses: Lay out the inheritance diagram with superclasses for each class above the class, but in the same left-to-right order that they appear in the definition of defclass. Now perform the following graph traversal:

1. Start at the bottom of the class graph.

2. Move upward, always taking the leftmost untraversed branch.

3. If a class node has a second branch, enter it from the right. If you can't center from the right, retrace until you get to a class node with an untraversed path leading upward. Move upward again, and repeat the preceding steps.

4. At the top of the graph, the node t, stop.

The order of the classes in the graph traversal is the class precedence list.

The precedence list for cookies-n-cream in the preceding example is cookies-n-cream vanilla ice-cream oreos basic-mix-in edible standard-object t. cookies-n-cream inherits the fat-content value from superclass vanilla. If vanilla did not have a fat-content slot, then cookies-n-cream would inherit the fat-content value from oreos, and if neither vanilla nor oreos had the fat-content slot, cookies-n-cream would inherit the fat-content slot from edible.

5.4.4.1. Inheritance Behavior for Slots
Different slot options have different inheritance characteristics. Slot options can be overridden in subclasses. For the purpose of inheritance,

the precedence of a slot specifier is determined by the precedence of the class that specifies it. The rules for inheritance are as follows:

:accessor, :reader and :writer specify methods that are inherited according to the way methods are inherited.

:allocation is inherited from the most specific class that provides a slot specifier, whether or not :allocation is specified.

:documentation is controlled by the most specific slot specifier that provides the :documentation option to the slot.

Any initarg in the class precedence list for the same slot can be used to initialize that slot.

:initform is controlled by the most specific slot specifier that provides the :initform option to the slot.

:type must satisfy all types specified in the class precedence list, so an inherited type can be more stringent than the types in its superclasses, but cannot be less stringent.

5.4.5. Methods and Generic Functions

A generic function is made up of one or more methods. You've already seen examples of generic functions and methods in section 5.3.3. There are two types of methods: *primary* methods and *auxiliary* methods. Primary methods do the main work of computation and return the value specified by the interface. Auxiliary methods can perform additional computation that is convenient to represent as a modular piece. You have already seen the use of an auxiliary method in adding a notification to the draw method in section 5.3.6. Auxiliary methods included are defined as before methods, around methods, or after methods, and are discussed further later.

Methods that apply to a class must have arguments specialized on the class or its superclasses. Arguments that are not specialized explicitly are specialized on class t.

In the basic ice cream example, suppose you want a method that actually adds sprinkles. The method may be more general than just adding sprinkles: You might like to add toppings as well and you might like to use it for edibles besides ice cream, such as low-fat frozen yogurt or fruit-ice. Therefore, you can add a generic function:

```
(defgeneric mix (x y)
```

You could have a method that doesn't specialize at all:

```
(defmethod mix (x y)
    ;; method 1
    (error "Don't know how to mix ~a and ~a" x y) )
```

The arguments are not specialized and this is equivalent to specializing the argument to t, the root class of everything. The definition

```
(defmethod mix ((x t) (y t))
    ;; method 1
    (error "Don't know how to mix ~a and ~a" x y) )
```

is exactly equivalent to the first definition.

A common technique is to define default methods that the system can always fall back on:

```
(defmethod mix ((x edible) (y edible))
    ;; method 2
    (format nil "Food ~a mixed with ~a"
            (type x) (type y)))
```

Specialize the method for ice-cream:

```
(defmethod mix ((x ice-cream) (y edible))
    ;; method 3
    (format nil "Ice-cream ~a with ~a"
            (type x) (type y)))
```

This specializes on the first argument only. Now specialize on the second argument:

```
(defmethod mix ((x edible) (y sprinkles-mix-in))
    ;; method 4
    (format nil "Food ~a with ~a sprinkles on top"
            (type x) (type y)))
```

Now specialize on both arguments using ice-cream and sprinkles-mix-in:

```
(defmethod mix ((x ice-cream) (y sprinkles-mix-in))
    ;; method 5
    (format nil "Ice-cream ~a sprinkles on top"
            (type x) (type y)))
```

CLOS determines which of these methods to call in any given situation by calculating the *applicable* methods. A method is *applicable* if each of the arguments matches the specialized parameters of the possible method definitions. Calling the following:

```
(setf *vanilla* (make-instance 'vanilla))
(setf *sugar-sprinkles* (make-instance 'sugar-sprinkles))

(mix *vanilla* *sugar-sprinkles*)
```

would result in every one of the preceding five methods being applicable. For example, method 2 is applicable because *vanilla* is of type ice-cream and *sugar-sprinkles* is of type edible. Method 5 is applicable because *vanilla* is of type ice-cream and *sugar-sprinkles* is also of type sugar-sprinkles. CLOS ranks these methods into an order from *most specific* to *least specific* and calls the most specific (in this case, method 5), which is what you would expect.

Redefining method 5 as follows:

```
(defmethod mix ((x ice-cream) (y sprinkles-mix-in))
    ;; method 5
    (call-next-method))
```

would result in the next most specific method being called. There are two obvious candidates: method 3 (specializing on ice-cream and edible) and method 4 (specializing on edible and sprinkles-mix-in). In fact, CLOS chooses method 3.

CLOS decides by using the following rule: The applicable methods are ranked in order of precedence using the class precedence lists for each argument (in left-to-right order).

If the first parameter of one of the applicable methods is specialized on a more specific class than the first parameters of the other applicable methods, then it is the most specific method. If there are ties, then they are broken using the second argument, and so on.

The class precedence list of *vanilla* is vanilla ice-cream edible standard-object t, selecting methods 3 and 5 as the most applicable. The class precedence list of *sugar-sprinkles* is sugar-sprinkles sprinkles-mix-in edible standard-object t, selecting method 5 as more specific than method 3. The next most applicable method is method 3, followed by method 4, method 2, and then method 1.

defgeneric has a keyword option :argument-precedence-order, which can be used to change the default left-to-right order of the arguments CLOS uses to calculate the applicable methods by specifying the new order for the parameters in the argument list.

Methods can also specialize on particular objects: For example, you can write the method:

```
(defmethod mix ((x (eql *vanilla*)) (y (eql *sugar-sprinkles*)))
    (format nil
        "Vanilla ice-cream with sugar sprinkles is my favorite"))
```

or

```
(defmethod mix ((x (eql 'cement)) (y (eql 'gravel)))
    'concrete)
```

Specializations on individual objects always take precedence over the class specializations.

The parameter list for methods follows the Common Lisp specification for functions (with the restriction that only the required parameters can be specialized).

CLOS defines that all methods for a generic function must have *congruent* parameter lists. They must have the same number of required arguments and the same number of optional parameters (zero or more), all use &rest (or none), and all use &key (or none).

5.4.6. Before, After, and Around Methods

Methods can be augmented by auxiliary methods: before methods, after methods, and around methods.

Before methods allow custom code to run before the primary method. They are called, most specific first, before the rest of the method runs. As an example, before methods might be used to inform the rest of the system about the priority for a shared resource the rest of the method will use. After methods are called, most specific last, as the final part of a method call. As an example, after methods are often used to notify other parts of the system that the method has run. The rest of the method (between the before methods and the after methods) is what is normally considered the method and is called the primary method. The value of the primary method is returned by a call to the method, even though the after methods are called after the primary method.

Before methods and after methods permit custom behavior to be prepended and appended to a method. Around methods can also replace the primary method. Typically, an around method calls the primary method using call-next-method (this is why they are called around methods), but this is up to the around method implementer.

The procedure described, known as *standard method combination*, is the default method combination prescribed by CLOS. Other method combinations exist (as described in the next section).

As an example, use the class hierarchy defined in the previous section:

```
(defmethod mix ((ic ice-cream) (sprinkles sprinkles-mix-in))
    (build-ice-cream-cone)

(defmethod mix :before (x y)
    (take-order)
```

```
(defmethod mix :before ((ic ice-cream) y)
   (pick-up-scoop))

(defmethod mix :after ((ic ice-cream) (sprinkles sprinkles-mix-in))
   (add-sprinkles sprinkles ic)

(defmethod mix :after ((ic ice-cream) y)
   (replace-scoop)
```

On calling

```
(mix (make-instance 'vanilla) (make-instance 'sugar-sprinkles))
```

which methods run? The effective method for this combination is obtained by calling in the following order:

- All before methods from most specific to least specific

- The most specific primary method

- All after methods from least specific to most specific

The value returned is the value of the most specific primary method. The effective method for this combination looks like this:

```
(multiple-value-prog1
   (progn (pick-up-scoop)          ; most specific before-method
          (take-order)             ; least specific before-method
          (build-ice-cream-cone)   ; most specific primary method
    )
   (replace-scoop)                 ; least specific after-method
   (add-sprinkles)                 ; most specific after method
   )
```

After methods don't have access to the value returned by the primary method. In many cases, you want to do some calculations, call the method, and then run another computation based on the value of the core method. As an example, you might only want to notify another part of the application that the method has run based on the return value of the core method. After methods won't let you do this.

An around method completely replaces the most specific method. For example, `build-ice-cream-cone` might fail if you are out of ice cream; otherwise, it returns the cone:

```
(defmethod mix :around ((ic ice-cream) (sprinkle sugar-sprinkles))
   (let ((cone (call-next-method)))
     (when cone (take-payment))
     cone))
```

Using `call-next-method`, this runs the next most specific method (i.e., `build-ice-cream-cone`)—in this case, the entire framework defined before, including all the before methods, after methods, and the primary method. The usual convention, illustrated here, is to return the value of the next most specific method.

5.4.7. Operator Method Combination

The method combination described in the previous section is known as *standard method combination.* CLOS supports combining methods in other ways. In particular, CLOS supports *operator method combination,* which can be most easily understood as a standard Lisp operator applied to all the applicable primary methods:

```
(defgeneric weight (x)
    (:method-combination +))
```

The `weight` method uses the + method combination and any `defmethod` on weight must have + as the second argument. Here's some code that defines classes with weights:

```
(defclass chassis () ())
(defclass engine () ())
(defclass wheels () ())
(defclass car (chassis engine wheels) ())

(defmethod weight + ((ch chassis)) 1500)
(defmethod weight + ((e engine)) 500)
(defmethod weight + ((w wheels)) 150)
```

Calling `weight` on an instance of `car` returns the sum of the individual weights:

```
(weight (make-instance 'car)) returns 2150
```

The operators supported are +, and, append, `list`, max, min, nconc, or, and progn.

5.4.8. Redefining Classes and Changing the Class of Instances

CLOS permits a great deal of flexibility in class redefinition. Evolving applications requires changing the design, sometimes radically. Getting the design right is usually an incremental process that can take many steps, and the ability to do this interactively greatly speeds the development process.

Many CAD applications permit classes to be redefined at runtime and the instances must be updated accordingly.

It is sometimes convenient to change the class of instances. For example, in a scheduling application, tasks may belong to classes that represent real resources, and in trying different schedules, you might not need to consider a particular task. The easiest way to handle this may be to change the class of the task to one where all the methods returning the resource constraints instead return no resource use.

5.4.8.1. Class Redefinition

Classes can be redefined at any time. The new class definition completely replaces the old one. The class redefinition may include adding or deleting slots, changing its superclasses, changing accessors, or changing any other option to defclass.

The new class redefinition affects not only all instances of the class, but all its subclasses and their instances, and CLOS automatically propagates the changes to all the affected elements. As with the rest of CLOS, the change can be customized (as discussed in the next section).

CLOS specifies that updating an instance happens before a slot of the instance is accessed, and CLOS only updates instances as needed. This lazy update model ensures that all instances appear correctly updated as soon as the class is changed while actually expending the cost of the update over only the instances that are used.

The slots of an instance are updated according to the following default rules:

- Slots occurring in both the old and the new definition keep their value. If they are unbound, then they remain unbound.

- Slots specified in the new definition but not in the old are added to the instance according the usual CLOS initialization protocol.

- Slots specified in the old definition but not in the new are discarded. The values of the old slots can be used before the update occurs by specializing the generic function update-instance-for-redefined-class.

- Shared slots in the old definition that become local slots in the new definition keep their value. If they are unbound, then they remain unbound.

- Local slots in the old definition that become shared slots in the new definition are initialized in the usual way.

As an example, I redefine `square`. The original definition is

```
(defclass square (convex-region)
    ((number-of-sides :initform 4 :allocation :class)
     (lower-left :initform (make-point :x 0 :y 0)
                 :initarg :lower-left
                 :accessor lower-left)
     (upper-right:initform (make-point :x 1 y 1)
                 :initarg :upper-right
                 :accessor upper-right)))
```

and making an instance is

```
(setf *s* (make-instance 'square
                :lower-left (make-instance 'point :x 2 :y 2)
                :upper-right (make-instance 'point :x 3 :y 3)))
```

Now I redefine it as

```
(defclass square (convex-region)
    ((number-of-sides :allocation :class)
     (xlow :initarg :xlow :accessor xlow :initform 0)
     (xhigh :initarg :xhigh :accessor xhigh :initform 1)
     (ylow :initarg :ylow :accessor ylow :initform 0)
     (yhigh :initarg :yhigh :accessor yhigh :initform 1)))
```

The only slot that is preserved is `number-of-sides`.

You need to update `*s*` properly, and you do it by putting an after method on `update-instance-for-redefined-class`. Note that the method definition has to be done before the new class definition; otherwise, if `*s*` were accessed after the class redefinition but before you defined the method, the slots would be defaulted to the new `initforms`:

```
(defmethod update-instance-for-redefined-class :after
            ((sq square) new-slots old-slots plist &rest initargs)
    (let ((ll (getf plist 'lower-left))
          (ur (getf plist 'upper-right)))
      (when (and ll ur)
        (setf (slot-value sq 'xlow) (x-coordinate ll))
        (setf (slot-value sq 'ylow) (y-coordinate ll))
        (setf (slot-value sq 'xhigh) (x-coordinate ur))
        (setf (slot-value sq 'yhigh) (y-coordinate ur)))))
```

On accessing the instance (`xlow *s*`), you get the value 2.

To preserve the original interface, you use the following:

```
(defmethod lower-left ((sq square))
    (make-instance 'point :x (xlow sq) :y (ylow sq)))

(defmethod upper-right ((sq square))
    (make-instance 'point :x (xhigh sq) :y (yhigh sq)))
```

Note that `make-instance` for `square` now takes new `initargs`. This interface can't be preserved. The convention is to define a constructor function that must be redefined to call `make-instance` with the new arguments, as in

```
(defun make-square (lower-left upper-right)
    (make-instance 'square :xlow (x-coordinate lower-left)
                           :ylow (y-coordinate lower-left)
                           :xhigh (x-coordinate upper-right)
                           :yhigh (y-coordinate upper-right)))
```

which would replace the original constructor function:

```
(defun make-square (lower-left upper-right)
    (make-instance 'square :lower-left lower-left
                           :upper-right upper-right))
```

5.4.8.2. Changing the Class of an Instance
When an instance is changed to a new class, the slots have the following update behavior:

- Shared slots in the original class are untouched, but the instance cannot access them any longer.

- Slots in the original class keep their values if they are local in the new class. If they were unbound, they remain unbound. If they are shared in the new class, they are changed to refer to value of the shared slot in the new class.

- New slots from the new class are added to the instance and are initialized according to the new class's slot initialization protocol.

- Slots only present in the original class are discarded.

As in updating an instance for a redefined class, instances can be updated by defining a method for `update-instance-for-redefined-class`. This generic function takes as arguments a copy of the instance before it was updated and the updated instance. Because the original class still exists unchanged, the copy of the instance before it was updated can be accessed using `slot-value` or any of the accessors defined in the original class.

As in updating an instance for a redefined class, this is normally done by using before methods or after methods.

5.4.9. Extending CLOS Using the Metaobject Protocol
This section shows some techniques for extending CLOS. These use the MOP and de facto extensions for CLOS described in Part II of *The Art of the Metaobject Protocol* (Kizcales, Rivieres, Bobrow, 1991),

implemented by most Common Lisp systems. For an excellent description of how a MOP is implemented, see *The Art of the Metaobject Protocol* (Kizcales, Rivieres, Bobrow, 1991). Note that this reference is a simplified form of the MOP for teaching purposes.

Every ordinary CLOS class is an instance of a system-supplied class metaobject class (or metaclass). This particular metaclass is called `standard-class` and, like all other CLOS objects, it has slots, values, and methods. When you made the class `cookies-n-cream`, an object was made that completely describes the `cookies-n-cream` class. The slots and values in this object are determined by `standard-class`. The following shows what the metaclass object might look like:

Slot	*Value*
Name	`cookies-n-cream`
Direct superclasses	`(vanilla oreos edible standard-object t)`
Direct slots	`()`
Effective slots	`fat-content`
Direct subclasses	`()`
Class	`standard-object`

5.4.9.1. Very Large Spreadsheets and Dependency Tracking
This section outlines two techniques often used in CAD applications.

As an example, Boeing designs very large planes using classes and instances to model the aircraft. Designers at Boeing iterate over a plane design by changing properties of objects in the model. It is often convenient to model the object properties as slot values of the object. However, many properties are often dependent on the slot values in other objects. For example, the seating capacity of the plane may be calculated from the height and width and length of the passenger compartment, but the length of the plane may be dependent on other dimensions of components of the plane.

Designing a plane is like manipulating a very large spreadsheet, where changing the value in a cell necessitates an update to other cell values that are calculated using the changed value. As in a spreadsheet, you want the system to automatically keep track of all the formulas defining the slot values of objects and their dependencies on other values.

Two cases have different semantics for tracking and updating such dependencies. In one case, when you change a value, you need to know all the dependent values immediately. For example, if a plane is being drawn on the screen, then changing a property should immediately result in all the dependent properties being updated correctly so that the view on the screen remains consistent.

Immediate update becomes impractical when the models are large. While working on one aspect of the model (say the seating arrangement), you may not need other parts of the model. In this case, to improve performance, it is better to defer updating the other parts of the model until they are needed.

We'll discuss the first case first.

Dependency Tracking Applied to Immediate Update

First of all, use the following code so that the functions for the metaobject protocols are visible in the current package:

```
(use-package :clos)
```

Now define a new type of metaclass by subclassing `standard-class`. All the classes in the model use the semantics of this metaclass:

```
(defclass dependency-class (standard-class) ())
```

At this point, you can make new classes of this type:

```
(defclass part ()
    ((dependency :initform nil
                 :accessor part-dependency))
  (:metaclass dependency-class))

(defclass body (part)
    ((length :reader lngth)
     (width :initform 0 :accessor width))
  (:metaclass dependency-class))

(defclass wing (part)
    ((length :initform 0 :accessor lngth))
  (:metaclass dependency-class))
```

Note that we use `lngth` instead of `length` to prevent a name clash with the system-supplied `length` function.

The `:metaclass` option specifies each class as a `dependency-class`. The terminology *metaclass* is historical syntax in the MOP for a class metaobject class. The following diagram helps illustrate the relationship between these classes:

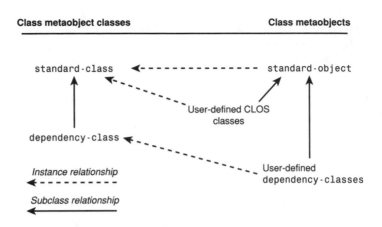

The dashed lines show instance relations and the solid lines show class relations. On the left of the diagram are the class metaobject classes, and on the right are their instances—that is, the class metaobjects themselves.

So far, not much has happened. `dependency-class` has exactly the same semantics as `standard-class`, so classes defined using the metaclass `dependency-class` have exactly the same behavior as regular CLOS classes. All subclasses of type `part` have a slot called `dependency` (which we will use a little later). You can make instances of the three subclasses as follows:

```
(setq w1 (make-instance 'wing))
(setq b1 (make-instance 'body))
```

What you want to do is model the value of the length slot of the plane as a derived quantity from the length slots of the wing and the width slot of the body. The formula might be the length of the plane is equal to the width of the body plus twice the length of the wing. In other words, you would like, for example

```
(setf (lngth w1) 3.5)
(setf (width b1) 0.3)
```

to automatically result in updating the plane length:

```
(lngth b1) => 7.3 (7.3 = 3.5 x 2 + 0.3)
```

The formula should be

```
(defun update-length ()
    (setf (slot-value b1 'length)
        (+ (width b1) (* 2 (lngth w1)))))
```

You want to make this possible for any type of dependency. You do this by adding custom behavior to the (setf slot-value) function in the CLOS MOP. Recall that this is a *function specifier* (a list representing a function that is used with setf syntax; it is the function called on an object with slot-name with a new value in the form (setf (slot-value object 'slot-name) new-value)).

(setf slot-value-using-class) is the method that implements the behavior of the (setf slot-value) function (called when you set the length slot of w1 or the width slot of b1). (setf slot-value) is the standard CLOS methodology for setting slot values.

When (setf slot-value) is called, the MOP specifies that it use the method (setf slot-value-using-class) to decide what it should do, so you specialize this method on dependency-class to implement dependency tracking. Here is the interface definition for generic function:

```
(defgeneric (setf slot-value-using-class)
    (new-value class instance slot)
    ;; generic function to set a slot-value
    )
```

(setf slot-value-using-class) is called by (setf slot-value) with the following arguments: the new value as its first argument, the class of the object as its second argument, the object itself as the third argument, and the metaobject representing the slot as its fourth argument (it's the argument slot above).

First, you need a function to find a slot from its name:

```
(defun slot-from-name (name class)
    (dolist (slot (class-slots class))
        (when (eq name (slot-definition-name slot))
          (return slot))))
```

Ignoring for now compiler optimizations and error-checking, (setf slot-value) is implemented in the following way:

```
(defun (setf slot-value) (new-value object slot-name)
    (let* ((class (class-of object))
           (slot (slot-from-name slot-name class)))
      (setf(slot-value-using-class class object slot) new-value)))
```

Here is the specializer on dependency-class:

```
(defmethod (setf slot-value-using-class) :after
    (new-value (class dependency-class) object slot)
    ;; Above is the argument list. Usage of this function spec:
    ;; (setf (slot-value-using-class class object slot) new-value)
```

```
(let*((name (slot-definition-name slot))

      ;; Look for a function fcn on the dependency slot of
      ;; object associated with the name of the slot argument.
      (fcn (if (slot-boundp object 'dependency)
               (getf (part-dependency object) name))))

  ;; Call the function fcn when it is present
  (when fcn (funcall fcn))))
```

You add an :after method that runs after the primary (setf slot-value-using-class) method runs. The primary method is inherited from standard-class and hence has the same semantics—that is, it sets the slot value. This :after method is specialized on the metaclass dependency-class, so it runs every time you try to set a slot of any instance of any class of the metaclass dependency-class. Recall that the value returned by the after method is ignored, so it does not affect the value returned by the primary method when the whole method runs.

Note that classes of ordinary type standard-class are unaffected.

What does this :after method do? It looks in the dependency slot of the object. It expects to see an association list—a list of pairs, each of the form (value, slot-name). The function getf looks up the value associated with slot-name of the metaobject representing the slot. If this value is present, it is run as a function that takes the object as its argument.

Note that (setf slot-value) may be called as part of the initialization of a new instance, so to prevent looking in the dependency slot before it gets initialized, you check it first to see if the initialization has happened using the standard CLOS function slot-boundp.

It's time to see it in action. Add a dependency to the model:

```
(setf (getf (part-dependency w1) 'length) #'update-length)
```

Now when you set the length slot of w1, the :after method runs the function update-length.

The effect of the :after method is purely a side effect resulted from running the function named update-length that is associated with the symbol length in w1's dependency slot. For example, it doesn't affect setting the slot value w1 in any way. In this case, because the length slot of b1 depends on the value in the length slot of w1, you want this side effect to change the length slot of b1.

The length slot of b1 is also dependent on the width slot of b1, so now you add that dependency as well:

```
(setf (getf (part-dependency b1) 'width) #'update-length)
```

When you try the following:

```
(setf (lngth w1) 6)
(setf (width b1) 1)
```

reading the value by calling (lngth b1) returns the value 13.

A diagram will help:

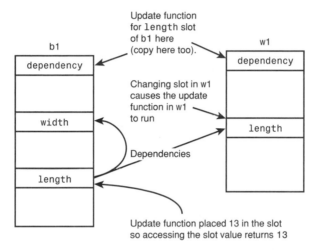

At this point, you can automate the preceding process by writing a function:

```
(defun add-dependency (this-object this-slot update-fcn
                       &rest objects-and-slots)
   (do* ((xx objects-and-slots (cddr xx))
      (newobj (car xx) (car xx))
      (newslot (cadr xx) (cadr xx)))
      ((null xx))
      (setf (getf (part-dependency newobj) newslot)
         #'(lambda () (setf (slot-value this-object this-slot)
            (funcall update-fcn))))))
```

This is all standard Common Lisp. It iterates over the pairs of objects and slot names and adds an anonymous function (defined as the lambda expression), which sets the slot named this-slot of the object named this-object with the value returned by update-fcn whenever one of the named slots of objects in the objects-and-slots list is set. This is cleaner than having to hard wire the to-be-updated object into the definition of update-fcn, as you did in the preceding example of update-length.

Note the similarity between this lambda expression and the original update-length function:

```
#'(lambda ()
   (setf (slot-value this-object this-slot)
      (funcall update-fcn))

(defun update-length ()
   (setf (slot-value b1 'length); <- set the dependent slot
      (+ (width b1) (* 2 (lngth w1)) ;<- the update function
   )))
```

Here you add the dependency of the length slot of b1 to the length slot of
w1 and the width slot of b1:

```
(add-dependency b1 'length
      #'(lambda ()(+ (width b1) (* 2 (lngth w1)))
      w1 'length b1 'width)
```

add-dependency adds the update function update-length for the length slot of
b1 whenever the length slot of w1 is set or the width slot of b1 is set.

Now you have spreadsheet semantics for slots. The semantics result in an
immediate update of all slots, which are calculated using other slots. This
type of semantics is exactly what is desired if you want to immediately
see the correct values of other slots, for example, where the slots represent dimensions of parts in an engineering diagram.

Dependency Tracking Applied to Lazy Evaluation

Consider a somewhat different problem: As part of the design, you need
to calculate the plane's vibrational characteristics to model its take-off
characteristics. Suppose that the calculation involves numerical algorithms that take a long time to compute and also depend on the dimensions of parts of the plane. Although you are modeling the plane, you
don't want the vibrational characteristics to be recomputed every time
you change the dimensions. In a way, you want the exact opposite
semantics for slot-value update that you just went through: You don't
want slots to recalculate their values *until you need to use them*. This
issue is not an academic one: Real-life planes, such as the Boeing 777, are
designed with Lisp-based software using techniques like those discussed
here (Phillips, 1997). The number of parts and dependencies in very large
models is enormous, so controlling the amount of recalculation is a critical performance consideration.

The system is the inverse of the one just designed, which recalculates values whenever something the slot is dependent upon changes. Instead,
here, you recalculate a value only when the slot is accessed. A simple
approach is to add a slot that keeps the update function and specialize
slot-value-using-class to call the update function whenever the slot is

read. As an example, use the weight of the plane as the sum of the weights of the wings, the engines, and the body. If the model has one engine per wing, then the weight of the plane is calculated using twice the weight of the engines, plus twice the weight of the wings, plus the weight of the body:

```
(defclass part ()
    ((updates :initform nil
              :accessor part-updates)
     (unused-updates :initform nil
              :accessor part-unused-updates)
     (dependency :initform nil
              :accessor part-dependency))
    (:metaclass dependency-class))

(defclass body (part)
    ((weight :initarg :weight :initform 0 :accessor weight))
    (:metaclass dependency-class))

(defclass wing (part)
    ((weight :initarg :weight :initform 0 :accessor weight))
    (:metaclass dependency-class))

(defclass engine (part)
    ((weight :initarg :weight :initform 0 :accessor weight))
    (:metaclass dependency-class))

(defclass plane (part)
    ((weight :initform 0 :reader weight))
    (:metaclass dependency-class))
```

You modify slot-value to recalculate values when the slot is accessed. When slot-value is called, as part of the metaobject protocol it calls slot-value-using-class. Like (setf slot-value-using-class), and ignoring for now compiler optimizations as well as error-checking, slot-value is implemented as

```
(defun slot-value (object slot-name)
    (let* ((class (class-of object))
           (slot (slot-from-name slot-name class)))
       (slot-value-using-class class object slot)))
```

slot-value-using-class is called by slot-value with the following arguments: the class of the object as its first argument, the object itself as the second argument, and the metaobject representing the slot as its third argument. Recall that slot-from-name was defined in the previous section.

You specialize slot-value-using-class on dependency-class using an around method because you set the return value from calling the method:

```
(defmethod slot-value-using-class :around
    ((class dependency-class) object slot)
```

```
(let((name (slot-definition-name slot))
     (result nil))
  ;; Call the primary slot-value method
  (setf result (call-next-method))

  (unless (eq name 'updates)

      ;; Look for a function fcn associated with name in the
      ;; updates slot of object
      (let ((fcn (getf (part-updates object) name)))

          ;; If we found fcn, run it and use that result
          ;; instead of the result returned by the primary
          ;; slot-value method called above.
          (if fcn (setf result (funcall fcn)))))
  result))
```

The :around method runs and uses the function getf to look up the function fcn associated with slot-name of the metaobject representing the slot. If this function fcn is present, it is run as an update function and its value is returned. If there is nothing there, you use call-next-method to retrieve the value using the semantics of standard-class. Because the protocol is present for all slots (including the updates slot), you suppress any infinite recursive calls to part-updates by ensuring that the slot being accessed is not the updates slot.

The update function needs to be added to the association list in the updates slot of the object containing the slot to be recalculated on access:

```
(defun add-update (object slot-name update-fcn)
  (setf (getf (part-updates object) slot-name)
    update-fcn))
```

You set up the rule for calculating the weight of a plane:

```
(setq w1 (make-instance 'wing :weight 500))
(setq b1 (make-instance 'body :weight 3000))
(setq e1 (make-instance 'engine :weight 1000))
(setq plane (make-instance 'plane))

(defun update-weight ()
    (+ (* 2 (weight w1))
       (* 2 (weight e1))
       (weight b1)))

(add-update plane 'weight #'update-weight)
```

(weight plane) returns the value 6000.

The disadvantage of what you have done so far is that the slot values are always being recalculated. As a next step, you add an optimization: Only recalculate slot values only when their dependencies change. The dependency tracking code uses the same version of (setf slot-value-using-class) defined in the previous example.

Whenever the weight slots of w1, b1, or e1 are changed, you want the
weight slot of plane to recalculate; otherwise, you cache the value from a
prior recalculation in the slot and just return it. Make a change to the
slot-value-using-class around method:

```
(defmethod slot-value-using-class :around
    ((class dependency-class) object slot)
    (let((name (slot-definition-name slot))
         (result nil))
      (setf result (call-next-method))
      (unless (eq name 'updates)
         (let ((fcn (getf (part-updates object) name)))
           (if fcn (progn
                    (setf result (funcall fcn))
                    (setf (getf (part-updates object) name)
                          nil)
                    (setf (slot-value object name) result)
                    (setf (getf (part-unused-updates object)
                          name) fcn)))))
      result))
```

Now on calling (slot-value plane 'weight), the :around method runs. You
check to see if there is an update function for the slot; if there is, you calculate the new value, remove the update function after it has done its
work, and stash it in the association list in the unused-updates slot. It needs
to be replaced in the association list in the updates slot of plane whenever
the weight slots of w1, b1, or e1 are changed again.

This work requires a change to the function that runs whenever (setf
slot-value-using-class) is called to change the weight slots of w1, b1, or e1.
You implement this work as an anonymous lambda defined in the function add-dependency. The anonymous lambda makes the update function
available after changing a slot the weight slot of plane depends on.

Now, when the update function is available, the weight slot of plane is
recalculated whenever you access the slot, and if it's not available there,
then you know the slot value is up to date and merely return the value in
the slot.

You are still missing a final piece of logic. If a slot in one object depends
on a calculated value in a second object, which in turn depends on a
value in a third object, changing the value in the third object does not
result in a recalculation in the first object (unless the value in the second
object has been recalculated after the change). The dependency has not
been propagated recursively.

The idea is simple: Set the slot value in the second object to any value
(e.g., 'unknown) at the same time the value in the third object is changed.
Changing the slot value in the second object triggers the after method to

make available the update function to the first object. Thereafter, the value in the first object is subject to recalculation as desired. If you do access the value in the first object, it accesses the value in the second object for its recalculation, which is also recalculated on demand. Here's the new version of add-dependency, which does the job:

```
(defun add-dependency (this-object this-slot update-fcn
                       &rest objects-and-slots)
  (do* ((xx objects-and-slots (cddr xx))
        (newobj (car xx) (car xx))
        (newslot (cadr xx) (cadr xx)))
       ((null xx))
    (add-update this-object this-slot update-fcn)
    (setf (getf (part-dependency newobj) newslot)
      #'(lambda ()
            (let ((fcn (getf (part-updates this-object)
                             this-slot))
                  (fcn1 (getf (part-unused-updates this-object)
                              this-slot)))
              (unless fcn
                (setf (slot-value this-object this-slot)
                  'unknown))
                (setf
                  (getf (part-updates this-object) this-slot)
                  fcn1)))))))
```

The change is in the lambda expression—that is, the function that gets run whenever (setf slot-value) is called on a slot that this-slot of this-object depends on. It checks to see if there is an update function that needs to be run when this-slot is read from. If there is, then it returns because the slot is out of date (i.e., someone else already installed the update function for the slot). Otherwise, it setfs the slot value to unknown (thus recursively notifying slots and objects that are dependent on this value) and then takes the update function out of the updates-unused association list and puts it back in the association list of the updates slot of this-object, where it is found and run next time this-slot is accessed.

This solution ignores many issues that robust code would have to deal with. More sophisticated implementations might want to set multiple dependencies on a slot of an object.

More customization might also be needed for dependency-class: For example, you would want to deal with the possibility of the slots being unbound. The following code indicates useful MOP generic functions:

```
(defgeneric slot-unboundp-using-class (class instance slot-name)
  ;; generic function for testing if a slot has a value
  )

(defgeneric slot-makunbound-using-class (class instance slot-name)
  ;; generic function to make a slot have no value
  )
```

5.4.10. Performance Considerations

In general, the default CLOS operations are highly optimized. Generic functions dispatch using caching techniques.

Build it right and get it working before you speed up anything. When you have to speed it up, profile your code! Profiling is really the only way to ensure you aren't wasting your time fixing things that matter little.

Here are a few hints for increasing speed when it is really necessary:

- Some implementations offer specialized CLOS semantics that are more restrictive than the default CLOS but that the compiler can use to optimize access. For example, a popular implementation, Allegro CL, offers a fixed-index metaclass that implements slot value as array memory accesses.

- If speed is really essential, consider recoding the performance critical section in straight procedural (non-CLOS) Common Lisp. This may add speed.

- Most implementations generate dispatching code for calculating which method to use based on the generic function. Because there is a large number of possibilities for different methods, many implementations generate the dispatching code at runtime. This needs to be compiled to run fast, introducing a delay the first time the method is invoked. Using the application before delivery precalculates the dispatching code.

- Many implementations have special cases for the dispatching code for common patterns of method arguments. For example, most CLOS operators dispatch only on the first argument and have fewer than 10 arguments overall. Of the remainder, most of the rest dispatch on either the second argument or on both the first and second arguments. Specialized methods that conform to these cases are likely to be faster.

- Never use the MOP to customize standard-class directly. Always subclass it first. In the presence of customizations, the compiler may not be able to optimize as efficiently.

For a more general book about improving performance in Common Lisp applications, you should look at *Paradigms of AI Programming* (Norvig, 1992), which has an excellent section on optimizing general Common Lisp programs.

5.4.11. Summary of CLOS Operators

We distinguish between generic functions, which are interfaces implemented with methods, and functions that are procedural interfaces. The notation arguments are italicized. When there is a list of a variable number of options in the argument list, it is surrounded by {}. When the list can be zero or more, you use *. When the list must be one or more, you use +. The &rest notation is a standard Common Lisp notation that takes arguments following the position in the argument list marked by &rest and makes them into a list bound to the name following the &rest. The &optional notation takes arguments following the position in the argument list marked by &optional, and if they are not present in an actual function call, the argument gets set to a (possibly user-defined) default value.

I don't attempt to handle all cases in this summary. For the complete specification of all CLOS operators, consult the ANSI standard (ANSI, 1996). However, the list given covers most of the common operations. The operations omitted here are used in parts of the MOP (except as used in the examples) and operations having to do with method combinations.

---

call-next-method &rest *arguments (Function)*

Returns the return value of the next method. call-next-method is used within the body of a method to call the next method, defined by the method combination type in use. If the next method is missing, then an error is signaled. The default behavior of signaling an error is implemented by the no-next-method generic function, called when the system detects the next method is missing. next-method-p tests to see if the next method exists.

Standard method combination permits use of call-next-method in around methods and primary methods. Operator combination types support call-next-method only in around methods.

call-next-method is normally called with no arguments, implicitly using the arguments of the method being used. Other arguments may be supplied as long as their types would cause the same applicable methods to be run as the types of the original arguments.

---

change-class *instance* new-class *(Generic function)*

Returns the instance. *instance* is an object and *new-class* is a class object, both with metaclass standard-class. This changes the class of *instance* to a new class and calls the generic function update-instance-for-different-class.

`class-name` *class (Generic function)*

Returns the name of the *class*. *class* must be a class object. `class-name` supports `setf` to change the name of the class.

`class-of` *object (Function)*

Returns an object that is the class of the object. Every object has a class.

`defclass` *name* (*{superclass}**) (*{slot-spec}**) *{class-option}** *(Macro)*

Returns the class object that is a new class or a redefinition of an existing class. The *name* of the class and the class object become type specifiers.

The arguments are

name	The symbol that is the name of this class.
superclass	A symbol that is the name of a direct superclass of this class.
slot-spec	The slot specification for a slot of the new class. *slot-spec* is either a symbol representing the name of the slot or a list containing the name of the slot followed with zero or more options that further specify the slot.

The possible options for `slot-spec` *are*

`:accessor` *accessor-name*	*accessor-name* is a symbol that names the reader generic function for the slot and (`setf` *accessor-name*) becomes the writer generic function for the slot.
`:reader` *reader-name*	*reader-name* is a symbol that names the reader generic function for the slot.
`:writer` *function-specification*	*function-specification* is either a symbol or a *function-specification* for writing the value of a slot. If *function-specification* is a symbol, then the writer generic function is called using normal functional syntax (`symbol new-value object`), but if the *function-specification* is a list such as (`setfsymbol`), then the writer is called with `setf` syntax: (`setf` (`symbol object`) `new value`).

`:initarg` *name*	*name* is a symbol, by convention a key word. By including *name* followed by a value in a call to `make-instance`, the slot is set to *value*.
`:initform` *form*	*form* provides the default initial value for the slot. *form* evaluates in the lexical environment where `defclass` is defined. When an `initarg` is present in a call to `make-instance`, `make-instance` uses the value provided by `:initarg` rather than the value of form specified in `:initform`.
`:type` *type*	This specifies the type of value of a slot. CLOS semantics do not specify an error if the value stored in the slot is actually of a different type.
`:allocation` *allocation-type*	This determines whether the slot is allocated as a local slot (the default) or as a slot shared among all instances of the class. The default *allocation-type* is `:instance`. Shared slots use `:class` *allocation-type*.

The possible options for `class-option` are

(`:documentation` *doc-string*)	*doc-string* is a string that should contain documentation for the class.
(`:default-initargs` {*initarg-name* *form*}*)	This option specifies the default values for initargs. Each form is used as an initial value form for the `initarg` of *initarg-name*. This option is the only class option inherited by subclasses.
(`:metaclass` *class-name*)	This specifies the name of the class of the new class. The default metaclass is `standard-class`.

`defgeneric` *function-name* *lambda-list* {*function-option*}* *(Macro)*

`defgeneric` defines a new generic function or redefines an existing one. `defgeneric` specifies the generic function interface using the lambda list. The options include documentation, `method-combination` type, and declarations. There are some variations on `defgeneric` that I do not describe here: `generic-flet`, `generic-labels`, `with-added-methods`, and `generic-function` (which defines an anonymous generic function):

function-name	Names the generic function using a symbol or a function specification such as (setf symbol).
lambda-list	Describes the argument list for the generic function. The argument list cannot contain &aux variables. Optional and keyword arguments may not have defaults or use supplied-p parameters. No parameter can be specialized.

The options for function-option *are*

(:argument-precedence-order order {*argument-name*}+)	Arguments are normally evaluated from left to right. This specifies a different for evaluating the arguments in the order supplied. If present, this list must include all required argument names.
(declare {*declaration*}+)	The standard Common Lisp declarations can be used, except for declaration, ftype, function, inline, and special.
(:documentation *doc-string*)	*doc-string* is a string that should contain documentation for the generic function.
(:generic-function-class *name*)	This specifies the class of the generic function object. The default is standard-generic-function.
(:method {qualifier}* specializer-lambda-list {decl ¦ doc}* {form}*)	Defines a method for the generic function. This is equivalent to defmethod.
(:method-class *name*)	This specifies the class of the methods for this generic function. The default is standard-method.
(:method-combination symbol {*arguments*}*)	This specifies the method-combination type with name *symbol*. *arguments* are the arguments needed by the method-combination type.

```
defmethod name {qualifier}* specializer-lambda-list
{decl | doc}* {body}* (Macro)
```

Returns the method object. `defmethod` defines a new method for a generic function or redefines an existing method:

name	This is the name of the generic function. It is either a symbol or a function specification such as (setf symbol).
qualifier	This identifies the role of the method. The standard method combination implements method qualifiers :before, :after, and :around.
specializer-lambda-list	This matches the standard Common Lisp argument list definition except that the name of a required argument can be replaced by a specialized parameter, which is a list of the form (arg *specializer-name*). Optional arguments cannot be specialized. *specializer-name* can be a list, for example, (eql form) or a symbol that names a class. Classes can be a user-defined built-in-class or a user-defined defstruct class declared without the :type option. A declaration about the method. A string that should contain documentation for the method.
decl	A declaration about the method.
doc	A string that should contain documentation for the method.
body	The code that implements the method.

```
describe object (Generic function)
```

Returns no value. Prints a description of *object* to standard output. A default primary method uses the standard method combination type.

```
find-class symbol &optional (errorp t) (Function)
```

Returns the class object with name *symbol*. If *errorp* is t (the default) and there is no class with this name, it signals an error; otherwise, it returns nil. This function works with setf to change the class name to a new symbol.

find-method *generic-function qualifiers specializers*
&optional *errorp (Generic function)*

Returns the method object associated with the generic function object (which, for example, is returned by symbol-function on a symbol) and its *qualifiers* and *specializers*:

> *qualifiers*   A list of the method qualifiers (such as :before).
>
> *specializers*   A list of the method's argument *specializer* objects. The list contains one specialization corresponding to each required argument. Arguments that do not have explicit specializations use the specialization class named t.
>
> *errorp*   If t (the default), signal an error if there is no method. If nil, return nil if there is no method.

make-instance *class* &rest *initargs (Generic function)*

Returns a new instance of *class* and initializes the slots by calling the generic function initialize-instance with the new instance and the *initargs*. There is a set of MOP operations that I do not describe here that can be used to customize make-instance (and redefine instances): initialize-instance, reinitialize-instance, shared-initialize, update-instance-for-redefined-class, and update-instance-for-different-class:

> *initargs*   Pairs of *initarg* names and values. The *initarg* names are defined in the :initarg option to defclass or are the names of keyword parameters defined in the MOP methods for make-instance, initialize-instance, or shared-initialize.

next-method-p *(Function)*

Returns t if there is a next method; otherwise, returns nil. It must be used in the body of a method and is used to make sure that call-next-method can be used. The method combination type is used to find the next method. For the standard method combination, in an around method, the next method is the next most specific around method (if it exists) or it is the current effective method; in a primary method, the next method is the next most specific primary method.

slot-boundp *instance slot-name (Function)*

Returns t if the slot in the instance is bound (i.e., has been initialized to a value). Otherwise, it returns nil.

slot-value *instance slot-name (Function)*

Returns the value of the slot specified by *slot-name* in the *instance*. *slot-name* must be a symbol naming the slot.

slot-value-using-class *class instance slot (Generic Function)*

This MOP function returns the value of the slot specified by *slot* in the *instance*. *slot* must be the effective slot definition metaobject. This generic function is used to customize slot-value.

update-instance-for-different-class old *new plist*
&rest *initargs (Generic function)*

This function is called by the system when an instance is updated after its class has changed. The return value is ignored. Conventional usage is to implement the method as an after method because the primary method calls shared-initialize to initialize the *new-slots*. Used to access information in the original instance to update the new version of the instance:

old	A copy of the original instance.
new	The new version of the instance.
initargs	The initarg names and their values. Valid initarg names are the same as for defclass and the names of key-words specified in methods for update-instance-for-different-class or shared-initialize.

update-instance-for-redefined-class *instance new-slots*
old-slots plist &rest *initargs (Generic function)*

This function is called by the system when an instance is updated
after a class redefinition. The return value is ignored. Conventional
usage is to implement the method as an after method because the
primary method calls shared-initialize to initialize the *new-slots*.
Used to access information in the original slots to update the new
version of the instance:

instance	The updated instance.
new-slots	The list of slots added to this instance.
old-slots	The list of slots removed from this instance.
plist	A list of alternating slot names and values. All removed slots with values appear on this list. No unbound slots appear.
initargs	The initarg names and their values. Valid initarg names are the same as for defclass and the names of keywords specified in methods for update-instance-for-redefined-class or shared-initialize.

with-accessors ({*accessor*}*) *instance-form* &body *body (Macro)*

Returns the last form of the body. This macro creates a lexical context for using *accessors* like variables. Each *accessor* must be a list
(variable-name accessors). Within the *body*, using setf or setq on a
variable defined in the *accessor* list calls the writer function associated with name of the associated *accessor*.

with-slots ({*slot-entry*}*) *instance-form* &body *body (Macro)*

Returns the last form of the *body*. This macro creates a lexical context for using slot names like variables. Each *slot-entry* must either
be a list (variable-name slot-name) or a slot name, specified by a symbol. Within the *body*, using setf or setq on a variable defined in the
slot-entry list calls the writer function associated with name of the
associated *slot-entry*.

5.5. References

ANSI. 1994. American National Standard for Information Technology Programming Language—Common Lisp. *ANSI X3.226-1994*. New York.

Bobrow, D. G., K. Kahn, G. Kizcales, L. Masinter, M. Stefik, and F. Zybdel. 1986. CommonLoops: Merging Lisp and Object-Oriented Programming. *ACM Sigplan Notices* 21(11).

Drescher, G. 1987. *ObjectLISP user manual*. Cambridge, MA: LISP Machines Inc.

Graham, P. 1994. *On Lisp: Advanced techniques for common Lisp*. Englewood Cliffs, NJ: Prentice Hall.

Keene, S. 1989. *Object-oriented programming in common Lisp*. Reading, MA: Addison-Wesley.

Kempf, J., W. Harris, R. D'Souza, and A. Snyder. 1987. Experience with CommonLoops. *ACM SIGPLAN Notices* 22(12).

Kizcales, G., J. des Rivieres, and D. Bobrow. 1992. *The art of the Metaobject Protocol*. Cambridge, MA: MIT Press.

McCarthy, J. 1981. History of Lisp. In R. L. Wexeblat(Ed.), *History of programming languages* (pp. 173–197). New York: Academic Press.

Norvig, P. 1992. *Paradigms of artificial programming: Case studies in Common Lisp*. CA: Morgan Kaufman.

Phillips, R. 1997. Dynamic Objects for Engineering Automation. *Communications of the ACM* pp.59–65.

Smith, B. C., and C. Hewitt. 1975. *A PLASMA primer*. Working Paper 92, MIT Artificial Intelligence Laboratory, Cambridge, MA.

Symbolics, Inc. 1985. *Reference guide to Symbolics Lisp*. Cambridge, MA: Author.

PART V
Prolog

CHAPTER 6

Prolog: Programming in Logic

by James H. Andrews

Prolog had a quiet birth but a tumultuous childhood. Developed in 1972, it became widely known only two years later and quickly became a topic of controversy. Even today, Prolog can provoke surprisingly strong feelings in some people, comparable to those around languages such as COBOL and Smalltalk.

Yet Prolog is just another programming language. It has its strengths and its weaknesses, application areas where it shines and application areas where it is best passed over. It brings a new perspective to many problems, and many programmers find it a useful addition to their toolkit. In these respects, it is no different from any other programming language.

However, in several respects, Prolog does differ from most other languages. It has a useful and powerful pure subset in which programs can be read as logical formulas. This pure subset allows us to solve problems by expressing the conditions under which a solution exists, without explicitly stating how to find the solution. This property allows a succinct and readable expression of tasks in problem domains with an inherently logical structure, such as deductive systems. Programs are naturally expressed using pattern-matching clauses, making Prolog ideal for such tasks as parsing and translating.

The programmer has to be aware, however, of how a running Prolog program does find a solution; this Prolog execution model, which is more complex than the imperative or functional model, is the main stumbling block in learning to use Prolog effectively. Prolog is not dogmatic about logic. Impure, extralogical additions allow us to circumvent the rigidity of logic whenever we need to, in the spirit of a truly pragmatic programming language.

6.1. History and Background

6.1.1. The Early Days

Prolog was invented in the early 1970s by Alain Colmerauer and was implemented by him and his group at the University of Marseilles around 1972. Its name was chosen as a contraction of *programmation en logique*, which translates to programming in logic. It was a practical embodiment of ideas that were being explored at the same time by Robert Kowalski in Edinburgh. Several other researchers, such as Elcock, Boyer, and Moore, had also studied programming involving logic, but mainly in a functional programming setting. When Kowalski encountered Prolog, he wrote an article for a prominent conference in 1974 that described these new ideas of "predicate logic as a programming language" to the world. Thus the logic programming paradigm was born.

At the time, the dialog in the artificial intelligence community was dominated by the battle of the "neats " and the "scruffies" in North America. The neats, typified by John McCarthy, wanted to do artificial intelligence (AI) by formulating broad theories based on principles; the scruffies, typified by Marvin Minsky, wanted to do AI by writing heuristic programs that worked, regardless of principles. Prolog quickly became a football in this battle. The neats praised it for allowing logical thought to be expressed more directly than in other programming languages, and the scruffies criticized it for being slow and pedantic.

Many neats became disenchanted with Prolog, however, when it became clear that most implementations used incomplete reasoning and had features that were not in accord with the neats' strict logical principles. That disenchantment, coupled with the perception that Prolog was exclusively an AI language and the lack of a strong academic tradition in Prolog in North America, led to it being largely rejected by North American computer science. It still enjoys popularity outside North America, however, and among a fair number of people in North America who are interested in symbolic computing.

Researchers interested in Prolog continued to develop the language after its initial release. The first implementation of Prolog to leave Marseilles was an interpreter written in Fortran. The early culmination of the development was the C-Prolog interpreter of the early 1980s, developed at the Artificial Intelligence department of the University of Edinburgh. C-Prolog was based on earlier work by David H. D. Warren, Fernando Pereira, Luis Pereira, and others. It was the first widely available Prolog with a usable debugger and extensive library. Its syntax and library became a de facto standard and are often referred to together as Edinburgh Prolog.

In the mid-1980s, the software company Borland marketed Turbo Prolog, a cut-down and somewhat modified version of the language for IBM PC-compatibles. C-Prolog and Turbo Prolog, although somewhat obsolete, were very useful and are still the first (or only) implementations of Prolog many people have encountered.

6.1.2. Progress on Prolog

Progress on Prolog has continued apace. The directions of progress can be classified into three groups: progress on implementation technology, progress on practical uses, and progress on variants and added features.

The earliest Prolog implementations were interpreters, but Prolog compiler technology has been widely available since the mid-1980s. The late 1980s and early 1990s saw great strides in making Prolog compilers and the code they generate more efficient. Modern Prolog compilers are comparable in compilation efficiency and code efficiency to functional programming compilers.

Prolog was applied originally to AI problems, and its most widespread commercial use still is as a language for programming expert systems. However, it has also been used as a basis for language translators, interpreters and compilers, automated design, deductive databases, computer-aided instruction, natural language front ends, schedulers, and so on. In fact, Prolog has been found to be suitable for many applications involving complex symbolic processing and search for solutions. A Practical Applications of Prolog conference is held every year to promote interaction among the users of the language.

Many added features, variants of Prolog, and similar languages to Prolog have been proposed over the years. The added feature that has met with the widest acceptance, even in commercial Prolog compilers, is definite clause grammars, which allow users to write parsers in a very natural style. Three of the more popular non-commercial languages in the Prolog mold in recent years are XSB Prolog, which offers more flexible search strategies, and Goedel and Mercury, which offer types to assist in compile-time processing. More academic add-ons include constraint processing (allowing more natural expression of arithmetic relations, among other things) and parallel processing, but these are available mostly in experimental implementations with limited environmental support. However, research on constraint processing in the context of logic programming has had the side benefit of leading to industrial-strength constraint tools for imperative languages, such as Ilog Solver.

Finally, an international Prolog standard has been developed, although as far as I am aware, no free implementation of the standard is available. Information on the standard can be found via the Internet.

6.1.3. Myths and Problems of Prolog

As a consequence of its history, Prolog is often known about, but seldom thoroughly known. Some myths have therefore arisen about the language and why it is not used in some circles. This is not to say that Prolog has no problems at all. Here I deal with some of the myths and discuss the real problems.

6.1.3.1. Myths

The biggest myth about current Prolog implementations is that they are slow. This impression may come partly from experience with old Prolog interpreters. As noted previously, with a proper compiler, Prolog is competitive with functional languages in speed. Another contributing factor may be the seductiveness of Prolog's logical syntax; it is possible to write a natural-looking program that is nevertheless executed by Prolog in a very inefficient manner. To use Prolog effectively, it is sometimes necessary to re-express parts of a program in a way that ensures efficient execution, but it is often possible to do so.

The second biggest myth is that Prolog's depth-first, backtracking search strategy makes it inadequate for the tasks it is supposed to perform. This is a holdover of the old AI debates about Prolog and only really applies if we expect to be able to code up our problem domain in logical formulas and have Prolog execute it as-is. We do have to take the search strategy into account when writing Prolog applications, but the same applies to imperative or functional languages, with their depth-first, non-backtracking execution model. Prolog's backtracking is a tool that we can use whenever we need it but set aside when we don't.

One of the strangest myths about Prolog, still spotted on the Internet from time to time, is that we can easily write a Prolog interpreter in Lisp but we can't easily write a Lisp interpreter in Prolog. This myth has been refuted several times, and various simple Lisp interpreters written in Prolog are now available on the Internet.

6.1.3.2. Problems

There do remain two major problems with most Prolog implementations. The first is that classic Prolog has no type system. This makes for great programmer freedom, but also for runtime errors similar to those that programmers in typeless Lisp variants have to deal with. Many logic programming systems have types, but these systems are rarely industrial-strength. Goedel and Mercury are two of the best.

The second problem is that classic Prolog has no notation for defining functions, just relations. For instance, the factorial function can be expressed easily in a functional language as a function fact(X) taking an integer X and returning an integer, but in Prolog, it must be expressed as a boolean relation fact(X, XFact) relating an integer X to its factorial XFact. Of course, any function taking N arguments can be defined as a relation of N+1 arguments. But it is often more convenient to define a function and then use a call to the function directly in an expression. Many proposals have been put forward over the years for merging functional and logic programming, but no one proposal has caught on and been widely accepted.

Prolog—or the languages that succeed it—will have to deal with these problems eventually as the logic programming paradigm evolves.

6.1.4. Prolog Resources

Many commercial and freeware versions and variants of Prolog are available, with the usual tradeoffs among power, cost, and usability. I recommend that interested users search for the *Prolog Resource Guide* on the Internet to get more information.

Many books have been written about Prolog from different perspectives. All of them go into more detail about the use and features of the language than this brief chapter is able to do. Some of the best, in my opinion, are the original classic, *Programming in Prolog*, by Clocksin and Mellish (1987); the more advanced books *The Art of Prolog* by Sterling and Shapiro (1986) and *The Craft of Prolog* by O'Keefe (1990); and the application-oriented *Prolog Programming for Artificial Intelligence* by Bratko (1990).

As well, online Prolog tutorials have been springing up on the Internet in various forms. Use your favorite search engine to find the latest.

6.1.5. The Structure of This Chapter

This chapter continues with an introduction to Prolog programming in section 6.2; section 6.3 concerns more advanced features. Section 6.4 is titled "Tips and Traps" and deals with useful hints and difficult problems. Finally, section 6.5 contains several sample programs, section 6.6 gives acknowledgments, and section 6.7 lists references.

6.2. Basic Prolog Programming

This section covers the basics of Prolog programming. It first looks at the operation of the Prolog interpreter and then explores a simple knowledge-base program with simple terms. It then moves on to studying the properties of the equality predicate and lists terms made up of simpler terms. Finally, this section looks at the execution model that Prolog uses in order to do what it does.

6.2.1. Hello World

Prolog is a declarative language, but it has a procedural subset to deal with input/output. Here, I introduce simple interaction with the Prolog interpreter using this procedural subset and the popular Hello World program.

When we start the Prolog interpreter, it prompts us with something like

```
¦?-
```

This prompt is referred to as the *query prompt*, and the things we type to it are referred to as *queries*. To this query prompt, type the query

```
¦?- write('Hello world.'), nl.
```

(**Bold** font indicates what the interpreter types, and `typewriter` font indicates what we type.) This query asks Prolog to write the text `Hello world.` and then output a newline character (`nl`). Prolog should respond with

```
Hello world.

yes
¦?-
```

It has written the string we asked it to, started a new line, reported on the success of its task with `yes`, and is prompting us again. On some interpreters, we may have to press Enter once to get the top-level prompt back. The interpreter goes through an infinite loop of reading a query, responding to it, and waiting for another query.

Prolog programs are generally stored in files. Create a file called `greet.pl`, containing just the line

```
hello :- write('Hello world.'), nl.
```

We can read this as saying the following to Prolog: To perform the task called `hello`, it should write the text `Hello world.` and output a newline. `hello` is called a *predicate*, and we have defined the predicate using a *rule*. A rule contains a *head*, in this case `hello`, and a *body*, everything after the `:-`. Back in the Prolog interpreter, we can now type the query

```
¦?- [greet].
```

This causes Prolog to "consult" the file `greet.pl`—that is, to read it as a Prolog source file. If we now pose the query

```
¦?- hello.
```

it responds exactly as if we had typed the rule body. We can also pose the query

```
¦?- hello, hello, hello.
```

This asks Prolog to perform the `hello` task three times, so Prolog prints the message three times:

```
Hello world.
Hello world.
Hello world.

yes
¦?-
```

Predicates can have parameters. Add the following definition to `greet.pl`:

This rule defines another predicate, `hello_age`, which takes one parameter, `N`. Now if we reconsult the source file using `[greet]` again and pose the query `hello_age(72)`, it should write

```
Hello 72-year-old.
```

We will explore I/O in more detail later, but for now, let's leave imperative programming aside and concentrate on declarative programming in Prolog.

6.2.2. The Genealogy Program

The Hello World program is the standard introductory program for imperative languages. However, the standard introduction to Prolog's declarative capabilities is the Genealogy program. Here we look at this simple knowledge-base program in detail.

LISTING 6.1. *A simple genealogy program in Prolog.*

```
% father(X, Y):  Y is the father of X
father(henry_viii, henry_vii).
father(margaret_tudor, henry_vii).
father(mary_queen_of_scots, james_v_of_scotland).
father(elizabeth_i, henry_viii).
father(james_v_of_scotland, james_iv_of_scotland).

% mother(X, Y):  Y is the mother of X
mother(james_v_of_scotland, margaret_tudor).
mother(james_vi_of_scotland, mary_queen_of_scots).

hello_age(N) :-

  write('Hello '),
  write(N),
  write('-year-old.'),
  nl.
```

Consider the text in Listing 6.1, which constitutes a perfectly valid Prolog program. This particular program concerns relationships among some people in the English and Scottish royal families in the Middle Ages. The program defines two predicates, father and mother, by listing pairs of people (X, Y) such that Y is the father of X and pairs of people (X, Y) such that Y is the mother of X. For instance, the text father(elizabeth_i, henry_viii) is intended to state that Elizabeth I's father was Henry VIII.

6.2.2.1. The Genealogy Program in Detail

Let's consider the features of this program in detail. The first line, beginning with a percent sign, is a comment. Prolog ignores everything after a percent sign on any line. This comment describes the intended meaning of the father predicate; if father(X, Y) holds true for some X and Y, then it is supposed to be the case that Y is the father of X. The other line beginning with a percent sign is a comment describing the intended meaning of the mother predicate. It is useful to have such a comment for every predicate in a program.

We have chosen a Prolog *constant*, such as henry_viii, to represent each person of interest. Any sequence of alphanumeric characters and underscores beginning with a lowercase letter is a constant. In the last section, we encountered two other kinds of constants: any sequence of characters between single quotes, such as 'Hello world', and any integer, such as 72. Here, obviously, henry_viii is supposed to represent Henry VIII, and so on. We don't have to declare constants; any use of a constant immediately makes the constant known to Prolog.

Each predicate is intended to be used to express some statement, as is usual in the realm of predicate logic. Predicate names have the same form as the alphanumeric or single-quoted constants (although the alphanumeric form is much more common to see).

The predicates in the genealogy program have two arguments each, but we can also have predicates with zero, one, three, or more arguments. As with constants, we don't declare predicates but simply use them with whatever arity we want. An example of a predicate with zero arguments might be rainy; the fact rainy in a Prolog program might be used to state that it is rainy today. rich might be used as a predicate with one argument: rich(henry_viii), for instance, might state that Henry VIII was rich. It is up to us to choose the predicate and constant names in a way that makes the resulting program readable.

In the genealogy program, the father relation is defined using five *facts*, each on a separate line and terminated by a dot; mother is defined using two facts. Facts, together with rules (such as the rule defining hello in section 6.2.1), are collectively known as *clauses*. A Prolog program, in general, is a list of clauses, each clause terminated by a dot. We can use any number of clauses to define a predicate, although most Prologs insist that the clauses defining a given predicate be grouped together. Because simple programs such as this in some sense sum up some knowledge about the world, they are often referred to as *knowledge bases*.

6.2.2.2. Querying the Genealogy Program

To see how Prolog uses such knowledge bases, we can load the genealogy program into a file named gene.pl and consult the file using [gene]. If we now issue the query

```
¦?- father(henry_viii, henry_vii).
```

we are essentially asking Prolog to confirm that that fact is true, according to what it knows so far. Prolog of course answers yes; to the query father(henry_viii, richard_iii), it answers no.

Prolog's strength is that it can not only confirm or deny facts, but also supply answers. When we pose the query father(henry_viii, X), we are asking Prolog to replace the variable x by something that makes the resulting fact true. Any sequence of alphanumeric characters and underscores beginning with an uppercase letter is a Prolog variable. When a variable x appears in a query, we can read the query as beginning "Does there exist an x such that...?" This sample query therefore says "Does there exist an x such that x is the father of Henry VIII?"

To this query, Prolog responds with

```
X = henry_vii ?
```

This output is not asking whether x can be henry_vii; rather, it is telling us that it can be and prompting us for whether we want to search for other xs that make the query true. This prompt is called the *solutions prompt*. At a solutions prompt, if we press Enter, we get back to the query prompt. To see a case where Prolog can find more than one solution, we can enter the query father(Y, henry_vii). This query asks rather if there is an Y such that Y is a child of Henry VII. It should come back with the solutions prompt

```
Y = henry_viii ?
```

But Henry VII has two children in the knowledge base. If we type the semicolon character (;) at the solutions prompt and press Enter, we get the other solution:

```
Y = margaret_tudor ?
```

If we type ; and press Enter again in this example, we get simply no, indicating that there are no more solutions.

Note that we can put as many variables as we like in Prolog queries; in fact, if we enter the query father(Kid, Dad) and then keep entering semicolons, we should get a list of all child/father pairs in the program.

6.2.2.3. Rules

Section 6.2.1 shows some imperative expressions called *rules*. Rules are usually used, however, to state general conditions under which predicates hold. Here we look at some simple rules.

Add the following text to the genealogy program:

```
% parent(X, Y): Y is a parent of X
parent(X, Y) :- father(X, Y).
parent(X, Y) :- mother(X, Y).
```

These rules define a new predicate, parent. The :- symbol can be read as "if"; the clauses can be read as "If Y is the father of x, then Y is a parent of x" and "If Y is the mother of x, then Y is a parent of x." If we reconsult the augmented program and issue the query parent(james_v_of_scotland, X), then we should get two answers, james_iv_of_scotland and margaret_tudor. Prolog has found the first answer by using the first rule and checking its collection of father facts. Because there is another clause defining the parent relation, Prolog then uses that clause and its mother facts to find the other solution.

Now consider the query parent(X, Parent), father(Parent, Grandfather).
This asks Prolog to find three values, X, Parent, and Grandfather, such that
Parent is the parent of X and Grandfather is the father of Parent. A comma-
separated list of predicate calls is a request to satisfy all of them. When
Prolog has finished looking, it should have been able to find four triples
of people satisfying those conditions, such as

```
Grandfather = henry_vii,
Parent = henry_viii,
X = elizabeth_i
```

We can encode the relation that this query reflects by adding the following rule to the program:

```
grandfather(X, Grandfather) :-
    parent(X, Parent),
    father(Parent, Grandfather).
```

After this addition (and a reconsult), we can pose the query grandfather(X,
Grandfather) and expect to get four answers again. Note, however, that
Parent is here a variable local to the definition of grandfather and thus
does not get reported in the result. As in other languages, local variables
can be used to hide details of the computation we are not interested in.
Any variable that appears in the body of a rule but not in the head is
local.

6.2.2.4. Recursive Predicates
Prolog does repeated computation by the usual method of declarative
languages—namely, recursion. We can add the following clauses to the
genealogy program:

```
ancestor(X, Y) :- parent(X, Y).
ancestor(X, Y) :- parent(X, Parent), ancestor(Parent, Y).
```

These clauses can be read as follows: If Y is a parent of X, then Y is an
ancestor of X; if Parent is a parent of X and Y is an ancestor of Parent, then
Y is an ancestor of X. Prolog can use these rules to find ancestors recursively—for instance, returning three ancestors of James V of Scotland for
the query ancestor(james_v_of_scotland, X): james_iv_of_scotland,
margaret_tudor, and henry_vii.

As with father, we can run this query in either direction, and in fact, it
might be useful to define the following predicate:

```
descendent(X, Y) :- ancestor(Y, X).
```

This rule says that Y is a descendent of X if X is an ancestor of Y. If we now enter the query descendent(henry_vii, Heir), we get the list of all Henry VII's descendants—just about everyone mentioned in the knowledge base.

Incidentally, this example explains why the monarchs of Scotland became the monarchs of England too; all of Henry VIII's descendants died out, so the monarchy passed to the descendants of Henry's sister Margaret, who happened to have married the King of Scotland.

6.2.3. A Grammatical Summary

Let's now summarize more rigorously the small subset of Prolog we have been working with:

- An identifier is a sequence of alphanumeric characters and underscores.

- A constant is an identifier beginning with a lowercase letter, a single-quoted sequence of characters, or an integer.

- A predicate name is an identifier beginning with a lowercase letter.

- A variable is an identifier beginning with an uppercase letter.

- A term is a constant or variable.

- An atom is an expression of the form p or $p(t_1, ..., t_n)$, where p is a predicate name and each t_i is a term.

- A goal is an expression of the form $a_1, ..., a_n$, where each a_i is an atom.

- A query is a goal terminated by a period.

- A fact is an atom terminated by a period.

- A rule is an expression of the form a :- g., where a is an atom and g is a goal.

- A clause is a fact or a rule.

- A program is a sequence of clauses.

This is only a subset of full Prolog, and as we go on, we will expand it.

6.2.4. Equality and Variables

Let's expand our syntax of Prolog now to include another kind of goal. This section explores the equality predicate and how Prolog solves equality queries involving variables.

6.2.4.1. Properties of the Equality Predicate

An expression of the form $s = t$, where s and t are both terms, is called an *equality* goal. = is technically a binary predicate, but it appears in an infix position in order to conform to the usual practice in mathematics and logic.

How does Prolog evaluate equality queries? As we might expect, the query a = a just returns yes. Here, a is a constant, and we are merely asking whether it is equal to itself. If we type the query a = b, however, Prolog returns no; two constants that do not have the same name are always treated as unequal. Thus the queries a = 37 and 'foo bar' = 9 also fail. However, the query 'archy' = archy succeeds, indicating that putting single quotes around an identifier that is already a constant results in the same constant, as far as Prolog is concerned.

This behavior has a natural extension to variables. The query x = b returns one solution, namely **x = b**. What we might not expect is that the query b = x returns the same thing. Equality is a symmetric relation; when it handles equality queries, Prolog is just trying, as it always does, to find a term to substitute for x that makes the query true. When we substitute x by b in b = x, we get b = b: a true query.

Now, what do you think the following query should return?

```
X = a, X = b.
```

If you answered **no**, you're right. Although equality has somewhat the flavor of the assignment statement of an imperative programming language, a Prolog variable can only ever be "equal to" one term. If we try substituting x by a in x = a, x = b, for example, we get a = a, a = b, which is false because a = b is false; and if we try b, we get b = a, b = b, which is false because b = a is false. There is no substitution for x that makes the query true, so no is the appropriate answer.

6.2.4.2. Equalities with More Than One Variable

Queries involving equality and more than one variable are solved in a similar way, by Prolog attempting to find a satisfying substitution of values for all the variables. Consider the following four queries:

```
X = a, Y = b.          % Query 1
X = a, Y = X.          % Query 2
X = a, Y = b, X = Y.   % Query 3
X = Y.                 % Query 4
```

The first query returns x = a, Y = b as a solution; and the second returns x = a, Y = a. But the third query returns no because there is no substitution that satisfies the query; x and y cannot be both equal to different constants and equal to each other. The fourth query does not put any constraint on the two variables other than that they are equal to each other; so the substitution that is returned is just x = y itself. This indicates that if we replaced x by Y, it would produce the trivially true query Y = Y.

6.2.5. Lists

The terms we have looked at so far have been just constants and variables. Now let's look at another class of terms, the list terms, and the equalities that hold over them.

[a,b,c] is a Prolog term that stands for the list of elements a, b, and c in that order. There can be as many or as few elements in a list as we want; for instance, [a] is a list, and [] is a list. This last list is referred to as the empty list. We can give variables as list elements too, intermixed with constants if we want, such as [a,X,b,Y]. We can put spaces before and after the commas if we want, but inside terms, it is traditional to leave out the spaces.

This comma-separated-sequence notation is really just a convenience. The underlying representation of a non-empty list in Prolog, as in Lisp, is a pair consisting of a term (the head of the list) and a list (the tail of the larger list). The list of one element [a] is thus seen as the list with head a and tail []. The expression [H¦T] is also a valid term and refers to the list with head H and tail T. The terms [a¦[]] and [a] are just two ways of writing the same term, and in fact the query [a¦[]] = [a] returns yes.

Let's look at some other equality queries involving lists:

```
[X,Y,c] = [a,b,Z].    % Query 1
[Hd¦Tl] = [a].        % Query 2
[Hd¦Tl] = [b,c,X].    % Query 3
[a,b,c] = [X,b,X].    % Query 4
[a,b,a] = [X,b,X].    % Query 5
```

The first query returns the substitution x=a, Y=b, z=c because that is the only substitution which makes the lists identical. The second yields Hd=a, Tl=[] because that substitution makes the left-hand term into [a¦[]], which as we have seen previously is identical to [a]. Similarly, Query 3 yields Hd=b, Tl=[c, X]; note that here, we have not put any constraint on the value of x at all. The fourth query returns no because no substitution for x makes the two lists identical, but the fifth query returns x = a.

There is a form of list that generalizes both the comma-style lists and the bar-style lists. The expression [a,b,c|X] denotes the list beginning with a, b, and c, whose tail after those first three elements is X. In practice, this mixed comma-and-bar style of list comes up fairly seldom but is useful occasionally.

Thus the full BNF for a list term is as follows:

```
<list-term>      ::= "[" [<list-contents>] "]"
<list-contents> ::= <term> [<rest-of-list>]
<rest-of-list>  ::= "," <term> <rest-of-list>
                  | "|" <term>
```

List terms can be used anywhere any other terms can be used. They constitute the basic data structure of Prolog programs and are used in just about every application.

6.2.6. Predicates on Lists

Lists are recursive data structures, in the sense that the tail of a list is also a list. Recursive predicates are therefore the natural things to use on them. This section explores some simple recursive list predicates.

6.2.6.1. member

Consider the following predicate definition[1]:

```
% member(List, X):  X is a member of List.
member(List, X) :-
  List = [Head|Tail],
  X = Head.
member(List, X) :-
  List = [Head|Tail],
  member(Tail, X).
```

Here we are using equality goals in the bodies of clauses in order to express what we want. (Soon we will see a much simpler version of this predicate that does not use equalities.) The first clause can be read as "x is a member of List if List consists of a Head and a Tail (that is, if List is not the empty list) and x is the head." The second clause can be read as "x is a member of List if List consists of a Head and a Tail and x is a member of the tail."

---

[1]This definition may lead to "singleton variable" warnings on some Prologs; we can ignore these warnings for now.

When you think about it, those are the only two cases in which we would normally consider an element to be a member of a list, so the predicate definition is correct and complete. If Prolog is given this definition, it correctly tells us that member([a, b, c], b), and the query member([faith, hope, charity], X) returns three possible solutions for X. Note that this member predicate can be used not only to confirm that something is a member of a list, but also to generate all the members of the list.

6.2.6.2. append

Now let's consider a definition of a predicate version of the traditional append function. In functional languages, append is a function that takes two lists as arguments and returns a list (which is the two lists appended into a single list). In Prolog, where we are defining relations, it is a predicate that takes three lists: append(List1, List2, Result) means that the result of appending List1 to List2 is Result. As in functional programming, the key question is whether the first list is empty or not. The clause

```
append(List1, List2, Result) :-
    List1 = [],
    Result = List2.
```

can be read as follows: "The result of appending List1 and List2 is Result if List1 is empty, and Result is just List2."

The clause

```
append(List1, List2, Result) :-
    List1 = [H¦T],
    append(T, List2, Temp),
    Result = [H¦Temp].
```

can be read as follows: "The result of appending List1 and List2 is Result if List1 consists of a head H and a tail T; the result of appending T and List2 is Temp; and Result is the list with head H and tail Temp."

The two clauses of the whole definition have the effect of the Lisp-style definition

```
(defun (append list1 list2)
  (cond ((null list1) list2)
        (t (cons (car list1) (append (cdr list1) list2)))))
```

However, because this is Prolog and we can use any pattern of variables and constants in queries, we can ask not only append([a, b], [c, d], R) and get R = [a, b, c, d], but we can also ask append([a, b], L2, [a, b, c, d]) and get L2 = [c, d]. In essence, we can "run the predicate backward" in a way that we cannot do with the function.

6.2.7. Complex Terms in Heads of Clauses

So far, although we have been working with *queries* with a mixture of constant and variable arguments, all the *clauses* we have seen have had either all constants or all variables in the heads. In fact, clauses—both rules and facts—can have a mixture of constants and variables in the heads as well. In this section, we will see how to derive such clauses from the simpler clauses I have been writing. The transformed clauses are usually much more concise and contain fewer equality goals in the bodies.

In the body of a predicate, whenever we see a variable being equated to another term, we can transform the clause by replacing all occurrences of the variable by the term and eliminating that equality.[2] After all, if two things are equal, we should be able to replace one with the other anywhere. For instance, consider the clause

```
member(List, X) :-
   List = [Head|Tail],
   member(Tail, X).
```

We can take List in this clause, replace it everywhere in the clause by [Head|Tail], and eliminate the equality, resulting in

```
member([Head|Tail], X) :-
   member(Tail, X).
```

Similarly, in the first clause defining member, namely

```
member(List, X) :-
   List = [Head|Tail],
   X = Head.
```

we can replace List by [Head|Tail] in the same manner, resulting in

```
member([Head|Tail], X) :-
   X = Head.
```

We can further replace X with Head and eliminate that equality; here, because we have eliminated the last part of the body, the rule turns into a fact:

```
member([Head|Tail], Head).
```

It is in fact a fact; for any list of the form [Head|Tail], Head is a member of the list.

---

[2]Strictly speaking, this applies only to clauses without cuts, a feature we will get to later. For the kinds of clauses we have been looking at so far, it holds true.

Thus the new definition of member that we derive from these clauses is simply

```
member([Head|Tail], Head).
member([Head|Tail], X) :-
  member(Tail, X).
```

We can read this new definition as follows: "Head is a member of the list [Head|Tail], and X is a member of the list [Head|Tail] if it is a member of the list Tail." It's a bit harder for a beginning Prolog programmer to see that this definition is also complete and correct, but we will get the hang of these definitions quickly. This is the standard definition of member that we are likely to find in other books (aside from the choice of variable names).

We can perform similar operations on the definition of append and derive the three-line definition

```
append([], List2, List2).
append([H|T], List2, [H|Temp]) :-
  append(T, List2, Temp).
```

This is also the standard definition of append and can be read as follows: "The result of appending the empty list and List2 is just List2, and the result of appending [H|T] and List2 is [H|Temp] if the result of appending T and List2 is Temp."

When we want to write our own predicates, we may find it useful to start out with an equality-style definition and then later massage it into the more concise format. Conversely, if we find a definition that we read hard to understand, it may be helpful to go backward to the equality-style definition.

6.2.8. How Prolog Does It

How does Prolog find the solutions it finds? The answer is with a fairly straightforward depth-first search algorithm. This algorithm can be considered to be the execution model of a Prolog program. This section explores this execution model.

The Prolog algorithm is given a query and systematically works its way through the query, guessing at which substitutions make the query true. The guesses are not arbitrary but are based on the facts and rules in the program in the order in which Prolog finds them. Every time Prolog comes up against an equality that cannot be satisfied, it knows it has guessed wrong some time in the past and backtracks to make another guess.

A simplified version of this algorithm, written in imperative-functional pseudocode, can be found in Figures 6.1 and 6.2. These figures have to do with three functions, each of which takes a goal as an argument.

```
solve(G):
```

- If the first subgoal in G is of the form $p(t_1, \ldots, t_n)$ and the rest of G is G'

  —Set result to redo, i to 1, and n to the number of clauses defining p in the program.

  —While $i \leq n$ and result is still redo

  - Set c to the ith clause defining p.

  - Set result to solve_clause($p(t_1, \ldots, t_n)$, C, G').

  - Set i to i+1.

  —Return result.

- If the first subgoal of G is of the form s=t and the rest of G is G', return solve_eq(s, t, G').

- Otherwise, G must be the empty query. Report on the current substitution and print a solutions prompt.

  —If the user presses the Enter key, return exit.

  —If the user types ; and presses the Enter key, return redo.

```
solve_clause(p(t₁, ..., tₙ), C, G):
```

- If c is a fact of the form $p(s, \ldots, s)$, return solve(($s_1=t_1, \ldots, s_n=t_n$, G)).

- Otherwise, c is a rule of the form $p(s_1, \ldots, s_n)$:- B. Return solve(($s_1=t_1, \ldots, s_n=t_n$, B, G)).

FIGURE 6.1. *A simplified version of Prolog's search algorithm: the functions* solve *and* solve_clause.

```
solve_eq(s, t, G):
```

- If s is a variable

  —Substitute s by t in G, yielding G'.

  —Return solve(G').

- Otherwise, if t is a variable

  —Substitute t by s in G, yielding G'.

  —Return solve(G').

- Otherwise, if s and t are identical, return solve(G).

- Otherwise, if s or t is a constant, the other term must be a list or a different constant, so return redo.

- Otherwise, if s or t is the empty list, the other term must be a non-empty list, so return redo.

- Otherwise, both s and t must be non-empty lists, where s is $[s_1|s_2]$ and t is $[t_1|t_2]$. Return solve((s_1=t_1, s_2=t_2, G)).

FIGURE 6.2. *The algorithm for* solve_eq *called by* solve.

Recall that a goal is any sequence of atoms (a_1, ..., a_n); for the purposes of these algorithms, it can also be the empty sequence of atoms, written (). The three functions are

- solve(G), which takes a goal G and returns either the token exit or the token redo. exit is intended to mean that the system has reported on an answer and the user has been satisfied with it; redo means the system should backtrack and try again, either because it has reached an unsatisfiable equality or because the user has requested it to backtrack with a semicolon at a solutions prompt.

- solve_clause(a, C, G), which takes an atom a, a clause C, and a goal G and tries to find a satisfying substitution for the goal (a, G) by using only clause C with a. It returns the same things as solve.

- solve_eq(s, t, G), which tries to find a satisfying substitution for the goal s=t, G. It also returns the same things as solve.

When a query Q is given to Prolog, it behaves as if it has called the function solve on the query. Note that solve may call the specialized functions solve_clause or solve_eq, both of which may call solve recursively. It is also worth noting that the comma separating atoms is essentially an associative operator so that the goal ((p, q), r) is treated the same way as (p, q, r).

6.2.8.1. An Example

As an example of how Prolog works, consider the query member([a,b], X), X=b. The sequence of calls to solve and solve_clause made during the start of processing of this query is as follows. (Calls to solve_eq are not shown for brevity.)

```
solve((member([a,b], X), X=b))
solve_clause( member([a,b], X),
              member([Head¦Tail], Head),
              (X=b) )
   solve(([a,b]=[Head¦Tail], X=Head, X=b))
   solve((a=Head, [b]=Tail, X=Head, X=b))
   solve(([b]=Tail, X=a, X=b))
   solve((X=a, X=b))
   solve((a=b))
```

At this point, we have reached a dead end. Our initial guess that the first clause of member was the right one to use has matched x to a, which is not equal to b. solve_eq returns **redo** and this return value gets passed back through all the levels of solve and solve_eq up to the topmost call to solve. We then try the second clause of member, with better results:

```
solve_clause( member([a,b], X),
              member([Head¦Tail], X) :- member(Tail, X),
              (X=b) )
   solve(([a,b]=[Head¦Tail], X=X, member(Tail, X), X=b))
   solve((a=Head, [b]=Tail, X=X, member(Tail, X), X=b))
   solve(([b]=Tail, X=X, member(Tail, X), X=b))
   solve((X=X, member([b], X), X=b))
   solve((member([b], X), X=b))
   solve_clause( member([b], X),
                 member([Head¦Tail], Head),
                 (X=b) )
      solve(([b]=[Head¦Tail], X=Head, X=b))
      solve((b=Head, []=Tail, X=Head, X=b))
      solve(([]=Tail, X=b, X=b))
      solve((X=b, X=b))
      solve((b=b))
      solve(())
```

This last call, asking to solve the empty goal, causes Prolog to report the solution and ask the user if she wants to find more solutions. If the user types ; and then presses Enter, Prolog tries again with the second clause of member and does not find any more solutions; the **redo** that results percolates up to the top level and causes Prolog to report **no** as its final verdict on the query. If the user presses Enter at the solutions prompt, **exit** is returned and Prolog ends up saying **yes**.

6.2.8.2. Some Terminology

Prolog programmers have developed a language that they use to talk about the execution of queries. Here we look at some of this terminology.

Prolog may succeed or fail to find a satisfying substitution for a query. This success or failure is often viewed as an action of the query itself or of a goal that is encountered during the processing of a query. Thus we say, for example, that the query member([a,b], X), X=b *succeeds* and that the query member([a,b], c) *fails*.

You may have noticed, in the execution model, that variables hang around during the processing of a query until a goal comes up that equates the variable to a term. When such a goal does arise, the variable is replaced everywhere by that term. This process of substituting a variable by a term is referred to as *instantiating* the variable; variables that have not yet been substituted for are referred to as *uninstantiated*. In fact, a variable, say X, may be replaced by a term that itself has uninstantiated variables in it, say [a,b,Z]. In this case, we say that X is *partially instantiated*, indicating that some but not all the "holes" in its pattern have been filled in.

The entire process of equating two terms—for instance, for processing [Head¦Tail] = [b] by substituting Head by b and Tail by []—is referred to as *unification*. Many texts present the Prolog "unification algorithm" as a separate entity; here we look at it as part of the wider algorithm that Prolog uses to execute a query. We say that two terms *unify* if the execution of an equality query between them does not result in failure. Thus a does not unify with b, but [Head¦Tail] does unify with [b].

6.2.8.3. Some Subtleties of the Execution Model

The Prolog execution model as given is a simplification in several ways:

- In matching a predicate call to a clause (as in solve_clause), Prolog actually renames the variables in the clause so that they do not clash with the variables in the actual query. The variables in the clauses are not intended to be the same as the ones in the query! This is particularly important with recursive calls because otherwise, the same variables would come up again and again.

- We need to keep track of the substitution of values for variables that is being built up, in order to report it to the user. I could have listed this as another parameter, but for simplicity, I have omitted that parameter in the pseudocode I presented.

- In solve_eq, we should make sure that a term that is being substituted for a variable does not contain an occurrence of variable somewhere within it. For instance, there is no substitution for X that makes the query X = [a,X] true. Most Prolog implementations actually do not do this "occurs check" for efficiency reasons. Although it is seldom a problem, we should still do it to be strictly in accord with logic.

- The execution model does not take into account some of the features we will look at later, such as function symbols and negation. Computations involving these features are described as they come up.

The algorithm as presented looks very inefficient because when substituting a variable by another term, we go through the rest of the query looking for all occurrences. Of course, real implementations don't do this. Rather, occurrences of variables are represented as pointers to structures, and only those structures are changed.

What about the output predicates write and nl that we met in section 6.2.1? These are handled by Prolog in a straightforward way: When a write or nl is the first atom in a query, the system simply does the output action and goes on evaluating the rest of the query. Consider the query member([a,b], X), write('Trying '), write(X), nl, X=b. The substitutions returned by Prolog are exactly the same as those in the example of section 6.2.8.1 because the output predicates have no effect on variables. The output of the query is

```
Trying a
Trying b
X = b ?
```

After the system backtracked to try the second clause of member again, it executed the write and nl atoms again, producing two outputs. The other I/O predicates of Prolog (which we will meet in section 6.3.5) behave in a similar way.

We can use these imperative features to debug programs in Prolog if we want. However, if your Prolog has an interactive debugger (the most common kind is described in section 6.3.8), it is probably better to use that because the output from a backtracking program is difficult to follow. It is better to use Prolog's I/O system for interacting with the user.

6.3. More Advanced Features
This section deals with some of the most important advanced features of Prolog. The logic and control constructs we look at here include negation, the Prolog "cut," the predicates for finding all solutions, and the predicates for manipulating the knowledge base. The forms of terms we explore include numeric terms, function-symbol terms, and strings. We also look at advanced usability features such as the Prolog interactive debugger, definite clause grammars, and operator declarations.

6.3.1. Negation

It is sometimes necessary to state not that a property holds, but that a property does not hold. Prolog provides the negation symbol \+ for doing this. \+ is a prefix operator that we can apply to any atom. For instance, if we want to find a term that is in the list [a,b] but not in the list [b,c], we can do so with the query

```
member([a,b], X), \+ member([b,c], X).
```

The only solution that Prolog returns is a because this is the only element of [a,b] that is not also an element of [b,c]. The \+ operator is of lower precedence than the comma that separates atoms in a goal, so it applies only to the next atom in a comma-separated sequence. Thus the query

```
member([a,b], X), \+ member([b,c], X), member([a], X).
```

would return the same thing. An atom or the negation of an atom is often referred to as a *literal*.

6.3.1.1. Computing with Negations

Prolog computes negated literals by the "negation as failure" method. For instance, \+ member([b,c], a) is computed by first computing member([b,c], a); because that query fails (is not evaluated as true), the negated literal succeeds (is evaluated as true). \+ member([b,c], b) is similarly computed by first computing member([b,c], b), but here, because that query succeeds, the negated literal fails.

Negation is also useful in predicate definitions. Negations can appear in queries and in predicate bodies, but not in predicate heads; the head always has to be a simple atom. Consider the following (faulty) code for the delete predicate:

```
% delete(L1, X, L2):   L2 is the result of deleting all
% occurrences of X from L1.
delete([X|Tail1], X, L2) :-
   delete(Tail1, X, L2).
delete([Y|Tail1], X, [Y|L2]) :-
   delete(Tail1, X, L2).
```

Why is this code faulty? The first solution that this code returns is correct; for instance, delete([a,b,c], b, L) returns L = [a,c]. But if we then ask for more solutions, it returns L = [a,b,c]. The problem is that although in the second clause, we named X and Y differently, in fact Prolog is happy to use that clause on backtracking even when the head of the first argument is the same as the second argument. What we really need is for the second clause to be

```
delete([Y|Tail1], X, [Y|L2]) :-
   \+ X = Y,
   delete(Tail1, X, L2).
```

This guarantees that the second clause is used only when x and y are distinct.

As another example, Listing 6.2 contains some code involving negation that might be found in a game-playing program. The predicate best_move_for is intended to compute the best move for player P given the current state of the game. Note that each negated condition is the negation of some condition that actually appeared in an earlier clause. This is a common pattern, and we will soon see how it can be done more efficiently.

LISTING 6.2. *Code from a game program that involves negation.*

```
% best_move_for(P, State, Move): The best move for player P,
% given the state of the game in State, is Move.
best_move_for(P, State, Move) :-
   winning_move_for(P, State, Move).
best_move_for(P, State, Move) :-
   \+ winning_move_for(P, State, Some_move),
   drawing_move_for(P, State, Move).
best_move_for(P, State, Move) :-
   \+ winning_move_for(P, State, Some_move),
   \+ drawing_move_for(P, State, Some_other_move),
   move_for(P, State, Move).
```

6.3.1.2. Negation and Unsoundness

One caution must be followed when using negation. Consider the query x=a, \+ x=b. It will succeed, as you might expect, with the substitution x=a. But now consider the query \+ x=b, x=a. The two queries are the same except that the order of the literals has been switched, but the second query fails! Prolog has succeeded in binding x to b in the computation of the first literal, so x=b succeeds and \+ x=b fails.

This is not in line with correct logical behavior; rather, it is a consequence of the negation as failure strategy, as implemented in most Prologs. However, there are ways of ensuring that the negations you use are logically sound. The rule of thumb is avoid situations where you have an uninstantiated variable *inside* a negation that also appears *outside* the negation. Thus the previous delete predicate is sound if the first two arguments (the list and the element to be deleted) are instantiated whenever it is used. Similarly, the best_move_for predicate is sound whenever the P and State arguments are instantiated whenever they are called (as presumably they would usually be); the local variables Some_move and Some_other_move in the second and third clauses, while uninstantiated, are not referred to outside the negation.

Some variants of Prolog, such as constraint logic programming systems, could deal with negations such as \+ x=b in a more intelligent manner, by remembering the fact that x is not supposed to be equal to b. But such features are not implemented in the most widely available Prologs.

6.3.2. The Cut Literal

In the definition of the best_move_for predicate, the second clause started out with a literal that negated the first clause. Essentially we were saying "If there is no winning move for P, then the best move is a drawing move." It is so common to want to take a predicate call appearing in one clause and negate it in a later clause that Prolog supplies a construct that is primarily used for this: the cut literal, !. Cut can appear in a rule body wherever any other literal can appear.

6.3.2.1. Using the Cut Literal to Simplify Code

Consider the following version of the best_move_for predicate:

```
best_move_for(P, Board, Move) :-
  winning_move_for(P, Board, Move),
  !.
best_move_for(P, Board, Move) :-
  drawing_move_for(P, Board, Move),
  !.
best_move_for(P, Board, Move) :-
  move_for(P, Board, Move).
```

This version computes the same thing as the original version but is more concise. The way it works is this. When Prolog gets to a cut literal !, it commits itself to the clause it has selected and refuses to use the remaining clauses for that predicate. Thus if there is a winning move for P, it never tries to claim a non-winning move as the best move; it is as if there is an automatic negation of winning_move_for before the other two clauses. Similarly, the cut in the second clause is like an automatic negation of drawing_move_for in the last clause. The name comes from the fact that it is in a sense "cutting away" a part of Prolog's potential search tree.

The main advantage of using the cut here is efficiency. In the first version of best_move_for, the first clause causes winning_move_for to be called; if it does not succeed, the second clause causes it to be called again (inside the negation). With the cut, winning_move_for is called only once. This can be a big timesaver. Similarly, the delete predicate is often expressed as

```
delete([X|Tail1], X, L2) :-
  !,
  delete(Tail1, X, L2).
delete([Y|Tail1], X, [Y|L2]) :-
  delete(Tail1, X, L2).
```

This guarantees that if the head of the first argument is the same as the second argument, the second clause is not used.

Because it has to do with negation, cut can also lead to unsound computations. You will often see dire warnings in Prolog texts about the dangers of using the "non-logical" cut feature. However, most of the uses of cut are to achieve exactly what we have been doing in this section: an efficient negation of some earlier condition. We just have to follow a similar rule of thumb to that which we use for negation. Avoid situations where a head variable is instantiated before a cut and the predicate then fails, because this pattern can cause an unsound negation. A call to the delete predicate is safe in this sense if the first two arguments are instantiated and the last one is uninstantiated at the time of the call because in that case, delete cannot fail.

Another useful rule of thumb for cut, as expressed by O'Keefe (1990), is to place a cut exactly where you first know that the clause being used is the right one. For instance, in best_move_for, as soon as we know there is a winning move, we know we can discard the other clauses; and in delete, as soon as we know the head of the first clause has been matched (that is, that the second argument is the same as the head of the first argument), we know we can discard the other clause. Placing the cuts earlier or later may result in unwanted failures or solutions.

6.3.2.2. Finding the First Solution
A secondary effect of cut is that it not only throws away alternatives to the current clause, but all the alternatives that have been built up since the predicate was called. This means that it can be used to find the first solution to a query. A predicate body that starts with

```
grandparent(X, Y),
rich(Y),
!,
...
```

finds the first rich grandparent of x.

This can be useful if it is sufficient for us to find just one rich grandparent. It can also be useful if all we want to establish is that some grandparent of x is rich because with the cut, if there is a later failure we will not go on finding other rich grandparents and retrying whatever comes after the cut. These uses of the cut are not as common but do arise occasionally.

6.3.3. Multi-Arity Predicates

Here we look briefly at defining predicates that have more than one arity. Such predicates are useful chiefly in situations where we want to have "default arguments."

Consider the following code:

```
ancestor(X, Y) :- parent(X, Y).
ancestor(X, Y) :- parent(X, Parent), ancestor(Parent, Y).

ancestor(Y) :- ancestor(me, Y).
```

This is just the definition of the ancestor relation with a new clause tacked onto the end. The different thing about the new clause is that the atom in its head has only one argument, as opposed to two for all other occurrences of ancestor, including the one in the body of the new clause.

Most Prologs do not raise an error message on such definitions but simply consider the last clause to be defining a new predicate—"ancestor with one argument"—in terms of an old predicate—"ancestor with two arguments." In Prolog parlance, the one-argument predicate is referred to as ancestor/1 and the two-argument predicate as ancestor/2. ancestor/1 here is useful if we expect to be calling the ancestor predicate a lot with the first argument me, and we want to save some typing. Two clauses are actually considered to be defining the same predicate only if both the predicate names are the same and the arities of the head atoms are the same.

In fact, expressions of the form predicate-name/arity are often used in Prolog reference material when talking about predicates, even if the predicates are not multi-arity. The arity serves to remind us of the format of the predicate call; thus we use append/3 to refer to the standard append predicate or write/1 and nl/0 for those output predicates.

6.3.4. More About Terms

We started out with only variables, constants, and integers as terms and then added lists to our collection of terms. In this section, we expand our set of terms even more.

6.3.4.1. Numeric Terms and Arithmetic Relations

We have seen that every integer is a term. Most Prologs also allow any real number to be a term; the standard input/output representation of real numbers is used, for instance 3.1416 or 1.86e5.

The standard arithmetic relational operators are all indeed relations, so they fit naturally into Prolog as infix predicates like the = predicate. Expressions such as x < 54 and 3 >= Y are valid goals and can appear in queries or clause bodies anywhere any other predicate call can. The "less than or equal to" operator is written as =< rather than <=, in order to avoid confusion with another operator.

We cannot mix arithmetic relations and uninstantiated variables indiscriminately, however. If Prolog encounters a call to one of these relations, and there are free variables in either of the arguments, it gives a runtime error. The problem here is similar to that with negated equalities. When processing x < 54, Prolog could remember that x is supposed to be less than 54 and use that information when processing future statements involving x, but this leads to slower and more complex processing, so such features are available only in constraint logic programming languages so far. Thus only instantiated variables can appear in arithmetic relations. This is no more of a restriction than in functional languages, where (because there are no logical variables) everything must be instantiated.

6.3.4.2. Arithmetic Operators and is
The standard arithmetic operators are also available. +, -, and * have the expected meaning; / is real division (treating the operands as real numbers), // is integer division returning the integer quotient, and mod is the modulo operation (the remainder after division). These cannot be used effectively in predicate arguments. Instead, a special binary infix predicate, is, is used for computing with the arithmetic operators.

The goal Fahrenheit = 77, Celsius is (Fahrenheit - 32) * (5/9) succeeds with Celsius instantiated to the appropriate value, 25. The variable on the left of is can be instantiated; the goal succeeds with no substitution if it is instantiated to the correct value already or fails if it is instantiated to some other value. The whole goal gives a runtime error if any of the variables on the right-hand side of the is are uninstantiated at the time Prolog processes it.

As an example, consider the following predicate for generating a list of all the natural numbers between M and N:

```
% all_numbers_between(M, N, List): List is all numbers between
% M and N, inclusive.
all_numbers_between(M, N, []) :-
  M > N,
  !.
all_numbers_between(M, N, [M|Rest]) :-
  M1 is M+1,
  all_numbers_between(M1, N, Rest).
```

We make the design decision that if M is greater than N, List is simply the empty list. Otherwise, List is M, along with the list of all numbers between M+1 and N. This predicate is used in a longer example that appears in section 6.5, "Examples," a prime number finder using Eratosthenes' sieve method.

Note that we could not simply pass M+1 as an argument to all_numbers_between. The operators only really make sense when used on the right-hand side of is, for reasons that will become apparent later.

6.3.4.3. Function Symbols

Lists are the basic data structure of Prolog; they are useful because of their flexible length. In many situations, we want to group a known number of values into a record-like data structure. For these situations, Prolog provides a notation that is internally represented more efficiently than a list.

For instance, the expression sq(e,2) is a valid term. This looks like a predicate call, but it can be used wherever any other term can be used—for instance, in the goal Square = sq(e,2) or empty(Board, sq(e,2)). We may choose this term to represent, for instance, the square at column e and row 2 of a chessboard.

sq, in this example, is referred to as a *function symbol*. This is a historical phrase from predicate logic that notes the resemblance between this form of term and the application of a function but does not imply that some defined function is being called when we use it. We can build up arbitrarily large terms from constants using function symbols. For instance, the term move(sq(e,2),sq(e,4)) is a term whose outermost function symbol is move; that outermost symbol has two arguments, namely sq(e,2) and sq(e,4).

The advantages of using function symbols over lists are space efficiency and readability. We could also choose the representation [e,2] for the square at column e and row 2, but this would be represented with a pointer to the e term, a pointer to the 2 term, and a pointer to the empty list. The representation of sq(e,2), in contrast, takes only two pointers. Moreover, if we notice the term sq(e,2) in program code or debugging output, it is easier to recognize what it is supposed to represent.

We can move back and forth between lists and function symbols by using the =.. binary infix predicate. The query X =.. [sq,e,2] succeeds with the substitution X = sq(e,2). This predicate goes the other way too; the query sq(e,2) =.. Y succeeds with Y = [sq,e,2]! The only instantiation pattern that is not permitted is for both sides to be completely uninstantiated. The decomposition of the function-symbol term only applies to the top level, so for instance, the query move(sq(e,2),sq(e,4)) =.. Y succeeds with the substitution Y = [move,sq(e,2),sq(e,4)].

Now for a surprise. Enter the query X = .(a,.(b,[])). You should get back the substitution X = [a,b]. Yes, lists are actually represented using a hidden function symbol (namely .). It is just that list terms are never output, and rarely input, using the dot-prefix notation. Thus function symbols are used in the basic representation of all complex terms in Prolog, although lists are more universally useful than any other kind of function symbol terms.

6.3.4.4. Strings

Any sequence of ASCII characters between double quote marks (" ") forms a Prolog *string*. As in most other languages, two double quotes in the sequence represent a double quote inside the string.

Prolog strings can be input (in queries and programs) as double-quoted sequences, but they are represented internally as lists of integers (the integers being the ASCII character codes of the characters of the string). That is also how they are output in answer substitutions. Thus the query Firstname = "Jamie" returns the substitution **Firstname = [74,97,109,105,101]** because those five numbers are the codes of the five characters of that name. This representation is useful for manipulation using standard Prolog list-processing predicates. No special string-processing package is needed.

What is the relationship between these character strings and the single-quoted sequences of characters we have met before, for instance, 'Hello world'? The latter are actually *constants* and are represented internally in the same way as other constants, such as a and 54. The single quotes allow us to use a constant name that has spaces or symbolic characters or begins with an uppercase letter (which would normally get it interpreted as a variable). These are what we normally use when we want to, for instance, write out some message to the user; write('Hello world') is thus a request to Prolog to write out the name of a constant, whose name happens to be Hello world.

We can move back and forth between the name of a constant and its Prolog string version using the name predicate. The query name(archy, X) returns the substitution X = **[97,114,99,104,121]**, and conversely name(Y, [97,114,99,104,121]) returns Y = **archy**. This works for integers as well as constants, so that name(42, Answer) returns **Answer** = **[52,50]**, those being the ASCII codes for the characters 4 and 2.

Consider the following predicate:

```
newword(Word, Number, Newword) :-
    name(Word, Wordstring),
    Wordstring = [Firstchar¦Restchars],
    Cap is Firstchar - 32,
    name(Number, Numberstring),
    append([Cap¦Restchars], Numberstring, Newwordstring),
    name(Newword, Newwordstring).
```

The predicate essentially capitalizes the string corresponding to first argument (which is supposed to be an alphanumeric constant), appends the string of the second (numeric) argument to it, and transforms the whole string back into a constant name. The result is that a query such as newword(car, 54, X) returns the substitution **X** = **'Car54'**.

6.3.5. Input and Output

Input and output are somewhat variable from one dialect of Prolog to another, but most dialects use some variant of the Edinburgh Prolog standard library of predicates. In general, I/O predicates are evaluated by Prolog once, as soon as they are called, and never take any action on backtracking.

6.3.5.1. Term I/O

The two simplest I/O predicates are read and write. Because they take terms as arguments, they are referred to as *term I/O* predicates. We have already encountered write, which simply writes out a standard ASCII representation of the term it is given. We have also encountered the specialized predicate nl, which writes the system newline character.

read(X) reads a Prolog term from the input and instantiates X to that term. (X must be uninstantiated when read is called.) The term that is read must be a valid Prolog term and must be terminated by a period, as a Prolog clause is. It is therefore not advisable to use read for interaction with a naive user: Prolog waits until the user types a period, and if the syntax of the term is wrong, it gives a compiler-like (that is, not very helpful) error message. It is better to use the character I/O described later for most interactions.

read is useful, however, for simple programs and for reading preformatted files of input terms. Section 6.5, "Examples," gives a program that reads a file of debugging output from a C program and checks it to see if the C program had any memory leaks.

6.3.5.2. Character I/O

Character I/O is done with the two predicates get0(X) and put(X). Both work with integers as character codes, get0 reading a character and put writing one. Here are two useful predicates that can be written with these character I/O predicates:

```
readstring(X) :-
  get0(C),
  readstring1(C, X).
readstring1(C, []) :-
  newlinechar(C),
  !.
readstring1(C, [C¦Cs]) :-
  readstring(Cs).

writestring([]) :-
  nl.
writestring([C¦Cs]) :-
  put(C),
  writestring(Cs).
```

The first reads a string from input up to the first newline character and returns a string consisting of all those characters except the final newline. (You have to program the newlinechar predicate yourself because this character varies from computer to computer; on UNIX systems, newlinechar(10) is usually correct.) The second predicate writes a string on output, terminating it with a newline character.

On end-of-file conditions, Prologs can be variable in what they report. (Check your Prolog manual.) Edinburgh Prologs usually return -1 as the character read after end-of-file by get0 and the constant end_of_file as the term read by read after end-of-file. Further reads after end-of-file may result in runtime errors. A safer version of readstring, which reports on whether it has reached the end of the file on its last read, is the following:

```
readstring(X, EOFflag) :-
  get0(C),
  readstring1(C, X, EOFflag).
readstring1(-1, [], EOFflag) :-
  !,
  EOFflag = eof.
readstring1(C, [], EOFflag) :-
  newlinechar(C),
  !,
  EOFflag = not_eof.
readstring1(C, [C¦Cs], EOFflag) :-
  readstring(Cs, EOFflag).
```

6.3.5.3. Reading from Many Files

Multiple-file I/O is also given standard support. The easiest way of switching from one input file to another is with the predicates see and seen. see(Filename) takes a constant as a parameter and opens the file by the same name for reading. Any subsequent reads and getøs come from that file. The argument to see must be a constant, so for instance, if there are any dots in the file name, the entire name must be single-quoted, as in 'data.txt' (not double-quoted because "data.txt" is a Prolog string). seen, which takes no arguments, closes the current input file and resets the input to come from the default source (generally, the terminal). A third predicate, seeing(X), instantiates its argument to the name of the file currently being seen.

The see/seeing/seen predicates have some state built into them. If you have previously been reading file A with see, then switch to file B with another see, and then later see file A again, you resume reading file A where you left off. Only when you have seen a file does it get closed completely and reopened again from the start with another see.

This behavior is particularly useful for including files in other files. Consider the following code:

```
process_file(Filename) :-
   seeing(Curr),
   see(Filename),
   process_lines,
   seen,
   see(Curr).

process_lines :-
   readstring(Line, not_eof),
   !,
   handle_include(Line).
process_lines.

handle_include(Line) :-
   append("#include ", Filenamestring, Line),
   !,
   name(Filename, Filenamestring),
   process_file(Filename),
   process_lines.
handle_include(Line) :-
   process_line(Line),
   process_lines.
```

This code processes lines in a file, using the previous readstring code and following include links to other files. On every line in the original or included files, the predicate process_line is called; this can be anything we want. Note the use of append in one of its other useful instantiation patterns—with the first and third arguments instantiated and the second uninstantiated.

The corresponding output routines to see/seeing/seen are tell/telling/told. They take the same number of arguments as the seen series and have similar behavior with regard to resuming previous I/O operations.

6.3.5.4. Stream I/O

It is also possible to open a file for reading or writing and obtain a handle with which to use it, called a *stream*. The predicate open(Filename, Mode, Stream) takes a constant file name and a mode (read, write, or append) and instantiates its third argument to a stream associated with that file.

The basic I/O routines read, write, nl, get0, and put all have variants that take a stream as an additional, first parameter. Thus read(Str1, Term) reads a term from stream Str1, and nl(Str2) writes a newline character on stream Str2. The one-parameter read is referred to as read/1, and the two-parameter version as read/2, consistent with the usual conventions for naming multi-arity predicates (see section 6.3.3). The predicate close(Stream) closes a previously opened input or output stream.

6.3.6. Other Logic and Control Constructs

Here we focus on four logic/control constructs that come in handy from time to time: fail, true, ;, and the if-then-else construct.

fail simply fails, and true simply succeeds without having any other effect. fail is sometimes useful after a cut to say that the predicate should fail without trying other clauses. true is mostly useful in conjunction with the if-then-else, to be described later.

The ; operator means simply "or." An example of its use is the following:

```
process_line(X) :-
   (X = "exit" ; X = "quit" ; X = "done"),
   report_termination.
```

This clause says that if x is either "exit", "quit", or "done", the clause succeeds and reports termination (whatever that may mean in this context). Without the or operator, we would have had to write this as three separate clauses:

```
process_line("exit") :-
   report_termination.
process_line("quit") :-
   report_termination.
process_line("done") :-
   report_termination.
```

The or thus allows us to usefully condense code. Note that the precedence of the semicolon is higher than that of the comma so that if we had omitted the parentheses, the clause body would have been parsed as x = "exit" ; X = "quit" ; (X = "done", report_termination).

Another useful condensing construct is the if-then-else construct. The expression (a -> b ; c), for instance, is a valid if-then-else goal. Its meaning is that if a succeeds, b must succeed, and if a fails, c must succeed. As you can see, it has the effect of performing a kind of cut within a single goal and can be used to avoid having to program the relatively meaningless auxiliary predicates that sometimes arise in Prolog code. For instance, the improved readstring predicate we wrote in section 6.3.5.2 can be simplified to

```
readstring(X, EOFflag) :-
  get0(C),
  ( C = -1 ->
      X = [],
      EOFflag = eof ;
    newlinechar(C) ->
      X = [],
      EOFflag = not_eof ;
    X = [C|Cs],
    readstring(Cs, EOFflag)
  ).
```

This packages up all the logic of readstring into one predicate, without requiring the auxiliary readstring1 predicate. Note that we have actually used if-then-else twice, with one occurrence nested inside the other. The comma has lowest precedence, so we should read the clause body as if there were parentheses around each comma-separated sequence of atoms.

6.3.7. Finding All Solutions

Prolog is useful for finding a solution to a logically stated problem. Occasionally, in doing so, we have to find *all* solutions to some subproblem. There are three main predicates that we can use to do this: findall/3, bagof/3, and setof/3.

6.3.7.1. findall

findall takes three parameters: The first is a term pattern, the second is a goal, and the third is a term that collects the solutions. For instance, the goal findall(Y, (grandparent(X, Y), rich(Y)), RichGrands) collects into RichGrands all the Ys such that (grandparent(X, Y), rich(Y)) is true—that is, all the rich grandparents of x. Here is a similar but more complex goal:

```
findall( wealth(Y,W),
         (grandparent(X, Y), (rich(Y) -> W=rich ; W=not_rich)),
         GrandsWealths
       )
```

This goal collects into GrandsWealths a list of terms of the form wealth(Y,W), where Y is a grandparent of X and W is rich if that grandparent is rich and not_rich otherwise. The predicate works in the way you might expect: It solves the goal in its second argument and then keeps retrying it and finding new solutions until the goal fails. If the goal goes into an infinite loop, or if it returns an infinite number of solutions, the findall call loops indefinitely as well. This predicate gives us a straightforward way of programming the union and intersection of lists:

```
union(L1, L2, L) :-
    findall(E, (member(L1, E); member(L2, E)), L).
intersection(L1, L2, L) :-
    findall(E, (member(L1, E), member(L2, E)), L).
```

The union of two lists is all the elements that appear in either of the lists, and the intersection is all the elements that appear in both of the lists. This is not the most efficient way of computing the union because the effect of the body is simply to append the two lists, keeping duplicates of any elements that appear in both lists, but it illustrates the potential of findall to help provide an elegant and readable expression of a problem.

Note that in findall, the variables in the first argument work in a rather different way from most variables in Prolog code. Usually, the appearance of a local variable X in the body of a predicate corresponds to the phrase "there exists an X"; here, it corresponds to the phrase "for all Xs." The uninstantiated variables that appear in the second argument but not the first are "there exists" variables, as is the third argument. The effect of this is achieved by special low-level code that inspects the internal representation of terms and goals; findall cannot be programmed by conventional Prolog clauses.

6.3.7.2. bagof **and** setof

One effect of the behavior of findall is that it always succeeds exactly once. It calls the goal in its second argument and compiles a list (which may be empty) of the successful patterns. Because of its treatment of uninstantiated variables, no variables get instantiated during a call to findall except the third argument.

This may not be exactly what we want. We may in fact want uninstantiated variables in the second argument to be instantiated to values that make the query succeed. This is what bagof and setof do. For instance, consider again the father predicate:

```
father(henry_viii, henry_vii).
father(margaret_tudor, henry_vii).
father(mary_queen_of_scots, james_v_of_scotland).
father(elizabeth_i, henry_viii).
father(james_v_of_scotland, james_iv_of_scotland).
```

If we ask the query findall(Child, father(Child, Father), Children), we get Children instantiated to a list of all the people who appear in the first argument in the father relation. However, if we ask bagof(Child, father(Child, Father), Children), we get four solutions:

```
Children = [henry_viii,margaret_tudor],
Father = henry_vii ? ;

Children = [elizabeth_i],
Father = henry_viii ? ;

Children = [james_v_of_scotland],
Father = james_iv_of_scotland ? ;

Children = [mary_queen_of_scots],
Father = james_v_of_scotland ?
```

As you can see, bagof treats the Father variable (and all uninstantiated variables in the second argument not appearing in the first) as if it is a regular Prolog variable, to be instantiated to whatever satisfies the query. Only the variables appearing in the first argument are treated as "for all" variables.

Because of this behavior, bagof fails if no solutions exist to the query in the second argument, and it can succeed multiple times upon backtracking. If this is not what you want—that is, if you just want a simple list of solutions, which may be empty—findall is the correct predicate to use.

setof is very similar to bagof but differs in its final processing of the list returned. bagof returns a list of solutions that may contain duplicates and is unordered (hence its name, because *bag* is another word for "set possibly containing duplicates"). In contrast, setof sorts its list and eliminates all duplicates. In a sense, setof is the most logical of the three all-solutions predicates because the list it returns is ordered not by the order in which the solutions were found, but by lexicographic order.

6.3.8. The Four-Port Debugger

Prolog was sometimes originally touted as a language in which you could write "executable specifications," text that was so obviously correct that it did not need to be debugged. Alas, as people wrote longer and more complex Prolog code, they found that it needed as much debugging support as any other programming language.

The debugging system of Edinburgh Prolog interpreters was developed originally by Lawrence Byrd. It is referred to as the *four-port debugger* or the *Byrd box debugger* because of the way in which it views predicate calls as boxes having four main input/output ports.

The execution of a Prolog goal can be difficult to follow because of the backtracking pattern of computation. An interactive debugger is therefore a useful tool. In Prolog debugging, it is not sufficient merely to have breakpoints on the entry and exit of a predicate; we must also be able to see when a predicate is being retried for this call due to backtracking and whether a predicate call has succeeded or failed.

The four-port debugger provides us with this information. There are four types of events associated with each predicate call that is processed by the interpreter: a *call* event, which occurs when the predicate is first called; a *redo* event, which occurs when backtracking causes other clauses to be retried; an *exit* event, which occurs whenever a solution has been returned by the predicate call (either on the first try or future retries); and a *fail* event, which occurs when the predicate has exhausted the clauses defining it. A call or redo event happens only when the predicate call has been successfully matched with a clause head; clauses that don't match the call are ignored by the debugger.

6.3.8.1. Creeping Through a Computation

Here is an example of a simple use of the debugger to "creep" through a computation. Consider again the standard definition of member:

```
member([X|Xs], X).
member([X|Xs], Y) :-
    member(Xs, Y).
```

We enter the Prolog interpreter, consult a file containing this definition, and enter the query trace. This predicate is a directive to the interpreter to begin tracing goals thoroughly; the query notrace turns this facility off. We then type the goal member([a,b], X), member([b,c], X). Prolog's first task is to evaluate the predicate call member([a,b], X). The first line returned from the debugger is something like

```
1   1   Call: member([a,b],_77) ?
```

This prompt is a debugging prompt, giving information on the current state of computation and asking us what we want to do next. The first number is the unique invocation identifier, which is different for every individual call to a predicate. The second number is the depth of the call—that is, how many times we have expanded a predicate call into its body from the top level in order to get to this call. call indicates that we are at the call port of the predicate. The last thing displayed is the internal representation of the predicate call. _77 is a machine-generated identifier that is Prolog's internal name for the variable x; this is different on every run of Prolog.

At this point, if we keep pressing Enter at the debugging prompts, Prolog keeps generating lines like this until we reach the last failure of the predicate. The next few lines, for example, are

```
1   1   Exit: member([a,b],a) ?
2   1   Call: member([b,c],a) ?
3   2   Call: member([c],a) ?
4   3   Call: member([],a) ?
4   3   Fail: member([],a) ?
3   2   Fail: member([c],a) ?
2   1   Fail: member([b,c],a) ?
1   1   Redo: member([a,b],a) ?
2   2   Call: member([b],_77) ?
2   2   Exit: member([b],b) ?
1   1   Exit: member([a,b],b) ?
```

Here, the interpreter has returned a as a member of the first list (the first line) and has tried to find it in the second list (the next three lines). The bottommost recursive call has failed, and that failure has propagated back to the top level of the second subgoal (the next three lines). The first subgoal has therefore been redone, and a recursive call results in b being returned. After this point, the output looks as follows:

```
3   1   Call: member([b,c],b) ?
3   1   Exit: member([b,c],b) ?

X = b ?
```

The interpreter has confirmed that b is a member of the second list and has given us a solution, with the solutions prompt. If we continue in this way, we will trace through another backtrack, which will ultimately fail, leaving us with only the one solution.

6.3.8.2. Some Other Debugger Commands

The fine-grained method used previously of tracing through an execution sequence is evocatively known as creeping, but Enter is not the only thing we can press at a debugger prompt. In fact, there is a whole set of commands we can use. Each command is issued by typing a single letter followed by pressing Enter.

The debug command s, for skip, can be used at a call or redo port to skip an entire computation. This leaves us at the exit or fail port at the end of its invocation without tracing what has happened in between. A useful technique is to look at the information that the debugger gives us and use it to decide whether to skip over the call. The debugger always tells us the predicate name and the arguments to the call, so if we know or can guess the outcome of the call, we may choose to skip over it. Some other simple debugging commands are

- a, for abort. This aborts the entire computation (for instance, when you think you have found the bug you were looking for) and returns control to the top-level interpreter.

- r, for retry. At a given port, this resets the state of the computation to what it was when the predicate call corresponding to the port was first invoked. This is useful when a call has been skipped but has failed unexpectedly or returned some unexpected result; retrying, followed by creeping, can help reveal the problem.

- f, for fail, forces the predicate call to fail. This can be useful for testing the behavior of the calling predicate on failure.

6.3.8.3. Spy-Points
If we know that a problem exists only once we reach a certain predicate, it is tedious to creep through a large number of levels until we reach the problem predicate. In the four-port debugger, we can set breakpoints, or "spy-points," on given predicates. We do this by issuing the top-level query spy p, where p is the name of the predicate we want a spy-point on. When we have done this, the debug command l, for leap, skips over (that is, executes without displaying any debugging information or prompts) all computation up to the next spy-point.

In addition to the trace mode used previously is a debug mode. When the interpreter is in debug mode (which is entered with debug and exited with nodebug), a query is executed as if the interpreter were in trace mode, except that there is an automatic l command given to the debugger. Thus no information is presented about the computation until the first spy-point is reached. This can be a useful timesaver.

Spy-points and leaping are useful but are tricky to use effectively. If we set spy-points at predicates at too low a level, leaping still gives us too much information; if we set them at predicates at too high a level, we may skip over the area where the problem occurs, perhaps failing back to the top-level interpreter without finding the problem we were looking for. A spy-point is most useful on a predicate that we suspect may be buggy or one that is called just before a known problem arises.

While at the debugging prompt, we can issue the command + to set a spy-point on-the-fly at the current predicate or - to remove a previously set spy-point. Both commands take effect immediately for the whole debugging session. An experienced Prolog programmer can use leaping, creeping, skipping, and on-the-fly spy-point setting to identify a problem relatively quickly.

Interactive debugging is available mainly in interpreters. Compiled Prolog code is sometimes able to use the four-port debugger but often can be debugged only with calls to the write predicate. Thus, a Prolog system with both an interpreter (and debugger) and a compiler, or with a compiler allowing debugging support, is the most useful configuration.

6.3.9. Definite Clause Grammars

One of the most useful features of modern Prolog systems is Definite Clause Grammars, or DCGs. DCGs allow us to write grammars in a natural style almost like traditional context-free grammars, but in such a way that the grammar is integrated with the rest of the Prolog program.

Grammar processing was, in fact, one of the original applications for which Colmerauer built Prolog. The idea of DCGs, which greatly simplify grammar processing, was first proposed by Fernando Pereira and David H. D. Warren (1980) and has now become a standard feature of Prolog.

6.3.9.1. Grammars in Conventional Prolog

Consider the following Prolog predicates:

```
beginning_is_sentence(List, Rest) :-
   beginning_is_noun_phrase(List, Rest1),
   beginning_is_verb_phrase(Rest1, Rest).

beginning_is_noun_phrase([evelyn|Rest], Rest).
beginning_is_noun_phrase([chris|Rest], Rest).

beginning_is_verb_phrase([sings|Rest], Rest).
beginning_is_verb_phrase([jogs|Rest], Rest).
beginning_is_verb_phrase([loves|Rest1], Rest) :-
   beginning_is_noun_phrase(Rest1, Rest).
```

These predicates can be seen as parsing the beginning of a list of constants as being a sentence, noun phrase, or verb phrase. beginning_is_noun_phrase takes two lists (List, Rest) and succeeds only if the beginning of List is a noun phrase we recognize (here, we recognize only two names as noun phrases) and the rest of List is Rest. The other predicates operate similarly. We can see whether the list [evelyn, loves, chris] is a sentence by posing the query

```
beginning_is_sentence([evelyn, loves, chris], []).
```

This requires that the "rest of the list after the sentence" is the empty list—that is, that the entire list constitutes a complete sentence. This query succeeds, but for instance, the queries

```
beginning_is_sentence([evelyn, loves], []).
beginning_is_sentence([evelyn, sings, chris], []).
beginning_is_sentence([evelyn, loves, chris, madly], []).
```

all fail. The query beginning_is_sentence([evelyn, loves, chris, madly], Rest) returns the substitution **Rest = [madly]**, although it is not as usual to give a non-empty list as the last parameter.

This technique can be used to write any grammar in Prolog. However, there are some straightforward and tedious aspects of the technique. In the predicate bodies, the second argument of one call is always the first argument to the next call, and the second argument of the last call is always the second argument in the head. The important information in the predicates is the sequence of predicate calls, and those are somewhat obscured by the rest of the definitions.

6.3.9.2. The DCG Version

Now consider the following text:

```
sentence -->
  noun_phrase,
  verb_phrase.

noun_phrase --> [evelyn].
noun_phrase --> [chris].

verb_phrase --> [sings].
verb_phrase --> [jogs].
verb_phrase -->
    [loves],
    noun_phrase.
```

This text constitutes a valid Prolog program as well; the --> expressions are DCG rules, and this text as a whole constitutes a DCG. When Prolog is reading a program, it automatically translates DCG rules into Prolog clauses in the style used earlier. For instance, the first three rules are essentially translated into

```
sentence(List, Rest) :-
  noun_phrase(List, Rest1),
  verb_phrase(Rest1, Rest).
```

```
noun_phrase(List, Rest) :-
   append([evelyn], Rest, List).
noun_phrase(List, Rest) :-
   append([chris], Rest, List).
```

Note that two arguments have been added to each identifier in the first rule. We use the DCG rules by calling these translated clauses, typically with the empty list as the last parameter. For instance, sentence([evelyn, loves, chris], []) is still the form of call we will use to parse that list of constants as a sentence.

Note also that the lists in the bodies of the second and third rules have been replaced by calls to append.[3] Lists of any length can be used in DCGs; for instance, the rule noun_phrase --> [the, bookstore, owner] would be translated into

```
noun_phrase(List, Rest) :-
   append([the, bookstore, owner], Rest, List).
```

6.3.9.3. Arguments in DCGs

The identifiers in DCG rules can have arguments as well. This is useful for returning a parse tree corresponding to the thing parsed. A parse-tree version of the preceding grammar might be

```
sentence(Meaning) -->
   noun_phrase(Subject),
   verb_phrase(Subject, Meaning).

noun_phrase(evelyn) --> [evelyn].
noun_phrase(chris) --> [chris].

verb_phrase(Subject, sings(Subject)) --> [sings].
verb_phrase(Subject, jogs(Subject)) --> [jogs].
verb_phrase(Subject, loves(Subject,Object)) -->
   [loves],
   noun_phrase(Object).
```

The extra arguments are added onto the end of the arguments already given so that the first rule is translated as

```
sentence(Meaning, List, Rest) :-
   noun_phrase(Subject, List, Rest1),
   verb_phrase(Subject, Meaning, Rest1, Rest).
```

---

[3]This is slightly inaccurate; most Prologs use the special predicate 'C', with a different argument order, rather than append because append is a library predicate that can be redefined. But the effect is the same as the standard definition of append.

6.3.9.4. Calling Prolog Goals

In some situations, it is useful to be able to call a Prolog goal within a DCG clause in order to test some condition. We can do this by enclosing the goal in curly braces ({...}); the goal simply gets copied into the clause translation as-is. For instance, the rule

```
uppercase(Character) -->
  [Character],
  {Character >= 65, Character =< 90}.
```

parses one character (and returns it as the meaning), but only if it is an uppercase letter. The translation is

```
uppercase(Character, Input, Rest) -->
  append([Character], Rest, Input),
  Character >= 65, Character =< 90.
```

Cuts are not excluded from the things we can do inside the curly braces. Here are grammar rules that parse a positive integer from a list of character codes and return the integer:

```
integer(N) -->
  [Ch],
  {digit(Ch), !, D is Ch-48},
  rest_of_integer(D, N).

rest_of_integer(Sofar, N) -->
  [Ch],
  {digit(Ch), !, N1 is (Sofar*10)+(Ch-48)},
  rest_of_integer(N1, N).
rest_of_integer(Sofar, Sofar) -->
  [].
```

These rules keep processing digits until there are no more in the input list and compute the integer represented. The cuts are useful for backtracking efficiency. Either with or without the cuts, a string beginning with "2345 foo" would first be parsed as the integer 2345 with the string " foo" left over. Without the cuts, on failure and backtracking, the string would next be parsed as the integer 234 with the string "5 foo" left over, and so on. The cuts allow us to take the entire integer in a "greedy" manner.

Note the use of the construct ... --> [] in the last example. DCG rules cannot be of the form atom. because that would be interpreted as a simple Prolog fact (without the extra arguments). If a DCG rule corresponds to parsing nothing, it must have a body consisting of at least the empty list.

6.3.9.5. Two-Level Parsing

The last two examples illustrate that DCGs can also apply to the lexical level of parsing. Because strings are just lists of integers, we can put strings into DCG bodies and they are treated just like any other lists. Here is part of a grammar to parse a simplified version of Internet URLs:

```
url --> transport, "://", machine, "/", path.
url --> "file:/", path.

transport --> "http".
transport --> "ftp".

machine --> ident, dot_idents.

dot_idents --> [].
dot_idents --> ".", ident, dot_idents.

path --> [].
path --> ident.
path --> ident, "/", path.
```

It is sometimes useful to have one DCG for the lexical level and another for the token level. The top-level loop of a program reads a file, tokenizing each line into a list of tokens with the lexical-level DCG; then it appends the token lists together and parses the whole thing with the token-level grammar.

6.3.10. assert and retract

Prolog is a largely declarative language, which means, among other things, that all information in a normal computation arises from the program or from parameters passed to and from predicates. However, occasionally it is useful to be able change the global state of the computation in order to store persistent data.

The Prolog assert and retract predicates allow us to do this. They are most useful in two situations: to record information that is used by only a small number of predicates and to save data from one query to another. Although we can use assert and retract to perform imperative-style computation, this is not advisable (see section 6.4.2).

6.3.10.1. Using the Predicates

assert does basically what its name suggests; it asserts that some fact or rule now holds, which may not have held before. Making the predicate call assert(outformat(verbose)), for instance, has the effect of immediately making the predicate outformat true of the atom verbose, even if it was not true before.

Subsequent calls to the outformat predicate reflect this change. After the call, it will be as if we had the clause outformat(verbose) in the program from the beginning. Consider the predicate definition

```
prompt(N, NGname) :-
    outformat(verbose),
    !,
```

```
      write(N), write(' articles in newsgroup '),
      writestring(NGname), write(' -- read now? ').
   prompt(N, NGname) :-
      write(N), write(' in '),
      writestring(NGname), write(' -- read? ').
```

The predicate outformat is treated as any other predicate, even though it has been manipulated by assert and may never have appeared in the original program. If prompt is called just after assert(outformat(verbose)) has been called, only the first clause of prompt is used.

In fact, the assert/retract database is usually implemented as a separate entity from the rest of the program clauses, although it is referred to in exactly the same way as the program clauses.

retract does exactly the opposite of assert. retract(outformat(verbose)) deletes that clause from the assert/retract database. Immediately after the retraction of this fact, for instance, a call to the prompt predicate uses only the second clause. If the clause that is the argument of retract does not exist in the database, the call fails. Conversely, if the argument to retract contains free variables and one or more facts in the database match the argument, the first fact is matched, the variables are instantiated, and the clause is deleted. This can be useful for retrieving an old stored value; for instance, the following code implements a useful switch-setting predicate:

```
   switch(Switchname, Newsetting) :-
      retract(switchvalue(Switchname, Oldsetting)),
      !,
      write('Old setting: '), write(Oldsetting), nl,
      assert(switchvalue(Switchname, Newsetting)),
      write('New setting: '), write(Newsetting), nl.
   switch(Switchname, Newsetting) :-
      write('Error:  switch '), write(Switchname),
      write(' not known'), nl.
```

These examples illustrate one of the main uses of assert and retract. An interactive system might benefit from implementing some kind of switch to record (for instance) whether the user wants verbose or terse output. We could do this by passing the switch as a parameter to all predicates, but this would be somewhat tedious because typically only the low-level output predicates would have to know the information. It simplifies the code (at the cost of a little non-declarativeness) to assert the switch value.

6.3.10.2. Declaring Dynamic Predicates
Most Prolog systems, especially compilers, require programmers to declare their intention to assert and retract clauses of a particular predicate with the dynamic predicate. To allow the asserts and retracts, for instance, we can type the query dynamic outformat/1 to an interpreter.

dynamic acts as a unary operator on a term of the form `pred/arity`, where `pred` is a predicate name and `arity` is a number indicating how many arguments it has.

The effect of this query can be achieved in a Prolog source file by including the following line in the file:

```
:- dynamic outformat/1.
```

The `:-` here is very important! If it is left out, then Prolog will think we are trying to give a clause for the predicate `dynamic` and we will probably get an "attempt to redeclare" error. As it is, we are asking Prolog to execute the goal `dynamic outformat/1` in the course of its reading the source file.

In fact, any goal can be executed during source file processing in this way; for instance, having the expression `:- write('Welcome to my system'),` `nl.` in a source file causes that string to be written out. However, the facility is most often used for the `dynamic` predicate and the `op` predicate (to be encountered soon).

6.3.10.3. Recording Persistent Data

Another main use of the `assert/retract` database is to record data that is maintained during a whole interpreter session. When we give an interpreter the query `x = 42`, it responds with `x = 42` but then discards that instantiation of x when processing the next query. The `assert` and `retract` data, in contrast, persist from query to query.

One of the useful applications of this feature is to convert a Prolog interpreter into a command interpreter for a kind of command subsystem. For instance, we might decide to write a game-playing program by implementing one predicate, `move`, which refers to a dynamic predicate, `current_board`:

```
:- dynamic current_board/1.

move(Move) :-
    retract(current_board(Curr_board)),
    board_after_move(Curr_board, Move, Mid_board),
    machine_response(Mid_board, Machine_move),
    board_after_move(Mid_board, Machine_move, New_board),
    print_board(New_board),
    assert(current_board(New_board)).
```

This predicate would remove the need for us to use the I/O predicates to interact with the user. The user knows that he has only to call the simple `move` predicate repeatedly in order to interact with the system.

6.3.11. Operator Declarations

We have encountered some examples of binary infix relations in Prolog, such as = and =.., and binary infix operators, such as + and /. We can declare such relations and operators ourselves; in fact, this facility is related to the representation of all goals and terms in Prolog.

6.3.11.1. A First Example

For instance, say that we wanted to represent a square on a game board. We could use the notation we adopted before, sq(Row,Column), but it would stand out more in our program if we could write Row::Column. We can achieve this with the following query declaring the symbol :: as an operator:

```
op(500, xfy, ::).
```

As with the dynamic declaration (see section 6.3.10.2), we can achieve the same effect by putting the following line in a source file and consulting it:

```
:- op(500, xfy, ::).
```

The first argument of the op predicate is the precedence of the operator, which we will look at more soon. The second argument is a fixity and associativity specifier; all we need to know about this at the moment is that xfy declares an infix operator. The third and last argument is the operator to be declared.

Immediately after processing one of these declarations, Row::Column is parsed by Prolog as a term and can appear anywhere a term can—as an argument to a predicate, for instance. Its internal representation is the same as if we typed ::(Row,Column), and in fact, the two terms are equal as far as Prolog is concerned. But terms of the form ::(Row,Column), after the declaration, can always be input and will always be output in the infix form.

6.3.11.2. What Can Be an Operator?

What sequences of characters can appear in the third argument of an op declaration? Actually, it turns out that the more relevant question is What sequence of characters can be a function symbol?

So far we have looked only at function symbols that start out with a lowercase letter and contain only alphanumeric characters and underscores, or the single-quoted sequences of characters. In fact there is a third class: all sequences of symbol characters. The set of symbol characters varies from one Prolog to another but typically excludes the alphanumeric characters and all forms of bracketing and includes such things as the colon, semicolon, slash, plus, and minus characters. We cannot mix symbol and non-symbol characters in a function symbol name, precisely because we would like to be able to write something such as a+b with no spaces and have the parser parse it as three separate tokens.

In fact, any function symbol can appear in the third argument of the op predicate. If we wanted to represent regular expressions in Prolog, for instance, we might want to use Exp1 bar Exp2 to mean either Exp1 or Exp2 and use Exp1 then Exp2 to mean Exp1 followed by Exp2. We could achieve this with the declarations

```
:- op(600, xfy, bar).
:- op(500, xfy, then).
```

This would ensure that the expression x then Y bar z would be parsed as exactly the same term as bar(then(X,Y),Z).

6.3.11.3. Precedences and Specifiers

Why, in the previous example, was x then Y bar z parsed as bar(then(X,Y),Z) rather than as then(X,bar(Y,Z))? The answer is in the precedence argument. In a complex expression involving many operators, the rule of thumb is that the operator with the highest precedence is the one that is the outermost operator. Because bar has precedence 600, and then only precedence 500, bar wins as the outermost.

This extends to built-in, predeclared operators such as the arithmetic operators. For instance, + and - are automatically declared by Prolog to be operators of precedence 500, and the * and / operators to have precedence 400, in order to achieve the desired grouping behavior.

As in arithmetic, we can always use parentheses to group operands in the way we would like. For instance, the term x then (Y bar z) is always parsed as then(X,bar(Y,Z)), regardless of the precedences of the operators.

Now, what about the expression A then B then C? Is it parsed as then(A,then(B,C)) or as then(then(A,B),C)? The answer is the former, and the reason lies in the fixity and associativity specifier xfy. Each specifier is a tiny picture of where the function symbol (f) is in relation to the operands and what kind of operands it can have (x and y). The operand code x indicates an operand whose outermost operator has strictly lower precedence to the operator being declared, and y indicates an operand whose outermost operator has precedence lower than or the same as the operator being declared. When then is declared using the specifier xfy, the only way to parse A then B then C that is consistent with that picture is then(A,then(B,C)).

Thus xfy declares an operator as being right-associative. This is a natural choice for then as a regular expression operator because we probably want to process the leftmost element of a then chain separately first. However, it would not be a good choice for the arithmetic operator - because we would like 10 - 6 - 4 to be parsed the same as (10 - 6) - 4. Hence the minus (and in fact all four of the standard arithmetic operators) are declared yfx instead, making them left-associative.

It is sometimes also useful to declare an operator as xfx, meaning that you cannot chain together sequences with that operator in between. This might have been a better choice for the Row::Column operator because we don't want to use it in any situation other than separating two numbers. Note, however, that it doesn't make sense to declare an operator as yfy because that would make terms such as A then B then C ambiguous. Hence yfy is not an allowed specifier.

6.3.11.4. Unary Operators
Unary operators are declared in exactly the same way as binary ones. The four possible specifiers are fx and fy, for prefix operators, and xf and yf, for postfix operators. fx would be the natural specifier for the \+ operator, for instance, if we wanted to disallow expressions such as \+ \+ in(Dict, X); if we did want to allow such expressions, fy would be the appropriate specifier. xf might be something we would want to declare star as for a regular expression package so that we could use the term x star to mean zero or more repetitions of x.

An operator can be declared as both a prefix or postfix operator and as an infix operator. This is especially useful for the - operator because we would like it declared both as an infix operator and as a prefix operator (for unary minus, as in -x). In fact, in most Prologs, it is declared as both, as if with the declarations

```
:- op(500, yfx, -).
:- op(200, fy, -).
```

6.3.11.5. Everything Is a Term
Now for another surprise, comparable to the surprise that lists are represented with function symbols (section 6.3.4.3). Most of the symbols we have encountered in the Prolog syntax are in fact operators, and everything that Prolog deals with is in fact a term!

Take the :- operator. We have not been accustomed to thinking of it as an operator, but it is treated as if declared with op(1200, xfx, :-). Moreover, the comma operator is treated as if declared with op(1000, xfy, ','). Thus a clause such as

```
grandfather(X, Y) :-
    parent(X, Parent),
    father(Parent, Y).
```

is treated just like the term

```
':-'( grandfather(X,Y),
      ','( parent(X,Parent),
           father(Parent,Y)
         )
    )
```

Note the rather odd and overloaded nature of the comma here. When it appears within parentheses immediately after an identifier, it separates arguments of that function symbol or predicate; elsewhere, for instance at the top level of a body of a clause, it is treated as an operator no different from + or =.

One advantage of this uniform treatment of Prolog syntax as built up with operators is that Prolog can use the same algorithm when reading clauses in a source file as when reading terms from a file with read. A program is just terms terminated by dots like a data file. Another advantage is that we can read clauses from a source file in programs in exactly the same way that Prolog does. This is a useful thing to be able to do for metaprogramming, where we write programs that manipulate programs.

6.4. Tips and Traps

Here we discuss some useful hints for Prolog programmers and annoying pitfalls that they sometimes run into. These tips and traps are presented in what I think is their approximate order of importance.

6.4.1. Style

As in all programming languages, following any given style of coding is a matter of taste, but it is helpful to follow *some* style. Here I list some recommendations for good coding and design style, which programmers can follow or not as they wish.

6.4.1.1. Whitespace, Comments, and Naming

Because predicates can appear with any arity in Prolog, interpreters do not check whether the number of arguments in a particular predicate call is accurate. Hence it is helpful to code so that the number and position of arguments to a predicate call is apparent. In this chapter, I have followed the common convention of not putting any spaces anywhere in terms, but putting spaces after each comma in lists of arguments to predicates. Some writers go further and put a space between the left parenthesis beginning the list of arguments and the first argument.

It is good technique to associate one comment with each predicate definition, except for predicates whose meaning is obvious. I generally try to make the comment start with text of the form `% pred(Arg1, Arg2):`, followed by the description.

It is useful to line up the predicate calls in a predicate body. Naturally, there are times when this is not so appropriate, such as when a predicate body contains a sequence of `write` and `nl` calls that would otherwise stretch down the page. When using nested constructs, such as `if-then-else`, predicate calls on the same logical level in the code should be lined up.

Because predicates are intended to represent something declarative, it somewhat misses the point to name them using verbs, which represent non-declarative actions. Aside from some classic predicates such as `append` and `delete`, and predicates with obviously non-declarative meaning, such as `write`, predicates are usually named using nouns and adjectives in highly declarative code.

Many predicates are actually functions, in the sense that they take `N-1` arguments as input and return their `N`th argument as output. The common style in these situations is to have the returned argument as the last argument. I have attempted to follow this style in this chapter.

6.4.1.2. Design Patterns

As in Lisp, the most common pattern for predicates is one of recursing down a list. Many predicates will have the pattern

```
p([], ...) :-
    ... .
p([X|Xs], ...) :-
    ... .
```

Programmers should not avoid such code simply because they have done it before and are bored with it. Prolog is in fact optimized in some ways for such code (see section 6.4.7), and programmers should take advantage of this optimization.

Many interactive programs have one or more top-level predicates that are highly imperative, writing to and reading from the user and asserting and retracting persistent data. However, below a certain point in the predicate calling hierarchy, even interactive programs should be highly declarative;

otherwise, there is little point in using a declarative language. It is useful to have interactive predicates grouped together in some source files and have other source files containing only declarative predicates. You can use the module facilities of your Prolog to link these together.

6.4.2. Overusing `assert` and `retract`

One of the most common mistakes of new Prolog programmers is to overuse `assert` and `retract`. It has been said that "a Fortran programmer can write Fortran programs in any language." Although not all programmers may be quite that bad, nevertheless it takes a programmer used to the imperative style quite a while to adapt to a programming language without imperative modification of data.

To avoid this trap, remember that Prolog predicates are typically going to have more parameters than the analogous procedures in an imperative language. Some of these parameters will be data structures that it is necessary to search at some point; it will not always be possible to dump data into Prolog predicates and get Prolog to do the searching for us. Prolog's searching is much more appropriate for structures of facts and rules that are common to the entire program execution, rather than for the changing data structures of a particular run of a program.

This trap is associated with a way of thinking that tries to understand and direct Prolog's execution strategy. This is like trying to ride a bucking bronco: Unless you are skillful, you will probably get thrown. Instead of thinking in these terms, it is often useful simply to try to express in logic the problem to be solved. You may end up with a solution that is inefficient, or even does not terminate due to the way it is coded. However, you can then proceed from the logic-based starting point to make the code more efficient as well as logical. This will help you understand the code much more thoroughly as it is being developed.

6.4.3. The Singleton Warning and Anonymous Variables

You may notice warnings of "singleton variables" from your interpreter concerning some of the examples in this chapter. Most Prologs check every clause that they encounter to see whether any variable has been used only once in the clause. The appearance of one of these singleton variables usually highlights a bug because experienced programmers use what are called anonymous variables to avoid singletons.

Any sequence of alphanumeric characters and underscores starting with an underscore is also a valid variable name. These underscore variables have the property that no two occurrences of the variable in a clause are connected with one another; the variable is in some sense nameless, or anonymous.

Anonymous variables are useful when we don't care about the value of some parameter. For instance, the member predicate can be re-expressed as follows:

```
member([X¦_], X).
member([_¦Xs], X) :-
   member(Xs, X).
```

This makes use of the simplest anonymous variable _ in two places where we don't care what the value of that part of the list argument is for the purposes of the clause. When we use anonymous variables in every place where we don't care about a value, every non-anonymous variable gets used at least twice.

Why does the Prolog system care enough to warn us about places where a variable comes up only once? Consider the following code:

```
process_list([], []).
process_list([X¦Xs], [NewX¦NewXs]) :-
   process_element(X, NewX),
   process_list(Xs, New_Xs).
```

You may not be able to see the problem with this code at first glance, but there is a problem. The variable name NewXs is used in the head of the second clause, but New_Xs is used later. The result of the recursive call does not get passed back, as was probably intended; instead, a list with an uninstantiated variable is passed back. Bugs such as these are very common and characteristically manifest themselves as one or (more commonly) two singleton variables in a clause. Prologs report on singleton non-anonymous variables but not singleton anonymous variables; so if we replace all intentional singletons with anonymous variables, the warnings we will end up with will highlight these misspellings.

_ is sometimes called *the* anonymous variable, but any identifier beginning with an underscore is an anonymous variable. Sometimes these other variable names are useful for reminding us what is supposed to go in that location while retaining their anonymity:

```
member([X¦_Xs], X).
member([_X¦Xs], X) :-
   member(Xs, X).
```

This code maintains the information that the members of the list are all the same kind of thing as far as the member predicate is concerned.

6.4.4. Infinite Terms and the Occurs Check

Occasionally, you may encounter a term in printout that literally goes on forever: The system keeps printing and printing until we break out of the program. This is usually due to a deficiency in most Prolog interpreters, which the program has happened to encounter.

When Prolog is given a query of the form x = [a|X], it should respond with **no**; after all, we can't find any term to substitute for x in that query that makes it true. Prolog should check to see whether x occurs in the term to the right of the = before trying to substitute.

Many Prolog interpreters do not perform this "occurs check" simply because it takes a long time and it very rarely results in a problem. Equality, and unification of terms for matching calls with clause heads, is one of the basic operations of a Prolog interpreter and is executed several times on each inference step. It must be made as efficient as possible.

Because variables are really represented by pointers, the incorrect processing of the query x = [a|X] takes the following form: x is set to a data structure with two pointers, of which the left pointer points to a and the right pointer points back to the term itself. Thus when Prolog goes to print the solution to the query, it typically prints

```
X = [a,a,a,a,a,a,a,a,a,a,a,a,a,a,a,a,a,...
```

and so on until we break.

The solution to the problem is either to turn on the occurs check on systems that have that option or else to code around the problem. The latter solution is more common because (except in application areas such as metaprogramming) problems with the occurs check very often result from bugs, rather than a genuine need to perform the check.

6.4.5. The Transitive Closure Problem

Consider the following code:

```
sibling(constance, cathleen).
sibling(cathleen, john).
sibling(X, Y) :- sibling(X, Z), sibling(Z, Y).
```

This code defines a relation sibling by two "base" clauses and a recursive clause. It does not seem like dangerous code because the two base clauses appearing first seem to block any potential infinite recursion; indeed, the code gives correctly the two first answers to the query sibling(constance, X). Unfortunately, however, when we type the semicolon for more solutions, the query does loop infinitely. This is a common problem encountered in knowledge-base applications; it is referred to as the *transitive closure problem* because we are trying to take the transitive closure of the base clauses.

What has happened here? Let's pick up the debugger trace after the second solution:

```
1   1   Redo: sibling(constance,john) ?
3   2   Redo: sibling(cathleen,john) ?
4   3   Call: sibling(cathleen,_732) ?
4   3   Exit: sibling(cathleen,john) ?
5   3   Call: sibling(john,_77) ?
6   4   Call: sibling(john,_1180) ?
7   5   Call: sibling(john,_1347) ?
8   6   Call: sibling(john,_1514) ?
...
```

This highlights the problem. As soon as we call sibling with a first argument (say, john) that does not appear as a first argument in the base clauses, we immediately skip to the recursive clause and call a goal of exactly the same form.

The solution is to separate the two levels of the predicate from each other and treat sibling as the transitive closure of some other relation, say sibling_base. The revised code looks very much like the parent and ancestor relations:

```
sibling_base(constance, cathleen).
sibling_base(cathleen, john).

sibling(X, Y) :- sibling_base(X, Y).
sibling(X, Y) :- sibling_base(X, Z), sibling(Z, Y).
```

This problem is made more complex when reflexive or symmetric relations are desired. A full treatment of the associated issues is found in O'Keefe's book (1990).

6.4.6. Tail Recursion Optimization

As in Lisp compilers, most modern Prolog compilers have *tail recursion optimization*. This means that if a clause defining p ends in a call to p, the recursive call is not compiled in such a way as to push an execution frame on a stack, but rather as a jump to the beginning of the code for the predicate. This means that a recursive predicate can execute without eating up stack space. Clauses that end with a call to the predicate being defined, without calling the predicate being defined anywhere else, are called tail-recursive; the method of compilation is called tail recursion optimization.

To make full use of this feature, it is sometimes necessary to re-express a predicate to pass a partial solution parameter to the recursive call. This parameter is often referred to as an *accumulator*. The classic example is the reverse predicate, which is coded most naturally as follows:

```
reverse([], []).
reverse([X¦Xs], Zs) :-
  reverse(Xs, Xsrev),
  append(Xsrev, [X], Zs).
```

Besides being inefficient in having calls to append that involve N recursive calls, where N is the length of the list being reversed, this code is not able to be tail-recursion optimized.

The usual tail-recursive version involves a call to an auxiliary tail-recursive predicate with an extra accumulator argument:

```
reverse(X, Y) :-
  revappend(X, [], Y).

% revappend(X, A, Y):  the reverse of X,
% appended onto A, results in Y.
revappend([], A, A).
revappend([X¦Xs], A, Y) :-
  revappend(Xs, [X¦A], Y).
```

Note that the second argument of revappend is in some sense a trick, but that the predicate nevertheless has a perfectly logical meaning. Whenever we write an auxiliary predicate, even if it arises from some coding technique such as this, it is useful to try to find the real meaning of the predicate and express it in a comment.

6.4.7. First Argument Indexing

Another optimization found in most compilers and many interpreters is *first argument indexing*. Prolog implementers discovered early on that the clauses defining a given predicate often differed from each other in the outermost function symbol of the first argument. They then developed strategies for exploiting this.

When executing a query of the form append(X, Y, Z), for instance, Prolog should theoretically try to match each recursive call to append with both clauses of the definition. However, if it remembers that the first clause of append has the empty list as its first argument, and the second clause has a non-empty list as its first argument, it can throw away any unnecessary backtrack points simply by looking at the format of the first argument, X. If X is an uninstantiated variable, it needs to look at both clauses; but if it is the empty list or a non-empty list, it needs to look at only one clause.

This is taken a bit further in most Prolog systems. When a predicate definition is processed, the clauses are classified according to the outermost function symbol of the first argument and then placed in an efficient data structure such as a hash table for easy lookup. Calls with partially instantiated first arguments can then be executed in much less time than before and with much less overhead because useless backtrack points are discarded before they are even reached. In compiled Prolog code, this can turn a backtracking call to a multi-clause predicate into a straightforward transfer to a single clause.

We can exploit first argument indexing by ordering the arguments of the predicates so that the outermost function symbol of the first argument is the one that is most likely to be different from clause to clause. For predicates that traverse a list, for example, this means putting the list being traversed as the first argument. Thus the revappend predicate as given in the last section can be executed efficiently, but not if we had made the accumulator the first argument, as follows:

```
reverse(X, Y) :-
  revappend([], X, Y).

revappend(A, [], A).
revappend(A, [X|Xs], Y) :-
  revappend([X|A], Xs, Y).
```

Even though the predicate definitions have the same logical meaning as before, many Prologs execute the second definition more slowly.

Some Prologs have the ability to index on any argument, although some of those need help from indexing declarations inserted into the Prolog code. However, it is still often useful to put the more unique argument first because it also helps in reading the program.

6.4.8. Reading Clauses from the Terminal

Prolog programmers occasionally want to type in clauses to the interpreter directly. It may seem natural to do this by simply typing the clause at the query prompt. However, because of the way that Prolog parses terms read in (see section 6.3.11.5), it parses a rule a :- b as a term :-(a,b) and takes it as a query on a (probably nonexistent) predicate :-.

The trick to know for typing in clauses directly is that the file called user is connected to the user's terminal. Thus to enter clauses from the terminal, it is possible to just consult the file user with the query [user], type in the clauses, and then end with an end-of-file indication. After the end-of-file, the interpreter returns to its top-level query loop, having processed the clauses.

6.4.9. Using the Dash in a Symbol

A common mistake, especially for Lisp programmers, is to try to use the dash (-) in a symbol such as a predicate or constant name. A dash is not a valid character to use in an identifier, but it is a valid symbol in its own right (see section 6.3.11.3). This leads to some subtle bugs.

When used in a predicate name at the beginning of a clause, the bug manifests itself as the user defining the dash predicate. For instance, the clause

```
new-value(X) :- read(X).
```

is parsed the same as the clause

```
'-'(new,value(X)) :- read(X).
```

This may go undetected even if the user calls the new-value predicate because the user will really still be calling the - predicate. With enough such names, the multiple clauses for the hidden - predicate will begin to interfere with one another, and the user will begin having obscure problems.

If, in a debugger trace of an execution of a Prolog predicate, you start encountering calls to the - predicate, this should be an indication that you have run afoul of this bug. The solution, of course, is to traverse your program and replace the incorrect dashes with underscores.

6.5. Examples

Seeing examples of a programming language is sometimes the greatest help in learning the language. I therefore present in the following sections five longer examples of Prolog code: a balanced tree package, a prime number finder, a utility for checking C programs for memory leaks, an implementation of the popular computer game Life, and a simple pure Lisp interpreter.

6.5.1. A Balanced Tree Package

In every programming language, we often want to associate keys with values. We could do this in Prolog by lists with elements of the form value(Key, Val), but this is the equivalent of using a linear list. Much more efficient for this purpose is a balanced tree, or Adelson-Velski'i-Landis (AVL) tree.

This Prolog treatment is based on Wirth's work (1976). A tree is represented either as the empty tree emptytree or as a tree of the form tree(Key, Val, Height, Left, Right), where Key and Val are the key and value of this node, Left and Right are the trees containing keys that are less (respectively, greater) than Key, and Height is the height of the tree. The user does not have to know about the representation, however; she can just call init/1 to get an empty tree and call predicates such as add/4 to add nodes and find/3 to find values of keys.

LISTING 6.3. *A Balanced tree package.*

```
%%%%%%%%%%%%%%%%%%%%
% Find
%%%%%%%%%%%%%%%%%%%%

% find(Tree, Key, Val):  Key appears, associated with Val, in Tree
find(tree(Key,Val,_,_,_), Key, Val) :-
  !.
find(tree(Thiskey,_,_,Left,Right), Key, Val) :-
  Key < Thiskey,
  !,
  find(Left, Key, Val).
find(tree(_,_,_,_,Right), Key, Val) :-
  find(Right, Key, Val).


%%%%%%%%%%%%%%%%%%%%
% Add
%%%%%%%%%%%%%%%%%%%%

% add(Tree, Key, Val, Newtree):  add Key associated
% with Val to Tree, yielding Newtree.
add(emptytree, Key, Val, tree(Key,Val,1,emptytree,emptytree)).
add(tree(Thiskey,Thisval,_,Left,Right), Key, Val, Newtree) :-
  Key < Thiskey,
  add(Left, Key, Val, Newleft),
  height(Newleft, LH),
  height(Right, RH),
  construct_balanced(Thiskey, Thisval, Newleft, Right,
                     LH, RH, Newtree).
add(tree(Thiskey,Thisval,_,Left,Right), Key, Val, Newtree) :-
  Key > Thiskey,
  add(Right, Key, Val, Newright),
  height(Left, LH),
  height(Newright, RH),
  construct_balanced(Thiskey, Thisval, Left, Newright,
                     LH, RH, Newtree).

% height(Tree, H):  H is the height of Tree.
height(emptytree, 0).
height(tree(_,_,H,_,_), H).

% construct_balanced(K, V, L, R, LH, RH, Newtree):  construct
% a balanced tree Newtree out of K, V, L, and R,
% where L and R are trees, all the keys of L are less than K,
% all the keys of R are greater than K, V is the value to be
% associated with K, and LH and RH are the heights of L and R.
construct_balanced(K, V, L, R, H, H, tree(K,V,H1,L,R)) :-
```

```
    !,
    H1 is H+1.
construct_balanced(K, V, L, R, LH, RH, Newtree) :-
    LH is RH+1, % left is one taller
    !,
    H1 is LH+1,
    Newtree = tree(K,V,H1,L,R).
construct_balanced(K, V, L, R, LH, RH, Newtree) :-
    RH is LH+1, % right is one taller
    !,
    H1 is RH+1,
    Newtree = tree(K,V,H1,L,R).
% Otherwise, tree would be out of balance if constructed as above.
construct_balanced(K, V, L, R, LH, RH, Newtree) :-
    LH > RH, % by more than one
    L = tree(LK,LV,LH,LL,LR),
    height(LL, LLH),
    height(LR, LRH),
    LLH > LRH, % left subtree is 1 taller than right
    !,
    H is LLH + 1,
    Newtree = tree(LK,LV,H,LL,tree(K,V,LLH,LR,R)).
construct_balanced(K, V, L, R, LH, RH, Newtree) :-
    LH > RH, % by more than one, but right subtree of L
             %  is taller than left
    !,
    L = tree(LK,LV,LH,LL,tree(LRK,LRV,LRH,LRL,LRR)),
    H is LRH+1,
    Newtree =
      tree(LRK,LRV,H,
        tree(LK,LV,LRH,LL,LRL),
        tree(K,V,LRH,LRR,R)
      ).
% Otherwise, tree would be out of balance, and right
% subtree taller than left
construct_balanced(K, V, L, R, LH, RH, Newtree) :-
    R = tree(RK,RV,RH,RL,RR),
    height(RL, RLH),
    height(RR, RRH),
    RRH > RLH, % left subtree is taller than right
    !,
    H is RRH + 1,
    Newtree = tree(RK,RV,H,tree(K,V,RRH,L,RL),RR).
construct_balanced(K, V, L, R, LH, RH, Newtree) :-
    R = tree(RK,RV,RH,tree(RLK,RLV,RLH,RLL,RLR),RR),
    H is RLH+1,
    Newtree =
      tree(RLK,RLV,H,
        tree(K,V,RLH,L,RLL),
        tree(RK,RV,RLH,RLR,RR)
      ).


%%%%%%%%%%%%%%%%%%%%
% newval
%%%%%%%%%%%%%%%%%%%%

% newval(Tree, Key, Val, Newtree):  replace the value of Key
```

```
% in Tree by Val, yielding Newtree.
newval(tree(Key,_,H,L,R), Key, Newval, tree(Key,Newval,H,L,R)) :-
    !.
newval(tree(Thiskey,V,H,Left,Right), Key, Newval,
tree(Thiskey,V,H,Newleft,Right)) :-
    Key < Thiskey,
    !,
    newval(Left, Key, Newval, Newleft).
newval(tree(Thiskey,V,H,Left,Right), Key, Newval,
tree(Thiskey,V,H,Left,Newright)) :-
    newval(Right, Key, Val, Newright).
newval(emptytree, Key, Newval, _) :-
    write('No value currently defined for '), write(Key), nl,
    fail.


%%%%%%%%%%%%%%%%%%%%%%%
% top-level utilities
%%%%%%%%%%%%%%%%%%%%%%%

% find_or_add(Tree, Key, Val, Newtree):  confirm that Key is
% in Tree associated with Val, or else add it yielding Newtree.
find_or_add(Tree, Key, Val, Newtree) :-
    find(Tree, Key, Val),
    !,
    Newtree = Tree.
find_or_add(Tree, Key, Val, Newtree) :-
    add(Tree, Key, Val, Newtree).

init(emptytree).


%%%%%%%%%%%%%%%%%%%%%%%
% test predicates
%%%%%%%%%%%%%%%%%%%%%%%

writetree(emptytree, _).
writetree(tree(K,V,H,L,R), Indent) :-
    Indent2 is Indent+2,
    writetree(L, Indent2),
    writeblanks(Indent),
    write(K), write('/'), write(V), write('/'), write(H), nl,
    writetree(R, Indent2).

% testree(L, Tree):  build a balanced tree out of the keys
% in list L, associating each key with itself as a value,
% printing out the intermediate stages along the way.
testree([], _).
testree([K|Ks], Tree) :-
    nl, write('Adding '), write(K), nl, nl,
    add(Tree, K, K, Newtree),
    writetree(Newtree, 2),
    testree(Ks, Newtree).

writeblanks(0) :-
    !.
writeblanks(N) :-
    put(32),
    N1 is N-1,
    writeblanks(N1).
```

6.5.2. Eratosthenes' Sieve

all_primes_less_than2, in this example, instantiates its second argument to a list containing all primes less than its first argument. It uses Eratosthenes' sieve method to do so:

```prolog
all_primes_less_than(N, List) :-
    N1 is N-1,
    all_numbers_between(2, N1, Initial_list),
    sieve(Initial_list, List).

% all_numbers_between(M, N, List): List is all numbers between
% M and N, inclusive.
all_numbers_between(M, N, []) :-
    M > N,
    !.
all_numbers_between(M, N, [M|Rest]) :-
    M1 is M+1,
    all_numbers_between(M1, N, Rest).

% sieve(Numbers, Primes): The result of performing an
% Eratosthenes' sieve sifting operation on Numbers is Primes.
sieve([], []).
sieve([Prime|Rest], [Prime|Primes]) :-
    delete_all_multiples_of(Rest, Prime, Next),
    sieve(Next, Primes).

% Delete from (sorted) List all multiples of M, giving Result.
delete_all_multiples_of(List, M, Result) :-
    delete_all_multiples_starting_with(List, M, M, Result).

% Delete from (sorted) List all multiples of M starting with X,
% giving Result.
delete_all_multiples_starting_with([], M, X, []).
delete_all_multiples_starting_with([X|Rest], M, X, Ys) :-
    !,
    XpM is X+M,
    delete_all_multiples_starting_with(Rest, M, XpM, Ys).
delete_all_multiples_starting_with([Z|Rest], M, X, [Z|Ys]) :-
    Z > X,
    !,
    XpM is X+M,
    delete_all_multiples_starting_with(Rest, M, XpM, Ys).
delete_all_multiples_starting_with([Z|Rest], M, X, [Z|Ys]) :-
    delete_all_multiples_starting_with(Rest, M, X, Ys).
```

6.5.3. A C Leak Checker

The following program illustrates term I/O and the use of Prolog for a task that is a bit awkward when done in simple pattern-matching languages. It helps in detecting memory leaks in C programs.

To use the leak checker on a particular C program, replace all calls to malloc and free in your C code with calls to new functions (say report_malloc and report_free), which call the original functions and also report information about the calls. At initialization, your C program should open a special log file; report_malloc should print a line of the form

```
malloc(Pointer, Description).
```

to the log file after its call to `malloc`, and `report_free` should print a line of the form

```
free(Pointer).
```

after its call to `free`. Here, `Pointer` is an integer representing the address allocated, and `Description` is a double-quoted string describing the block being allocated; for instance,

```
malloc(4372, "B-tree node").
malloc(4400, "Parse tree leaf").
free(4372).
free(4400).
```

After a run of your program, call the `leakcheck` predicate on the log file. `leakcheck` reports on any pointers allocated but not freed and also on any memory that may be allocated twice or freed without being allocated:

LISTING 6.4. *A C leak checker.*

```
% leakcheck(Filename):  top-level predicate.  Takes filename
% (e.g. single-quoted constant) as argument.
leakcheck(Filename) :-
   see(Filename),
   read_process([]),
   seen.

% read_process(Allocated):  given the pointers known to be
% Allocated so far, read and process the rest of the reports in
% the log file.
read_process(Allocated) :-
   read(Report),
   process(Report, Allocated).

% process(Report, Allocated):  process Report and the rest
% of the reports in the file, given the pointers known to be
% Allocated so far.
process(end_of_file, []) :-
   !,
   nl,
   write('No leaks detected.'), nl.
process(end_of_file, Allocated) :-
   nl,
   write('Pointers allocated but not freed:'), nl,
   report_allocated(Allocated).
process(malloc(Pointer,_), Allocated) :-
   member(Allocated, malloc(Pointer,_)),
   !,
   write('* Memory allocated twice at address '),
   write(Pointer), write('.'), nl,
   read_process(Allocated).
process(malloc(Pointer,Desc), Allocated) :-
   read_process([malloc(Pointer,Desc)|Allocated]).
process(free(Pointer), Allocated) :-
   delete(Allocated, malloc(Pointer,_), Rest_allocated),
   !,
   read_process(Rest_allocated).
```

```
process(free(Pointer), Allocated) :-
    write('* Attempt to free memory not allocated at address '),
    write(Pointer), write('.'), nl,
    read_process(Allocated).

report_allocated([]).
report_allocated([malloc(Pointer,Desc)|Reports]) :-
    write('  Address '),
    write(Pointer),
    write(': '),
    writestring(Desc),
    nl,
    report_allocated(Reports).

% Standard predicates.

member([X|_], X).
member([_|Xs], Y) :-
    member(Xs, Y).

delete([X|Xs], X, Xs) :-
    !.
delete([X|Xs], Y, [X|Zs]) :-
    delete(Xs, Y, Zs).

writestring([]).
writestring([C|Cs]) :-
    put(C),
    writestring(Cs).
```

6.5.4. The Game of Life

This program implements John Horton Conway's Game of Life, as described in Gardner's work (1983). The implementation incorporates suggestions by William Clocksin, for which I am very grateful. Note the use of an operator declaration and multi-arity predicates and some exploitation of first-argument indexing to achieve efficiency.

The life "game board" is represented as the list of cells that are alive. Each cell is represented by the notation R::C, where R is the row and C is the column of the cell. The live cells are sorted into reading order—that is, left to right and top to bottom—for most of the processing.

To play the game, call life(Num_R, Num_C, Live_Cells, Some_future_gen), where Num_R and Num_C are the number of rows and columns on the desired board, Live_Cells is a list of live R::C cells, and Some_future_gen is an uninstantiated variable. Some_future_gen is instantiated first to the original list of live cells; keep entering the semicolon on the solutions prompt to get succeeding generations. At each solution, the board is printed out.

LISTING 6.5. *The Game of Life.*

```prolog
% Operator for separating row::column in square specifiers.
:- op(200, xfx, ::).

% Top-level predicates

% life(Max_R, Max_C, Live_Cells, Some_future_gen):
% Given a board with Max_R rows and Max_C columns,
% where Live_Cells is a list of Row::Column cell specifiers,
% Some_future_gen is some future generation of the board.
life(Max_R, Max_C, Live_Cells, Some_future_gen) :-
  % you don't have to use "sort" if you make sure Initial_RCs is
  % always in "reading order".
  sort(Live_Cells, Board),
  future_gen(Board, Max_R, Max_C, Some_future_gen).

% A future generation is either this generation (in which
% case the board should be printed), or some future generation
% of the next generation.
future_gen(Board, Max_R, Max_C, Board) :-
  printboard(Board, Max_R, Max_C).
future_gen(Board, Max_R, Max_C, New_Board) :-
  next_gen(Board, Max_R, Max_C, Mid_Board),
  !,
  future_gen(Mid_Board, Max_R, Max_C, New_Board).

% printboard/3
printboard(Board, Max_R, Max_C) :-
  printboard(Board, 1, Max_R, 1, Max_C).

% printboard/5
% Could be made more efficient if make use of "reading order".
printboard(_Board, R, Max_R, _, _) :-
  R > Max_R,
  !.
printboard(Board, R, Max_R, C, Max_C) :-
  C > Max_C,
  !,
  nl,
  R1 is R+1,
  printboard(Board, R1, Max_R, 1, Max_C).
printboard(Board, R, Max_R, C, Max_C) :-
  ( on(Board, R, C) ->
    write(' @') ;
    write(' .')
  ),
  C1 is C+1,
  printboard(Board, R, Max_R, C1, Max_C).

%%%%%%%%%%%%%%%%%%%%%%%%%%%%%%%%%%%%%%%%%%

% Basic engine

% Board, Adds, and Deletes are all lists of pairs R::C,
% ordered in "reading order" (top to bottom, left to right).

% next_gen/4:
next_gen(Board, Max_R, Max_C, New_Board) :-
  updates(Board, 1, Max_R, 1, Max_C, Adds, Deletes),
  updated_version(Board, Adds, Deletes, New_Board).
```

```prolog
updates(_Board, R, Max_R, _C, _Max_C, Adds, Deletes) :-
  R > Max_R,
  !,
  Adds = [],
  Deletes = [].
updates(Board, R, Max_R, C, Max_C, Adds, Deletes) :-
  C > Max_C,
  R1 is R+1,
  !,
  updates(Board, R1, Max_R, 1, Max_C, Adds, Deletes).
updates(Board, R, Max_R, C, Max_C, Adds, Deletes) :-
  number_of_neighbours(Board, R, C, N),
  updates1(N, Board, R, C, Adds, Later_adds, Deletes, Later_deletes),
  C1 is C+1,
  updates(Board, R, Max_R, C1, Max_C, Later_adds, Later_deletes).

% 2 neighbours: do nothing.
updates1(2, _Board, _R, _C, Adds, Adds, Deletes, Deletes) :-
  !.
% 3 neighbours, one already there: do nothing.
updates1(3, Board, R, C, Adds, Later_adds, Deletes, Later_deletes) :-
  on(Board, R, C),
  !,
  Later_adds = Adds,
  Later_deletes = Deletes.     % unifs at end for efficiency
% 3 neighbours, none there right now: add.
updates1(3, _Board, R, C, [R::C|Later_adds], Later_adds,
          Deletes, Deletes) :-
  !.
% < 2 or > 3 neighbours, one there: delete.
updates1(_N, Board, R, C, Adds, Later_adds, Deletes, Later_deletes) :-
  on(Board, R, C),
  !,
  Adds = Later_adds,
  Deletes = [R::C|Later_deletes].
% < 2 or > 3 neighbours, none there: do nothing.
updates1(_N, _Board, _R, _C, Adds, Adds, Deletes, Deletes).

% Does a merge of 1st and 2nd args, ignoring deletes.  Exploits
% the fact that all the lists are in "reading order".
updated_version([], Adds, _Deletes, Adds).
% If first add is before first in board, use it first
updated_version([R::C|Board], [R1::C1|Adds], Deletes, New_Board) :-
  (R1 < R ; (R1 = R, C1 < C)),
  !,
  New_Board = [R1::C1|New_Board1],
  updated_version([R::C|Board], Adds, Deletes, New_Board1).
% Otherwise, try first in board, but if it is really to be deleted,
% the delete will be the first in the list of deletes
updated_version([R::C|Board], Adds, [R::C|Deletes], New_Board) :-
  !,
  updated_version(Board, Adds, Deletes, New_Board).
% Otherwise, use first in board.
updated_version([R::C|Board], Adds, Deletes, [R::C|New_Board]) :-
  updated_version(Board, Adds, Deletes, New_Board).
```

%%%

% Utilities

```
number_of_neighbours(Board, R, C, N) :-
  sum_number_on(
    [ (R-1)::(C-1),(R-1)::C,(R-1)::(C+1),
      R     ::(C-1),         R     ::(C+1),
      (R+1)::(C-1),(R+1)::C,(R+1)::(C+1) ],
    Board,
    0,
    N
  ).

sum_number_on([], _Board, Sofar, Sofar).
sum_number_on([Row::Col|Pairs], Board, Sofar, N) :-
  R is Row,
  C is Col,
  ( on(Board, R, C) ->
    ( Sofar1 is Sofar+1,
      sum_number_on(Pairs, Board, Sofar1, N)
    ) ;
    sum_number_on(Pairs, Board, Sofar, N)
  ).

% Requires R and C to be input; exploits the fact that the board
% is ordered in "reading order".
on([R::C|_], R, C) :-          % found it
  !.
on([R::C1|Board], R, C) :-     % same row, later column
  C1 < C,
  !,
  on(Board, R, C).
on([R1::_C1|Board], R, C) :-   % later row
  R1 < R,
  on(Board, R, C).
```

6.5.5. A Simple Lisp Interpreter

Finally, here is a simple pure Lisp interpreter.

In this interpreter, each Lisp s-expression (a b c) is encoded as a list [a,b,c]; thus, for instance, [append,x,y] for (append x y). Quoting must be done explicitly, as for instance [quote,[a,b]] for '(a b). I encourage you, as an exercise, to write a two-level parser using DCGs (section 6.3.9.5) to parse a Lisp source file into the form expected by this interpreter.

To evaluate an expression E, pose the query eval(E, Result); Result is instantiated to its value. Functions are defined by adding clauses of the form defun(Funcname, Arglist, Funcbody) to the program; they could instead be asserted after being parsed from an input file. Nexpr functions, which do not evaluate their arguments, are similarly defined using defun_nexpr.

LISTING 6.6. *A simple Lisp interpreter.*

```
% Main predicate.
% eval(S, Result):  Result is the result of evaluating S.
eval(S, Result) :-
  eval1(S, [], Result).

% eval(S, Env, Result):  Result is the result of evaluating
% S in the context of the variable bindings in Env.
eval1([F¦Args], Env, Result) :-
  !,
  eval_appl(F, Args, Env, Result).
eval1([quote,Arg], _, Arg) :- !.
eval1(A, Env, Result) :-
  eval_atom(A, Env, Result).

% eval_appl(F, Args, Env, Result):  Result is the result
% of applying function F to Args, in environment Env.
eval_appl(F, Args, Env, Result) :-
  ( defined_func(F, Nargs) ->
    ( length(Args, Nargs) ->
      eval_appl1(F, Args, Env, Result);
      ( write('Wrong number of arguments: '),
        write([F¦Args]), nl,
        Result=nil
      )
    );
    ( write('Undefined function: '),
      write(F), nl,
      Result=nil
    )
  ).

% defined_func(Funcname, N):  Funcname is the name
% of a defined function with N arguments.
% Builtins...
defined_func(eq, 2).
defined_func(car, 1).
defined_func(cdr, 1).
defined_func(cons, 2).
defined_func(cond, _).
defined_func(quote, 1).
defined_func(eval, 1).
% ...and user-defined functions.
defined_func(Func, Nargs) :-
  defun(Func, Args, _),
  length(Args, Nargs).
defined_func(Func, Nargs) :-
  defun_nexpr(Func, Args, _),
  length(Args, Nargs).

% Evaluate a function with the right number of arguments.
% Builtins...
eval_appl1(eq, [S,T], Env, Result) :-
  eval1(S, Env, Sval),
  eval1(T, Env, Tval),
  decide_eq(Sval, Tval, Result).
eval_appl1(car, [S], Env, Result) :-
  eval1(S, Env, Sval),
  ( Sval = [Result¦_] ->
    true;
    Result = nil
  ).
```

```prolog
eval_appl1(cdr, [S], Env, Result) :-
  eval1(S, Env, Sval),
  ( Sval = [_|Result] ->
    true;
    Result = nil
  ).
eval_appl1(cons, [S,T], Env, [Sval|Tval]) :-
  eval1(S, Env, Sval),
  eval1(T, Env, Tval).
eval_appl1(cond, Clauses, Env, Result) :-
  eval_cond(Clauses, Env, Result).
eval_appl1(quote, [S], _, S).
eval_appl1(eval, [S], Env, Result) :-
  eval1(S, Env, Sval),
  eval1(Sval, Env, Result).
% ... and user-defined functions.
eval_appl1(Func, Aparams, Env, Result) :-
  defun(Func, Fparams, Body),
  map_eval1(Aparams, Env, Evalparams),
  build_env(Fparams, Evalparams, Newenv),
  eval1(Body, Newenv, Result).
eval_appl1(Func, Aparams, _Env, Result) :-
  defun_nexpr(Func, Fparams, Body),
  build_env(Fparams, Aparams, Newenv),
  eval1(Body, Newenv, Result).

% Decide on the result of an eq
% decide_eq(S, T, Result):  Result is t if S and T are
% identical (for Lisp purposes), and nil otherwise.
decide_eq(S, S, t) :- !.
decide_eq([], nil, t) :- !.
decide_eq(nil, [], t) :- !.
decide_eq(_S, _T, nil).

% eval_cond(Cond_clauses, Env, Result):  Result is the
% result of evaluating a cond expression whose list of
% clauses is in Cond_clauses.
% If have reached end of cond, return nil.
eval_cond([], _, nil).
% Otherwise, evaluate the test and decide on the result.
eval_cond([[Test,S]|Clauses], Env, Result) :-
  !,
  eval1(Test, Env, Testval),
  eval_cond1(Testval, S, Clauses, Env, Result).
% We could consider a list after the test in a cond clause
% to be correct, and return the last one evaluated, but in
% a pure Lisp this is probably erroneous.
eval_cond([[_Head|Rest]|_], _, nil) :-
  !,
  write('Error: list after cond test: '), write(Rest), nl.
eval_cond([Atom|_], _, nil) :-
  write('Error: atom instead of cond clause: '), write(Atom), nl.

% eval_cond1(Testval, S, Clauses, Env, Result):  if Testval
% is non-nil, Result is the value of S; otherwise, Result is the
% value of a cond expression containing Clauses.
% Interpret nil as false, non-nil as true.
% If test value is nil, go on with other clauses
```

```
eval_cond1(nil, _, Clauses, Env, Result) :-
  !,
  eval_cond(Clauses, Env, Result).
% If test value is not nil but rest of clause is empty,
% return test value
eval_cond1(Testval, [], _, _, Testval) :-
  !.
% Otherwise, evaluate rest of clause
eval_cond1(_Testval, S, _, Env, Result) :-
  eval1(S, Env, Result).

% map_eval1(Exprs, Env, Values):  Values is the list of
% the values of Exprs, when evaluated in binding
% environment Env.
map_eval1([], _, []).
map_eval1([S¦Ss], Env, [T¦Ts]) :-
  eval1(S, Env, T),
  map_eval1(Ss, Env, Ts).

% build_env(Varnames, Values, Env):  Where Varnames is
% x1, ..., xn and Values is v1, ..., vn, build the
% environment bind(x1,v1), ..., bind(xn,vn).
build_env([], [], []).
build_env([F¦Fs], [A¦As], [bind(F,A)¦Env]) :-
  build_env(Fs, As, Env).

% eval_atom(Atom, Env, Value):  Value is the value of
% Atom, according to Env.
eval_atom(t, _, t) :- !.
eval_atom(nil, _, nil) :- !.
eval_atom(S, Env, Result) :-
  getval(Env, S, Result).

% getval(Env, Atom, Val):  bind(Atom,Val) is a member
% of Env.
getval([], S, nil) :-
  write('Undefined atom: '), write(S), nl.
getval([bind(S,T)¦_], S, T) :- !.
getval([bind(_S1,_)¦Env], S, Result) :-
  getval(Env, S, Result).


% Declare functions as dynamic, since don't have
% to have them if we don't want to.
:- dynamic defun/3.
:- dynamic defun_nexpr/3.


% Some sample function definitions

defun(null, [x],
  [eq,x,nil]
).

defun(append, [x,y],
  [cond,[[null,x],y],
        [t,[cons,[car,x],[append,[cdr,x],y]]]]
).
```

```
defun(member, [x,y],
   [cond,[[null,y],nil],
         [[eq,x,[car,y]],t],
         [t,[member,x,[cdr,y]]]]
).
```

6.6. Acknowledgments

Thank you to my editor, Peter Salus, for his patience and understanding. Thanks also to Veronica Dahl and Fernando Pereira for their feedback on earlier versions of this chapter. I would also like to acknowledge that I have benefited greatly over the years from the illuminating articles of Richard O'Keefe on the Usenet newsgroup comp.lang.prolog. Naturally, any errors and omissions that remain in this chapter are solely my responsibility.

6.7. References

Bratko, I. 1990. *Prolog programming for artificial intelligence*. Reading, MA: Addison-Wesley.

Clocksin, W. F., and C. S. Mellish. 1987. *Programming in Prolog* (3rd ed.). Berlin: Springer.

Gardner, M. 1983. *Wheels, life, and other mathematical amusements*. New York: W. H. Freeman.

O'Keefe, R. A. 1990 *The craft of Prolog*. Cambridge, MA: MIT Press.

Pereira, F., and D. H. D. Warren. 1980. Definite clause grammars for language analysis—A survey of the formalism and a comparison with transition networks. *Artificial Intelligence* 13:231–278.

Sterling, L., and E. Shapiro. 1986. *The art of Prolog*. Cambridge, MA: MIT Press.

Wirth, N. 1976. *Algorithms + data structures = programs*. Englewood Cliffs, NJ: Prentice Hall.

INDEX

Symbols

G

H

I-J

R